Someone more Like Myself

THE INDIGO LEWIS SERIES

janay harden

Someone More Like Myself
The Indigo Lewis Series

Copyright © 2021 by Janay Harden

All rights reserved. No part of this book may be reproduced or transmitted in any form or by any means without written permission of the author.

Ebook ISBN: 978-1-7365412-4-1
Paperback ISBN: 978-1-7365412-5-8

"This life is mine alone.
So I have stopped asking people for directions
to places they have never been."

Glennon Doyle

PROLOGUE

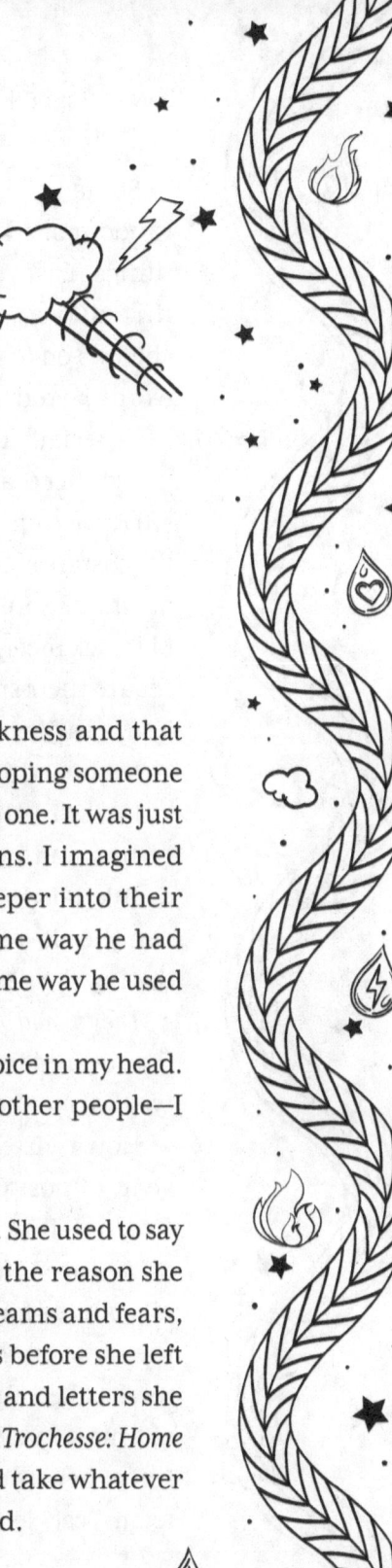

I WATCHED HIM SINK further into the darkness and that made me want to giggle. He was probably hoping someone would come and save him, but there was no one. It was just me and him here at this dock in New Orleans. I imagined beautiful, Black mermaids pulling him deeper into their clutches where they preyed on him, the same way he had preyed on us. They would rule over him the same way he used his position to rule over others.

"Well done, my girl. Well done," I heard Mom's voice in my head. Her instructions were clear, and contrary to other people—I was a mama's girl.

"I got it," I whispered back.

Thoughts of mom swirled through my mind. She used to say all the world's magic was in water and it was the reason she loved to live by the lake. "You can find your dreams and fears, all right there," she pointed one day. That was before she left us. These days, all I had were thoughts of her and letters she sent every few months from her new abode at *Trochesse: Home for the Criminally Insane*. To be with her—I would take whatever time I could get, even if it was only in my head.

Sonia Lewis, the crazed killer some people called her, had random one-liners that often prophesized the most random things. Last year, after I killed Jaxon, she asked me how my first kill was. I quickly changed the subject and thankfully, she was on to the next topic in a matter of seconds. Still—her words jarred me and everything she said had meaning.

Especially today.

I glanced around the wharf, and it was quiet. Nothing stirred except for the water he disturbed by his presence. In the distance, I heard music bumping from somewhere. After all, it was Saturday night. Titus University had just won their big track meet, which brought us to New Orleans, and it would secure their spot at nationals. I had just left the Libra Festival hours earlier.

My how things change.

I'm sure the track team was waiting for their coach to return and impart some congratulatory speech while they drank, laughed, and celebrated. They would joke about who ran the slowest and giggled about things that went wrong during the day.

They would be waiting a while, I smirked. He would forever be the revered track and field coach of the great Titus University—the one that went missing and was never found.

How twisted life could be. This was my second kill. Last year, almost twelve months to the date, I had killed Jaxon Green. I didn't plan that one and the same for this one. The difference? He showed up and violated my new life. Out of all colleges for him to get a job, how did we make our way to the same one? He and I both hailed from a sleepy, Louisiana town called Tunica Rivers. His wet demise was at the bottom of a man-made lake now. Surely, they would come looking for him when he didn't show up to celebrate the big win with his team. I cackled out loud, amused by their imminent confusion.

When I was a kid, man, I loved to read. I had so many books around me and I relished the stories about faraway places like islands and big city skyscrapers. I read about vacations and being outside all day long on a beach. I waited for the day when the sun hit my skin right and my melanin glowed against the rays. It was a delirious type of happy I had yet to experience in real life, only in books I read.

Until today.

That's what this moment felt like for me. I felt bad about killing Jaxon. I had nightmares about it, even. I worried if people saw it on me. On my skin. Indigo Lewis, the teenaged murderer.

Worry didn't live here anymore.

It was insane to think this excited me, but it did. Watching him sink to the bottom; his arms outstretched grasping for someone... anyone... no one. Men underestimated me and those I loved—and I would continue to show them exactly who Indigo was.

I surveyed the scene. I paid special attention to the light posts for cameras. I heard The Bus purring a few feet away from me, which was ironic because it was usually loud and sounded like it was coughing. Ever since Grandpa Ez gave me his old car—an Oldsmobile Cutlass, I had called it The Bus. Most days it came roaring down the street with a deafening noise. It hummed softly behind me in the distance, waiting to take me back to safety in the other direction, where we had just sat and scoped out the scene. It was the way I needed it to be while I finished what I had to do.

We played cat and mouse for months and tonight—here we were. Only I wasn't the mouse. The voices directed me. Guided me. I felt them cheering me on. The urges coursed through me like wildfire, and every inch of my body tingled in anticipation of what was to come.

JANAY HARDEN

He angered so many parts of me. "Who do you think you're dealing with, girl?" he had sneered. I didn't hear him say it, but I saw the way his nasty mouth curled, and his lips formed the words. I read all of them, every syllable. I saw his eyes as he stood in front of The Bus and without one ounce of fear. He threw his head back and laughed, exposing all thirty-two teeth in his mouth. He snickered like I wasn't worth the time or energy. He waved me away like some frivolous child that didn't concern him. Was he worried now? At the bottom of all that water?

When I was in high school, I planned, primped, and prodded. I tried to make sure I arranged everything in a way for me to do well. A college student and a working girl, living on a hope and a prayer; making her own decisions. How do you prepare for murder? How do you prepare for the feelings that come with it? I mean, it's not like there is a support group for college girls who have a penchant for this kind of stuff. If your oppressor was right there within your reach, and within your grasp—what would you do? Would you take the bait? That was a funny word: bait. I guess he was the one who was now bait; sitting at the bottom of a lake.

I pulled my jacket tighter around my waist and shivered. I wasn't physically cold, but my soul sent chills up my spine. It was a late, May evening in Louisiana—that meant it could be ninety degrees at night. Beads of sweat formed at my hairline. I shivered again. My hands ached, and they were raw from rubbing against the graveled blacktop. My braids swung wildly at my shoulders and they too were wet from puddles where it had rained days earlier. I had them up in a bun, sitting high on top of my head when the day started, but I wasn't sure where my hair tie was at this point. I poked my chest out and stood with my hands on my hips, staring over the ledge into the dark, menacing water. It was crashing up against the rocks, not caring how hard or how many times it hit the wall. Its intensity never let up; it repeatedly came back for more. That was how I wanted to be. When you come for me and mine, I would never let up. I took one last look into the darkness and saw nothing.

Why did men think women were inferior? Weaker? When did that idea start? I was fighting with myself and the parts of me that protected me the most. The voices in my head were trying to keep me safe. They sensed danger even before I did most times, but I stood in their way. I was not weak, and I could take care of myself. If someone hurt me or someone I loved—well, clearly, they were dealt with.

I turned on my heel, with my braids cascading down my back and head held high, I strutted back to The Bus.

I could do this.

I would do this.

I was this girl—this person.

We were the same.

In the words of famous poet, Fat Joe, *"Yesterday's price, was not today's price."*

The price was his life.

PART 1

NEOPHYTE

CHAPTER 1

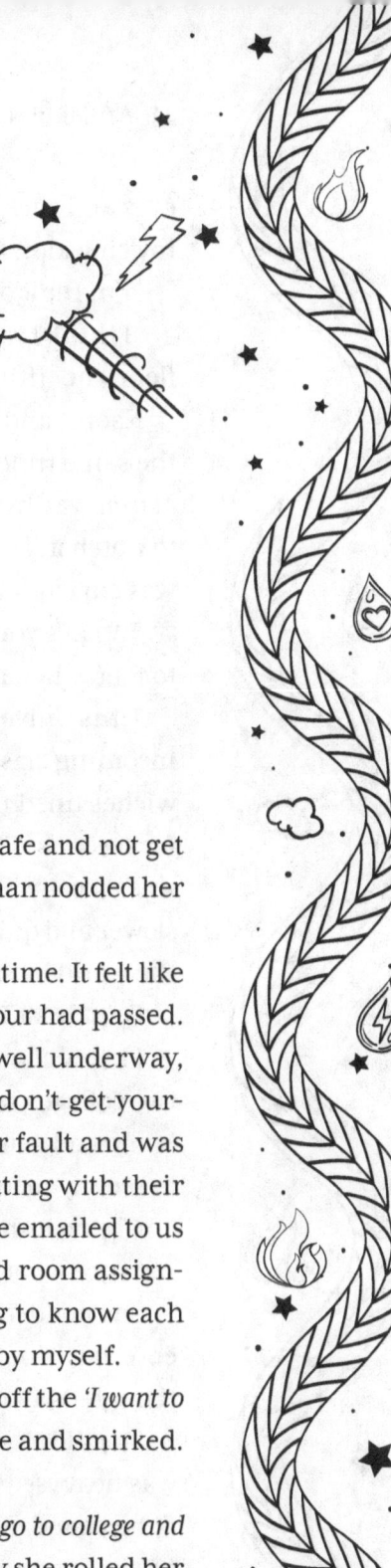

8 MONTHS AGO

"AND THAT, LADIES, is how you stay safe and not get yourself snatched up," the older woman nodded her head with a dramatic pause.

I sighed and checked my phone for the tenth time. It felt like I had already been there forever, but only an hour had passed.

Dorm orientation for Titus University was well underway, and we were learning the ins and out of the don't-get-yourself-raped spiel. As if it could somehow be our fault and was preventable. I was alone; everyone else was sitting with their roommates. The orientation instructions were emailed to us and stated we should line up by our floor and room assignments, and spend the next few hours getting to know each other. My roommate was absent, and so I sat by myself.

"She acts like we come to college and check off the *'I want to be assaulted box.'*" A white girl leaned close to me and smirked.

I giggled.

"Never have I ever thought, *'man, I want to go to college and get raped.'*" The girl dug a little harder. The way she rolled her

eyes and sucked her teeth made me cover my mouth to hide my chuckles. "I'm Naomi—Naomi Holland," she beamed.

"I'm Indigo, they call me Indy."

"I think I saw your name somewhere. I think you're on my floor, the fifth?"

Naomi and I paused for a second before we exclaimed at the same time, "on the fifth floor!" and held up four fingers. *Martin* was life, and I hoped they had the channel I needed to watch it. I was surprised a white girl knew the reference. I was curious about this Naomi girl on the fifth floor.

"What's your major?" Naomi asked. She motioned for me to follow her, and we walked to the food table.

Titus University set up an elaborate spread to welcome the incoming class of 2025: cakes, pies, fruits, coffee, and sandwiches lined the room, and we weren't the only ones in line for seconds. They packed students inside the building, and it was already a hot September day when the old folks moved slower and quieter while us youngins' were hellbent on taking the world by storm.

Or at least I was.

I knew choosing this school was a great choice. I applied to two colleges, but Titus University was three hours away from home and using The Bus; I could go home whenever I needed to see my sister, Sidney, and my dad.

Giving a shrug, I whispered, "Liberal Arts right now. I'm not sure what I want to do. I just know I'll find it in college."

She nodded. "I feel the same. I'm majoring in Political Science, but I don't know the first thing about it. Sounds important though. Maybe I could be like Abby Phillip or something."

She didn't say Tomi Lohren—that was a good sign. Naomi was heavyset with her hair pulled back into a tight ponytail at her nape. She had on these bad ass Jordans I could never afford, not with my sad work-study job they assigned me.

When I got the letter in the mail and it said I was to work in the Theatrical Arts department this school year, my dad laughed and said, *'they're gonna have my baby opening and closing the curtains.'* He and his girlfriend, Ms. Arletha, thought that was hilarious and fell out in stitches.

I hoped they weren't right.

"Then why are you majoring in Political Science?"

Now it was Naomi's turn to shrug. "Parents just don't understand, right?"

She had a point there. "Where are you from?"

"New Jersey. You?"

"Right here in Louisiana. A couple hours away in Tunica Rivers, even though this place seems like an entire world away."

"Yeah, it's pretty different from Jersey too." Naomi's face softened.

As the presenter began handing out condoms to the boys, we found a small corner and sat our food across the table. We shook our heads in disgust at the fiasco. We both had two plates topped with all kinds of sweets and treats. Naomi was already grinning at me as I looked at her and our impromptu picnic.

I had a forkful of rice ready, and my mouth was watering when my cell phone rang.

Crap! I thought I put it on vibrate. An ugly boy with bug eyes at a different table spied me when my phone rang, interrupting the woman's shrill voice up front. "I'll be right back. Can you watch my food?" I mouthed to Naomi. She nodded; her mouth full of salad.

"Hey Dad!" I breathed into the phone, rushing into the hallway.

"Indy Lindy!" Different voices screamed.

I smiled. Dad, Ms. Arletha, Grandpa Ez, and Sidney were on the phone.

"What are you doing, Indy?" Sidney constantly wanted to know my whereabouts.

"I'm in orientation. They're teaching us how not to be assaulted."

"What, now?" Dad shouted. I could hear his frown through the phone.

"Who assaulted my Indy?"

"Hush Grandpa Ez, I'm fine!"

"And what's this Grandpa Ez, business girl? Don't go to that crackerjack school and start acting funny now."

Grandpa Ez insisted Sidney and I call him Ez. Every now and then I slipped in a Grandpa on him, and he shut it down. I heard some muffled sounds, and Ms. Arletha's voice came through loud and clear. "Indy, you tell them people your team is hashtag *'Me Too,'* okay?"

"Me too, what? I want it too," Sidney whined.

"You stay away from them parties, Indy. Me and 'Letha been watching SVU, and we know what goes on at the colleges on Thursday nights."

"Oh, hush boy, and leave that girl alone!" Ms. Arletha spat.

"Indy, I saw Will at the carwash last week. That boy love him some you," Ez laughed.

This was my family.

I made a mental note to call Will, my best friend from home. I figured some things would change with me being hours away, but we hadn't talked in a few weeks and that wasn't like us.

Chatter erupted and students shuffled out of the auditorium. "I have to go, love you guys," I whispered.

"We love you, Indy! And have a good time in college!" Sidney shouted.

"And you call me if you need me to tinker with The Bus, Indy!" Ez's voice boomed.

When I re-entered the room, Naomi was still waiting. She had taken a napkin and placed it over my food. "Got anywhere to be?" She gave a devilish grin.

I had to run to the store and pick up more stuff for my dorm room. I wanted to walk around and figure out where my classes were so I wouldn't get lost on the first day. I also wanted to search for a beauty supply store because, well—every Black girl needed to live within five miles of a beauty supply store—that's law. Finally, I wanted to scope out the theater and meet my supervisor for my work-study job. The way Naomi looked at me, I knew whatever she had in mind was more fun.

"No, nothing really. What about you?"

"Omega Psi Phi fraternity is having a welcome BBQ; I saw it on this flyer." Naomi pushed a crumpled paper into my hand and sure enough, they were grilling close to the campus. They called themselves the Ques.

"You want to go?" Naomi raised her eyebrows at me.

"Sure, why not?"

Naomi squealed with delight, and we were off in search of purple Ques and free hot dogs. We trotted the short walk to the center where the campus met in the middle from five different directions. The smell hit me before I saw anything. Naomi and I smirked and picked up the pace. The aroma of barbequed meat, and the smoke from spareribs turning over an open flame, hit my nostrils and reminded me of home. How was that? Is barbeque a Black rite of passage? I barely got to eat at orientation and the scents emanating from the pits hit my soul and the ancestors sang out. I had to at least eat a hotdog.

I inhaled deeper, taking it in. It reminded me of Mama Jackie and Ez on the lake back in Tunica Rivers. Sitting at the water's edge with baked beans, mac and cheese, and gumbo. There was lots of meats and sides; I wondered who cooked it

all, especially the potato salad. My stomach growled and at this point, I really didn't care. I needed a rib.

Naomi grabbed a couple of sodas from the nearby cooler. "Are these free?" she asked the guy grilling.

"Yeah, baby, you can have anything here, whatever you want," a tall, fine ass brown-skinned man said. His white teeth gleaned against his skin and his hair was cut low, like he spent some time brushing those waves into existence and he was proud.

I chimed in. "Good, we'll just take four then, two for her and two for me."

"Ladies, I'm Booker Knoll, a senior here at Titus University. Everything you see before you is free, your student tuition paid for even those four sodas, so take as many as you want. College rule 101 they don't teach you in that orientation over there," he motioned with his pitchfork. "When there's free food you take as much as you can carry."

"I'm Indigo, and this is Naomi." I smiled at Booker.

He glanced us up and down over his eyeglasses and wiped sweat forming at his brow line. "Nice to meet you beautiful ladies. I'm a Q from the best fraternity known to man, and this is our event. If you need anything, please let me know."

Naomi and I stared at each other before following orders and taking as many sodas as we could carry. I stuffed some in my backpack just in case I would need them later. I thought about Ez and chuckled; he hoarded everything. If someone told him to take as many as he wanted, well he would put that offer to the test.

I popped open my can of soda and before I could take a drink, someone bumped me hard. "What the..." I started. My lip hit the rim and blood quickly found its way to the surface and tasted coppery. Swinging around, I was face to face with the deepest set of light brown eyes piercing mine. His long face was filled with apologies, but mine didn't read forgiveness.

SOMEONE MORE LIKE MYSELF

I dabbed at my lip and frowned. "What the hell!"

Naomi handed me a napkin from the table where Booker grilled food.

"I'm sorry, I didn't see you standing there. My fault," the man said.

Booker wiped his hands on a dish towel and scampered to the three of us. "Chaquille, what's going on here?"

Chaquille... a voice in me whispered. *Chaquille.*

"I ain't mean nothing by it, Book. I was carrying the watermelons and bumped into her."

"This is Indigo and Naomi." Booker placed a hand on Chaquille's shoulder. "They are freshmen."

Booker said freshmen like we were children and didn't know any better.

"You tried to take my girl out," Naomi glared. In just an hour, Naomi and I were girls.

We will see.

"Ya'll wildin'! It wasn't that serious. I just bumped into her! And she's not saying anything; are you speaking for her?" Chaquille frowned.

My fists balled, and I wanted his head on that open flame behind Booker. *Calm down, Indy. It's not that serious*, I told myself. This thing with Jaxon had me on edge and triggered. But he wasn't Jaxon, and I wasn't that same Indigo.

My body trembled as I simmered down. "*Her*, is right here. And I can speak for myself. You busted my lip, thank you very much."

Chaquille's eyes softened as he examined my face. "My bad, yo.' I really didn't see you." He picked up the watermelon he was carrying and stood behind the grill. He avoided my eyes as he unpacked.

"Let's go over there." Naomi pointed to an empty table. We grabbed our sodas and a few ribs before making our way out

of the scorching sun. I held a napkin to my busted lip, and it stung against the barbeque sauce from the rib.

"Indigo? Indigo Lewis?" I heard someone ask from behind.

I looked up and saw the tallest, most beautiful Black girl standing in front of me. She had to be at least six feet with deep mocha skin clear as day. Dressed in a white pants suit with the sun bouncing off her clothes, she seemed to shimmer with every shake and catch only the sun's best rays. She looked like new money. I heard snippets of an African accent.

"I'm Theodora Nkosi—I think we're roommates." Theodora pulled her phone from her pocket and tapped it while her manicured nails clicked and clacked. "See? Right here," she said.

Sure enough, a picture of me popped up on Theodora's phone. When I first applied to the college they asked for a headshot, and this was the same picture Theodora showed me. The Indigo in that picture took my breath away. She was a different girl, and I didn't want to go back to her.

"Hi, nice to meet you." I smiled. "This is Naomi, I just met her at orientation. Sit down with us."

Theodora took a seat and checked out the mob scene. Black, white, and everything in between was in the center of the campus. True to Booker's word, people were carrying heaps of plates and sodas, taking all they could carry. Music bellowed from somewhere, and Frankie Beverly and Maze crooned. While Booker cut a rug with a woman and two-stepped, smoke billowed from the pits.

"Were you at orientation?" I inquired.

"No, I drove down from Maryland with my family. I'm the first Nigerian child to go to college in the States, so my entire family decided they were coming to drop me off. It got so crazy! We ended up running behind and missing orientation entirely! I'm glad we got here late, though. I was dreading all of them there." Theodora shook her head, and her eyes widened.

Naomi and I chuckled at Theodora's words. I saw a few parents and grandparents front and center with their college-aged students, and I wondered how her Nigerian family would react to the condom and rape warning. I shuddered to think of Ez here in a room full of judgmental eyes. He was as loud as ever, and his voice matched his almost seven-foot frame.

"My room is on the fifth floor too," Naomi chimed in. She held up four fingers to Theodora, and we laughed. At least Theodora liked *Martin*—I felt relieved. We wouldn't have to fight over the tv.

A quick breeze snapped by, and I took in the air. It smelled different at Titus University—felt different. *'It is beautiful here, Indy, this will be good for us,'* a voice in my head said.

'Don't forget to meet your supervisor and see about your classes, Indy,' another voice popped in.

I closed my eyes for a second to drown them out. I wasn't sure what my life would look like here, but I wanted it to start at the Titus University Wellness Center, where I made an appointment to talk to a counselor. The paper had asked the reason for counseling services, and I paused. I didn't know how to write, *well last year I killed a man and I kind of sort of liked it. But I know that's wrong. But if it's wrong, I don't want to be right.* Nah, I couldn't write that. I settled on my anxiety. That was a good buzzword these days. Mom's schizophrenia was a family trait, and by the looks of it, may have passed down to me. Most days I felt worried about someone knowing what I did and them whispering and pointing at me. Other days I couldn't quiet the voices and wanted to feel the rush of taking someone's life once more.

JANAY HARDEN

I didn't know how to talk about the things that go on in my head all the time but one thing I knew for sure was I couldn't tell anyone about Jaxon Green. To me, it was self-defense, but I knew no one would see it that way. I had to keep my mouth shut and focus on controlling the thoughts in my head. I was looking forward to my first session coming up. Someone could help. They had to.

CHAPTER 2

"**DON'T BE LATE** to my class again," Mrs. Winifred balked. She sat behind a desk, scowling, and pointed at me with her cane. This was my first time being late for her class, but I was late for my Intro to Biology class last week.

"I-I'm sorry," I stammered. I rushed into the auditorium, thirty minutes after it started, and felt the weight of the heavy book I just bought for this very class. The damn thing cost me one-hundred twenty dollars. I did a double take when they rang me up at the bookstore. Surely this book could not be over a hundred bucks.

It was.

I had no money left for the week.

Rushing from the bookstore, I missed the first shuttle back to campus and had to wait for the second. Much to my chagrin, Mrs. Winifred noticed.

"Excuse me—I'm sorry," I whispered, scutching and squeezing past everyone. I plopped down in a corner of the nosebleed section of the room.

Mrs. Winifred kept her eyes on me with an icy glare. "And if any of you are thinking about going to homecoming and

not finishing my ten-page paper, you've got another thing coming," Mrs. Winifred rolled her eyes. She leaned back in her seat like we were annoying her and slammed her hands down on the desk.

'Who does she think she's talking to?' Mom's voice came through in my head loud and clear. Mom had been visiting me in my head right along with the other voices for the past year, and now that I was in college—she showed no signs of slowing down.

"Mrs. Winifred, we have other classes too, not just yours," a girl in the front of the class complained. I couldn't see her from my vantage point, way up in the we-are-late-to-class section of misfits, but I heard her voice crack. She sounded unsure of herself and if I had learned nothing about Mrs. Winifred in the past few weeks—unsure was one thing you couldn't be with her.

"You want to be writers, don't you? You want to be taken seriously, right?" Mrs. Winifred raised her voice to make sure I could hear from my seat. "Those other classes will help you with your writing, but this one—this one will help you see the story. So, no darling, you are incorrect. In my mind, this *is* the only class you have."

I checked my watch and rubbed my eyes. This was going to be a long class, and I was already exhausted.

'Get some sleep Indy, we can stay up later.'

'No Indy, you stay awake, you can't sleep in class!'

The voices came through hushed and in distress. I wished they gave me some space and didn't bother me while I was supposed to be concentrating, but no, they were arguing.

I sighed.

Last night I stayed up late, and I made a pros and cons list like all those mainstream magazines say you should do. If I told someone about the voices, I'd have to tell them about Jaxon. I'd have to tell them the whole story.

I also thought about medication. I had little experience with meds, but since I read about it in the pamphlet I picked up from the Wellness Center, maybe that could help. A couple years ago when Grandpa Ez was having trouble sleeping, Mama Jackie took him to a doctor who put him on something. For a moment in time, Ez was not Ez. He was moody and mean. He was a zombie, and he moved throughout the house with drool hanging from his lips. You know that white stuff old people have at the corner of their mouth? Ez had that too. Mama Jackie took those pills and flushed them down the toilet and a few days later, Grandpa Ez was back to normal. I didn't want to be like that. Like... like a zombie. Taking the first appointment they had available, I was supposed to meet with a woman named Jill tomorrow.

Jill.

Sounded decent enough. She was probably white; I didn't know any Black girls named Jill. At home, I didn't have insurance. Now, since I was a student, I had health insurance, food, and really—a future. I wasn't sure if I was going to tell the truth about hearing the voices, or maybe I would wait and get to know this Jill better. I wasn't telling her about Jaxon. They locked people away for stuff like that—word to my mother. No, we wouldn't talk about Jaxon.

When I returned to my dorm room, minutes turned into hours and before I knew it, it was time for my Freshman Seminar class. I yawned and wondered if I should skip tonight. I hadn't missed a session yet, and all we ever talked about was how to be successful in college. The microwave dinged as Theodora showed me how to make her famous Nigerian jollof rice with a few oodles and noodles packets, jasmine rice, and some herbs she kept in a bag gathered from the campus center.

One missed class couldn't hurt.

When I awoke the next morning, the sun shined through our dorm window, which could be described as a cinderblock cell. Theodora and I tried decorating. She hung string lights, while I hung my Meg Thee Stallion poster because, well—Meg was life. A Tiwa Savage poster rested across Theodora's bed. The walls in the old building sweat when the heat was too high and the posters slid down the slick walls. It seemed to happen at night, and the loud smack of the laminated pictures hitting the floor made me jump in bed. The space we shared was a square. When we moved the furniture around to see how it would look, we ended up keeping it the way it was originally with our twin beds directly across from each other.

Theodora stirred when I stretched, and my bones cracked. I glanced at my phone, and it was at three percent, and I forgot to set my alarm. Searching for my charger, I found it right next to my phone and where it was supposed to be. I was too tipsy last night with Theodora; I couldn't even put my phone on the charger, even though I was right next to it. I had to shake my head at my damn self.

"What time is it?" Theodora croaked. Her voice was raspy first thing in the morning.

"It's late. I missed my first class." I jumped up, searching for my clothes.

"Did we finish the entire bottle of wine last night?"

"Yes, we did," I chuckled.

"You brought it in. I told you I'm a lightweight," Theodora threw her hands up in defense.

"Don't you have class too, Ms. Pre-Med." I tossed her Titus sweater over to her side of the room then I threw the leftover rice and empty wine bottle into the trash. Pulling my chunky braids into a low bun on top of my head, I searched for a toothbrush to lay my edges.

"Yes, Ms. Pre-Med has missed class, so sue me." Theodora fell back onto the bed and covered her face in her fluffy, pink pillow. Theodora's parents rode her hard and she was expected to be the doctor of the family. I'm not sure she had a choice, but she did as she was asked. With our families planning to visit for homecoming, Theodora barely mentioned hers while I gushed about Ez.

"Where is your family staying when they come?" I moved around the room, clearing a pathway to the door.

"They got a hotel right outside of town, thankfully. It's at least ten of them coming," she groaned.

"I'd love to have a big family like that," I admitted. It had been me, Sidney, and Dad for so long that I forgot what a regular family looked like. Not with a strange grandfather and a mom locked away in an insane asylum.

Theodora's face fell, and she relaxed her shoulders. "I love them. They're great. I'm not complaining..." She shook her head and looked like she wanted to say more.

"Girl, get up, let's go, crazy." I kicked a few socks and empty soda cans. Theodora and I rushed to get dressed. I had just enough time to grab lunch before my next class and then my work-study gig this afternoon.

The dining-hall was packed and everyone was buzzing around us. The salad line was jumping and the dining-hall workers behind the glass swirled enormous bowls of lettuce. The burger line was just as long on the other side of the hall and next to that sat tacos, spaghetti, fried chicken, and sushi. Titus was notorious for not having all the grills working at the same time, like McDonald's and their ice cream machine situation, but they were running at full speed today.

JANAY HARDEN

Everyone around me was fresh-faced with loads of energy. My face felt puffy from just waking up, and I was still foggy from the wine.

"It's so bright," Theodora whispered. She wore large sunglasses to cover her red eyes and a fleece sweatsuit. We stood in the center of the hall in a stupor, taking in all the sights and sounds around us.

Through my sunglasses, I saw a familiar face and my eyes bulged out of my head. He soared above the pack. He wore a Titus University tracksuit, and he was walking toward us, gliding through the crowd with his eyes on me and Theodora. His face reminded me of Tom Brady: calm, patient, and ready to pounce. *What the hell is going on?*

"Shit, here comes my track coach!" Theodora shifted and took off her sunglasses. Her eyes were bloodshot red. She smoothed her hair and fidgeted with her sweater.

Her track coach? Mr. Chestnut was Theodora's track coach?

"Ms. Nkosi, how are we today?" Mr. Chestnut nodded. He looked Theodora up and down, doing a double take before his eyes landed on me.

"Mr. Chestnut." I swallowed, returning his gawk.

A familiar smile flashed across his face. Mr. Chestnut was the track coach at my old high school. He was notorious for messing with the female students and he seemed to get away with it. One of the students was my friend, Joya. He got her pregnant and left her to figure it out. How or why was he here though? His haircut was shorter than I remembered, and it was dyed deep brown. I didn't know grown men dyed their hair, unless they were trying to become a different person. Isn't that why everyone dyed their hair?

"Please, help me? I remember your face, but I'm terrible with names," he asked.

SOMEONE MORE LIKE MYSELF

I opened my mouth to speak and before words came out, Theodora said, "this is my roommate, Indigo. You know each other?"

"He was the track coach at my high school... But what are you doing here?" I frowned.

"Opportunity knocks," he smiled. "A position opened here, and I've wanted to train at the collegiate level. So, I'm here. I didn't know you were a student."

Why would he know? Mr. Chestnut kept a tight leash on the girls he trained, and now he had fresh meat—at the collegiate level. How lucky for him. I stared at Theodora, and she was gawking at Mr. Chestnut with a dazzling, flirty smile. I hoped she wasn't falling for his bullshit but from the dreamy look on her face, she already had.

I ogled him with less dazzle and more disgust. We clearly didn't see the same person.

"Well, I'll let you ladies get back to your lunch, Theodora. I'll see you later for practice."

"Yes, Mr. Chestnut." Theodora's eyes grazed his backside when he walked away.

"Yes, Mr. Chestnut," I mocked. Theodora shoved my shoulder.

When I decided what I wanted to eat, I darted toward the burger bar when I felt a cold wetness run down my back. "What the hell?" I swung around. The same set of light brown eyes and skin that almost ran me over at the campus center spilled a milkshake on me. "You again!" I spewed. It was like time stopped and everything moved in slow motion.

'Punch him in his face Indy!'

'Don't let him get away with it!'

'Make him respect you!'

The voices were coming in fast, but when I looked around, they came from no one.

Theodora's eyes were wide with concern. "Chaquille! What is your problem?" She hissed.

"Oh, my bad, I didn't see ya'll standing there. My fault."

"How many times is it your bad, Chaquille—damn!" I grabbed tons of napkins from the concession stand behind us. I patted the wet spots where Chaquille's chocolate shake doused my sweater, but it just spread the mess. He must've had the biggest sized shake he could get, and he spilled most of it on me.

"Well, you were standing in the middle of the aisle. What was I supposed to do?" Chaquille's voice rose, and he slapped his hands together as he talked.

"Indy, are you okay?" I heard from behind.

Naomi.

I spun around, and Naomi's eyes widened as she looked me up and down covered in chocolate. The surrounding people were stopping and laughing. Some of them took out their phones, and I saw the flash from cameras. They were laughing; they were all laughing at me.

'Run Indy, leave this place!'

'College isn't for you!'

"I really didn't mean that. My fault, I didn't see you." Chaquille locked eyes with mine. He seemed sincere, but damn this was the second time. Naomi and Theodora formed a small circle around me to shield people from recording. "I'm sorry. I-I- I got to do better at uh, playing around and watching where I'm going." Chaquille's cheeks were red.

"Whatever, Chaquille." Theodora grabbed my shoulder and pushed past him. She rolled her eyes in his direction over the top of her sunglasses.

"Not cool, not cool at all." Naomi shook her head at Chaquille and wagged her finger in his face.

My head was low when we headed back to our dorm room to change my clothes. After I showered and checked my watch, I fumed. I would be late for work-study at the theater.

Naomi and Theodora made sure I was okay before they left for class. I sat down at my desk, where my opened computer stared back at me. There was no point in going to work late, and I was already in a bad mood. I had to write a short story for Mrs. Winifred's class, anyway.

When I received my research paper grade, I was blown away when I saw a large, red, *C* written. A *C*?! When words were so near and dear to my heart? I told Naomi and Theodora how I was the editor of my high school newspaper, and I was kind of a big deal. Here I was, pulling a C in English Lit 101! I was a small fish in a big pond in college. With weeks under my belt, I had to try harder.

Days ago, I visited Titus' art gallery alone to get a feel for the place. One artist created a painting of Audre Lorde's poem, *A Woman Speaks*. The artist took the composition and drew the poem in cursive, starting in the corners of the square canvas. He drew the words vertically from the bottom in red, and then he swapped out the red for green and drew horizontally. He drew the top with a black paint brush. Shades of red, green, and black formed a square until the center filled in and the artist wrote:

Our blood.

Our money and resources lost.

Our skin.

That's what he wrote in the center of the square in red letters. The red paint was bold against the white canvas, and it dripped down into the center, resembling blood. I was taken by the painting, and I craned my neck to read every word. I had read Audre Lorde before and liked most of her pieces.

Not this one though—this one I had never heard. The words swirled in my mind and read like a song. She was the catalyst for my short-story. Her spiciness and sharp tongue jarred me. She talked about men in a way that made me proud to be a woman and nothing else. If she could talk like that and not feel bad about it, well I could too. Thinking about the red paint made my stomach jump. Parts of me ached to kill again and those thoughts also kept me up at night.

I wrote for about an hour before I looked at my clock. I realized I didn't grab my mail from the student center downstairs. They were about to close, and I was expecting a letter from Mom. I slipped into my Crocs and when I flung my door open, Mr. Chestnut stood before me with his knuckles up, ready to knock.

I glared up at him. "Can I help you?" *How did he even know where my room was?*

"Indigo. Indigo Lewis," he said my name and stared at me, not waiting for a response. "I'm the new dormitory representative in addition to track coach, which you're already aware. I just wanted to come and say hello. I am here to help with any dormitory needs that you may have." He tucked his hands into his pockets.

"How can I help you?" I asked again. I said it really snooty, not a hint of honey in my words. *And what the hell happened to Mr. Bill, our current rep?*

Mr. Chestnut focused his gaze at me and broke into a half smile. I shifted my weight to another leg and cowered under his stare. "Listen, Tunica Rivers is home for the both of us. Titus is also now home for the both of us. Whatever you think I've done and whatever rumors you may have heard from back home are false. The previous rep stepped down. Actually, both of the reps stepped down some time ago and they asked me to take on the position. I recently accepted, so here we are.

Again, I just wanted to come and officially introduce myself. I hope we don't have any problems. I know how you college girls can get," he gave a chuckle.

"Excuse me?" I croaked. *How us college girls could get?*

'He's next on the list, Indy!' Mom shouted in my mind while I gritted my teeth.

And with that, Mr. Chestnut flashed a million-dollar, bullshit grin. His pearly, white teeth were long and too large for his mouth. If you stared hard enough, you could see the lies behind the smile, at least I could. "You have a good evening, Ms. Lewis, and do tell Ms. Nwosi I stopped by and said hello."

"Whatever," I mustered.

I hoped he didn't hear my voice cracking or my heart beating because I surely felt it pounding through my shirt. How could he be here? In my space? This was my safe place and he easily gained access like it was nothing. Women were never safe from men. One way or the other, our safety was inevitably—ours.

'Are you lying to yourself again, girl?' Mom's shrill voice pierced through my thoughts. I rested my head on the back of my door. *'You know what we need to do, Indy. He's a lot smarter than Jaxon was.'*

My hands shook as I locked the door and sat back at my desk, staring into space. I would have to get the mail later after my stomach wasn't in knots.

CHAPTER 3

THE TITUS UNIVERSITY Wellness Center was tucked away at the far end of campus. The free STD Clinic was on the third floor, mental health on the second, and the police station on the first, go figure. I wore a large, fuzzy turtleneck which covered my chin and cheeks. Even though it wasn't cold, I looked cute paired with my gold hoop earrings. I dabbed a little gloss on my lips. I wanted to look nice, so they didn't think I was crazy. Strange things happened in my mind, but I could at least look decent.

Today was the day I met Jill—my new therapist. I Googled what to do during a first session, so I knew she was probably going to ask a bunch of questions. When my dad told me Mom had schizophrenia, it made sense to me. She had killed a man, ran him smooth over with her car. When I first heard the voices, her voice in particular, my fingers tingled. She was undoubtedly with me, even though I knew better, and *this* wasn't normal. Hearing voices, being angry at the dumbest things, wasn't normal. Maybe I was just used to it, but I would damn sure fight against it and do everything I could to make myself better. I wanted to be a writer. Maybe even have my own magazine one day. I wanted to visit Dad, Sidney, and Ez on the weekends and then go home to my penthouse apartment in the big city. Eat delicious foods and go to yoga classes Saturday mornings. I wanted to be loved. Be in love. Being a killer wasn't in my plans, but here I was anyway. *Trochesse: Home for the Criminally Insane* couldn't be in my future.

I walked down the long hallway and was met with posters telling me I had options if I didn't want to keep my baby, and another poster that said mental health matters. I wrote my name down at the front desk before taking a seat in the waiting room. The Wellness Center had a pleasant view of the campus from its corner point. I could see our dorm, most of my classrooms and the campus center from this high up.

"Ms. Indigo Lewis?" a woman asked.

I turned around and eyed a middle-aged, white woman. "I'm Jill Rambone." She extended her hand.

Now that Jill was in front of me, I gripped the sides of the chair and wanted to make a dash for the door. I chewed my gum harder. "Hi-Hi," I stammered and followed her to her office.

"Take a seat anywhere you're comfortable." Jill motioned to a couch and a lounge chair.

I opted for the couch, which was the furthest seat from where was sitting. Nothing against her, but if the voices showed up while we were talking... well, I was looking out for her.

"Give me one second to pull your chart." Jill clicked on her computer.

I took in Jill's office. It was light purple with shades of grey. Everything on her desk matched from her pencil holders, file cabinets, and wall accents. Jill's walls were lined with pictures of women with their arms stretched to the skies that said, *"God will make a way,"* and *"pray to him."*

"Okay, got it." Jill stopped clicking, and I heard the printer in her office rumble awake. "So, what brings you in?"

JANAY HARDEN

I swallowed and twirled a braid in my hand. My mind wandered to everything but her question. I wished I sprayed my scalp this morning. It felt dry as I scratched it and looked away from Jill. I wondered what grade I got on my biology test. Theodora and I stayed up late studying equations. I snooped down at Jill's pictures on her desk and noticed all the frames were different. They looked expensive and personal. Jill and a few other women stood together, grinning away. Their undereye concealer shone under the flash of the camera and didn't cover their raccoon eyes. They looked happy, not a care in the world. I bet none of them had mental health issues.

"Sometimes, I...feel things."

"So, you're depressed," Jill nodded. She grabbed a clipboard and began writing.

"No, it's more than depression...I..."

"It could also be anxiety; you know that's common in college students."

"It's more than anxiety too...my thoughts..."

Jill's shrilling office phone rang out, interrupting my thoughts. I jumped in my seat and felt a prickle at the back of my neck.

"One moment, Ms. Lewis." Jill held up a finger to me and she answered the phone. "I'm not sure, that's not my client. I don't have access to that file. You have to check with billing, they handle those things," Jill gave a high-pitched laugh and smiled into the phone before hanging up. "Sorry about that, Ms. Lewis. You were saying you are anxious?"

I gulped before continuing. "I feel different all the time. And my mom, she has these issues too, it's hard to talk about because—"

"You know, depression runs in families sometimes. How about this, we can bring your mom in for a future session?

SOMEONE MORE LIKE MYSELF

You know, the last time I had a family session, I think it went well. And I've done it with my family and children too."

If I can just get a word in! My God this lady can talk. "That's nice, Jill. No, my mom can't come to a session. I have to do this on my own."

"Independent woman. I like that, Ms. Lewis. Tell me, is your dad in your life. Do you know who that is?"

"What?" I frowned.

"Oh, I'm sorry. I didn't mean to offend. I just assumed you lived with your mom since you mentioned her."

I took a deep breath, and my ears began to ring. "Yes, I know who my father is." Jill scribbled in her book, and I winced. *What is she writing?*

"Okay, that's good. And any issues there?"

"No, no issues." I shifted in my seat. I stared at the pictures on her desk, wishing the time passed by.

"Any drugs, alcohol. Have you ever been sexually abused?"

My throat was tight, and I choked back a cough. "No, none of that. That's not really why I'm here, I have these thoughts and—"

"I understand, Ms. Lewis. Let's get through the intake first, and then we can get to the good stuff. And look on the bright side, this is the easy part." She gave a forced smile before her eyes darted to the clock above my head that I peeped on the way in.

Jill's phone rang again, and this time she answered it without raising a finger to ask me to hold on. Remnants of the same conversation as before were recycled and I shrunk into my seat. When she gave her last laugh on the call and hung up, I was on autopilot answering yes and no to every question she asked. My baby hair was lifting under my edge control because my temple was damp with sweat.

I got this one so wrong. I was so wrong about therapy.

JANAY HARDEN

    I walked back to my room in a daze, replaying the conversation in my mind. I left her office with a headache and upset stomach. I knew I would have to deal with the voices in my head on my own. If my interaction with Jill was any sign of therapy, well, I wanted no parts of it. Did she stand in my way of addressing the voices, or did I stand in my own way?

CHAPTER 4

MY INDY LINDY! *Have you attempted to make contact with me, my dear daughter? If you twist my arm, I am remiss to tell you I have been placed in confinement. They attempt to control my body, thoughts, and emotions by placing restrictions on who I talk to and for how long. They want me to suffer. I have to be careful about what I say in my letters, they're listening to everything these days.*

How is the weather? This is my first time out in about one month, so you should now be one month as a college girl at Titus, right fresh meat? Don't you go gaining no Freshman 15. Your curves is perfect, girl, shaped just like your Mama Jackie. You keep 'em that way as long as you can. Are you having sex in that college? I know what goes on in those dorm rooms, girl.

When they locked me in confinement, all I thought about was Ez. Did I ever tell you that Ez used to make candles? Strange right? One day a lady came to our house, and she was selling homemade candles. Ez just about fell in love with the scents and different colors, and the names of them. He would smell one and say, "this one here smells like Tunica Rivers when the ground thaws and the trees is shaking the cold off of 'em." I laughed and thought, you can't name a candle that. It was strange but he loved it. He would stay outside in the cold and in the heat,

stirring a large pot of wax next to the boathouse. Ez wasn't all bad, Indy. He really wasn't. He put up with me, didn't he? And I gave him grief. You should give a man grief in your life, Indy, at least just once. Don't let your dad make you think Ez is bad. You see where he allowed them to put me. What might he do to Ez?

Love you my oldest child,
Mom

"Too slow!" Naomi snatched the last French fry off my tray.

We were in the dining-hall eating lunch. My morning class was a breeze, now that I made sure my alarm was set before I went to sleep the night before. After reading Mom's letter my appetite quickly dissipated. Theodora was across from me, but she looked to be in an intense conversation with a guy at the table behind her. They were leaned in close, whispering. Theodora's long flowing weave hung down her back and swayed effortlessly when she tilted her head and smiled. Naomi was eating fried chicken wings and the last of my French fries. Her hair was pulled into her signature low ponytail and her gold earrings said *Omi*.

"You can have them." I pushed my tray toward her.

"What did she say?" Naomi asked.

I dropped my shoulders. When Naomi asked about my mom months ago, I didn't hold back. I told her they locked her away in Trochesse. Naomi asked why, and again—I told the truth. She killed a man. I waited for Naomi to walk out. To leave and go back to the fifth floor and not return. Who wanted to be friends with the killer's daughter? Mom was suffering from schizophrenia and Dad failed to tell me and Sidney until it was too late. Mom liked talking in an English accent, and that's exactly how I read her letter. My temples got hot. What I didn't know about my family meant I didn't know about myself. I didn't know what I didn't know, and I didn't like that.

"Nothing. She's just her usual self." And that was the truth. Mom was her usual self, and she was usually all over the damn place.

"Fascinating." Naomi's eye twinkled. When I was honest with Naomi about my mom, she didn't leave or walk away. She said she was thinking about switching her major to Psychology and she'd love to meet my mom.

Go figure.

"So, you know I'm coming for winter break, right?" Naomi nodded.

"I'm coming too," Theodora chimed in. She finally turned around from her friend.

They thought it would be cool to visit me in Tunica Rivers for a few days. With Homecoming this weekend, the next event was winter break and we were already making plans. A whole month off from school; what a treat! If I was back in high school I would've thought that was way too much time off, but with college kicking my ass these days; I welcomed all four weeks.

"You know your parents are not letting their precious Theodora skip the holidays to go hang out with her friends," Naomi teased.

"I'll have to come up with something, but I wouldn't count it out," Theodora said with a slight smile. She spent many days on the phone debating with her parents about the choices of her life.

Theodora was excited at the thought. "I've never been further than Titus University. You live in the south south. Are there ghosts?" Her eyes danced.

Naomi was more interested in Mom. "Can we go see her? I'd love to pick her brain."

I wouldn't be planning *any* visits to Trochesse with them, but I did plan to see Mom. Showing my girls Tunica Rivers and where I came from could help me open my heart and take a step in the right direction. I was still salty about little miss Jill. Maybe my expectations were too high; I don't know.

I folded Mom's letter and put it back in my pocket. I spotted Chaquille's frame in my peripheral. Someone was throwing a football, and he was diving through the air trying to catch it. In the dining-hall, at that. He caught the ball then turned to me and smiled. I rolled my eyes and turned to my friends. "What time do your next class?"

"Mine is later. I have nothing on the schedule right now," Naomi tossed her food in the trash.

"I'm heading out. I'm going to walk with Dylan." Theodora pointed to the boy behind her.

"I have to get to the theater." I added.

I had officially been to work-study once, and that was only to complete tax forms. I *had* to make an appearance today. The last time I worked at a job, it ended with Jaxon being cremated before he was dead. I pushed those thoughts out of my head even though my heart started beating faster. I mapped out my afternoon the night before and I even bought a calendar. In college, there was no school bell ringing telling me where to go. In college, I had to *know* things. Like how to study and when. Submitting assignments with little to no reminders. All the high school things I took for granted. Here, I had to be on my game.

"I'll catch you guys later," I said, clearing my space and grabbing my bag. The theater awaited.

"In-dee-goh!" the woman read from the paper.

I blinked. It wasn't that hard.

"Indigo. But they call me Indy."

"Indy," she repeated. "Are you from Indiana? I've been to Indy, honey, it's not that great." She leaned in with a smirk, like we shared some forbidden secret.

"What's been taking you so long? I've been holding your work-study file open for as long as I could." I inspected her desk where she sat. Her name tag read: **Harper O'Sullivan**.

"Huh?" I knitted my brows.

"You were supposed to sign your work-study contract two weeks ago. You only came in that one time, and I tried to call and email you. You didn't get my messages? Anyway, the bosses wanted to let you go, but I kept putting your file at the bottom so they would skip it. They wanted to fill your position and report you to the Financial Aid Office for job abandonment."

I groaned and tapped my foot, kicking myself for not planning for college better. But wait—why was Harper O'Sullivan helping me? I glanced her over. She was an olive-skinned older woman with unruly hair stopping at her chin. Her bangs fell over her eyes, and she shook them out of her sight when she talked. She wore an oversized men's blazer cuffed at the elbows, blue jeans, and penny loafer shoes. She attached a pin to her blazer that read, "Stamp out Karens."

"Why did you hold my file?" I inquired.

"Because, girl," Harper huffed and rubbed her eyelid like the answer was clear. "Every year we take part in the Libra Festival and we're pretty good, if I say so myself." Harper's eyes danced with delight as she leaned in. "I told Rita and them, I said, '*Rita, we only win the big prize when the tables are balanced. We have two girls and two boys on the team this time.*'"

"Two boys and two girls on the team?" My stomach fluttered.

JANAY HARDEN

"Yes, you work-study kids. When we have two boys, and two girls, then we win the big prize." Harper wrung her hands and thrust her chest out. Her large breasts shook from side to side, and she looked like she liked it that way. "Last year we had all boys. It was a snooze fest. We came in dead last at the festival. The year before that, we had all girls. That one almost drove me to drink." Harper held her palm up to me and closed her eyes. "That's the year we don't speak of. This year we got lucky. You are the fourth crew member. We already have two boys, one girl, and now you. They were going to request another candidate, but I did my part and saved the day, per usual." Harper tilted her head back and tossed her hair out of her face, not hiding her smirk.

"What's the big prize?"

"Bragging rights, girl! And you kids get your pick of the nicer dorm rooms next year."

"You did that for me?" I blinked.

"Did I tell you my name, honey? I'm Harper O'Sullivan, and I've been working at this theater for ten something years. I lost track because one of them years I threw my back out and was gone for months while I took myself an FMLA vacation." Harper leaned back in her chair and clapped her hands. She looked around like someone heard her. "If I didn't learn something in these ten years, it's that we need a balanced team to win. And besides, I don't want to work with all boys or all girls. You balance us, but you just don't know it yet." She waved her hand in front of her face. "You're here and that's all water under the bridge. Time for you to fill out this paperwork so we can officially get you on payroll. You'll have to do orientation again since you missed that the first session." Harper pulled her glasses up from the long lanyard around her neck. Her voice changed and became professional as she discussed tax codes, all kinds of different W-2 forms, and work hours.

"What will your work hours be?" Harper asked.

Tapping my pen against the clipboard, I narrowed my eyes. "I'm not sure. I have to talk to Theodora. Oh, that's my roommate. And Naomi, I have to check their schedules in case they have something planned." Before I could even mention my actual classes, Harper scowled.

"Honey, I thought you was here to get the education—not to follow these other people you just met."

My toes curled in my shoes. What was I really doing? I hadn't been here in weeks. My student refund check was running out from buying these expensive ass textbooks. Harper was right, I had to buckle down and do what I came here to do. I was about my money, and I couldn't fall off my game in college. My penthouse in the city was calling my name.

"Let's see your class schedule." Harper studied her computer screen, while I pitied myself.

"Here. You have classes three days a week, so how about we schedule work two days per week?"

"I guess that works." I nodded. Harper slid from around her desk to stand and I could see she was a shapely older woman. She looked to be in her fifties. She was medium build, and she wore more pins and buttons attached to a crossbody purse around her waist. And she was dragging that wagon!

I had met Ms. Harper O'Sullivan for all of five minutes, and her giddiness tickled me.

"This is how things work around here. You and the crew have important jobs. When the actors are on stage; they are performing and creating art. I like to think they are the painters. But us, us little people behind the scenes make it happen. The painters need paint, right? And all their materials? And inspiration? And guidance? That's where we come in. We're the actors behind the curtains." Harper sat close to me on the bench. I could smell the coffee and a hint of something

stronger on her breath. She's probably told this story a million times, but her eyes still lit up like it was the first.

"So, it's our job to make them shine?" I lamented.

"Yes, but not in a bad way."

"I don't think it's a bad way." I shuffled on the bench. "I don't mind playing in the background. Fewer eyes on me."

"Well, honey, with a face like that I'd make sure the world sees what I have to offer."

I blushed. I got my hair done in my signature long braids to my waist the day before. Theodora and I stayed up all night while she braided. I was wearing my black fleece jacket; it was long and came down to my knees. In my ears were pearl studs, and around my neck was my locket of Mom. I looked cute today.

"She ain't all that," I heard a male voice say.

My neck whipped up in a flash and Chaquille stood in front of me, smirking. He was standing next to another girl and guy, peering at Harper and I before they turned away and disappeared behind Harper's desk. My cheeks were red all over again, but now from the tightness that had formed in my jaw. I ungritted my teeth.

"Don't mind him, that's our Chaquille. He's our other stagehand. That's also June and Fredo, the other soon to be Libra Festival winners and stagehands!" Harper beamed.

"He works here too?" My eyebrows raised, not paying attention to June or Fredo.

"Yes, this is his second year."

My mouth dropped open before I quickly closed it. I had to work with this tool.

Chaquille, Fredo, and June disappeared in the back, and I grimaced.

"Ohh, is there something we should know?" Harper's eyes widened.

I didn't want to become the next talk of the town and besides, Chaquille had apologized. There really was nothing to say. "No, there's nothing you should know. "And what exactly do we do at this Libra Festival?"

Harper clapped her hands and poked her chest out again. "Good." She smiled. "Now, the Libra Festival. We compete against other colleges in the southern states. It's kind of like ComiCon for the theater arts program. We are judged on the quickest set turnaround time, make-up and costume application, and breaking down the stage."

'Opening and closing the curtains, Indy. Just like your dad said,' Mom cackled in my head.

Harper continued. "Next order of business... Rita. Our fearless leader and supervisor," Harper slowly released a deep breath. "Our Rita is an acquired taste..."

Harper spent the next hour teaching me how to figure out what type of mood Rita was in by the way she jingled her keys in the morning, but I half listened. I thought about the mounds of homework I still had to do and now, speculated about working Chaquille.

CHAPTER 5

"MS. INDIGO LEWIS?" a man asked.

I recognized the voice but couldn't place it. Racing from my dorm to the theater for work was my focus this morning. I forgot to set my alarm and was running late, per the usual. I just couldn't bring myself to wake up on time and be everywhere I was required to be.

"Yes?" I spun around and zipped my jacket. I flipped my head over and put my braids up in a messy bun on top of my head when I saw who the man behind the voice belonged to.

Khalil Jamison.

He was the officer from Tunica Rivers who was investigating Jaxon Green's murder. He showed up to our over the summer when I was seventeen and still needed a parent present. I was eighteen now, and he knew it. What was he doing here? Hours away? Did he know something? I cleared my throat.

"I'm not sure if you remember me or not, but I came to your house last summer and spoke to you and your dad about Jaxon Green."

Jamison waited for my response, and I gave him none. He continued. "I hope I can speak to you again regarding newly found information."

"I have to get to work," I sputtered. My stomach was suddenly in knots. I began the short walk to the theater without waiting for him to say or do anything else. I was hoping he would go away, but he didn't.

"Well, I'll walk with you. I can use the exercise," he said with a half-smile. I picked up my speed and pulled my jacket drawstrings tighter around my neck.

"What do you want to know?" I asked. "You could've just called." The lump sat at the base of my throat and hardly let me speak. Jamison took out a small notebook where he kept all his secrets and a tiny pen. I wondered if they were taught to keep a notebook and pen to catch people in their lies in cop-school.

'He won't catch anyone, Indy. Don't worry—we got this one,' the voices in my head said.

I almost smiled. They didn't play about me, but he would find out.

"When was the last time you actually saw Mr. Jaxon Green?"

Even though I answered this question for him before, I thought back; I knew exactly when I had seen him. I stuffed him into Shelby, the incinerator at the funeral home where I worked last year. They searched for him for months. They were still searching for him. Hence, Jamison's appearance. Over the summer I ran across flyers his parents had plastered everywhere. They were offering a cash reward for any information.

My jaw twitched and I worked to keep a straight face next to Jamison. I would be lying if I didn't think of ways I could feed them information, receive the cash reward, and *not* go to jail. Seemed like too much to think about when college was already taking a beating to my time. But still, I let the thoughts play in my mind. Did I feel bad about it? I wasn't sure. I killed someone; I took a life, and that conclusion left

me with a shivery feeling all over, and a pain—a pain in my chest that wouldn't go away.

When Theodora, Naomi, and I were hanging out in our room the night before, we had a great time, but something in the back of my mind turned to Jaxon. What had I done? Did I have legit reasons? I believed I did. He used those pictures to blackmail me. For months, I wrote all his papers to help him graduate from high school because he couldn't read, and his rich parents would rather cover up the issue instead of addressing it. He took advantage and tried to force me to do the same for him in college. When I had asked about money, he baulked at me. I spent my last dime scraping money together for application fees, while my dad slaved at the retirement home. Yet, the opportunity was so easily given to Jaxon.

He owed me money.

He used me—with money.

Jaxon had cut my hair. This mofo took scissors when I was drunk and snipped off a few of my braids. I was mindful of my drinking since that night. My hair still hasn't fully grown back in that spot. I also didn't like the way he looked at me. Like I was naked, and he was imagining all the things he could do when he thought he had me over a barrel with the pictures. He was not Thomas Jefferson, and I was not Sally Hemings. I grumbled when I thought about the tough time I was having adjusting to college life, and how harder it would be if I agreed to extend our little arrangement beyond high school, had I not killed Jaxon.

I did what I had to do when I had no other options.

"Ms. Lewis?" Jamison raised an eyebrow.

I came to and realized I had been walking to the theater without speaking. "I guess the last time I saw him was our high school graduation."

"Yes, you guys graduated the night before. I guess what I really want to know is about these?" Jamison pulled out two Polaroid photos, and before he turned them toward me, I already knew what they were. "Care to discuss?"

Me. They were pictures of me, and this was the real reason Jamison came all this way to see. Jaxon had used those pictures to blackmail me. As I took the photos from Jamison, I thought back to the last time I saw them sitting in Jaxon's car when he brandished them on his phone. I remembered his smirk when he realized he had me. In the first photo, I was wrapped around the toilet with vomit on my shirt and around my mouth. In the second photo, Jaxon was standing over top of me with a pair of scissors, either he already cut my hair, or he was about to.

I was also topless.

My eyes darkened as I passed them back to Jamison with a shaky hand and heavy heart. "Those are from Spring Fling, the senior party before graduation," I managed to say. I felt faint when we reached the theater.

"So, this isn't your first time seeing these photos? Ms. Lewis, when was the first time you saw these pictures? And why would Jaxon have them?"

Jamison scribbled fast in his little notebook and shot out questions. I wanted to snatch it from him and rip it to shreds. My ears started ringing as I bit the inside of my cheek. It reminded me of Jill and her writing when I tried to share my shame. My eye jumped, and I heard laughter over Jamison's shoulder. Scanning over him, Chaquille was walking up with his headphones in and rapping along the way.

"I have to go to work. Is there anything else you need from me?"

"You didn't answer my questions." He cleared his throat. "Why would Jaxon have these pictures of you?"

'*Because he was an asshole, and he was going to hurt our Indy, that's why,*' a voice in my head exclaimed.

'*Keep calm, Indy, remember what you did. They will never find Jaxon, and nothing connects to you. Don't let him scare you. Keep calm,*' another voice said. This one was softer and spoke in a lower tone.

I relaxed my face and swallowed away the flutters in my stomach. "It was just a party." I smiled. "Just a couple of teenagers having one last fling before all of this." I waved my hands around. Chaquille walked past us and nodded at me before he stole a glance at Jamison. I was a Black girl talking to a cop first thing in the morning. I didn't want the eyes on me. That was the good thing about being away from home; I could create a new Indigo. How could I do that if Jamison was showing up randomly, asking questions about things I was trying hard to forget?

"One last question, Ms. Lewis. Did you and Mr. Green date? Have any relations? I'm just curious as to why he would have these pictures of you, share them with his friends, and you don't seem surprised?"

I felt like I had been gut punched. *Sharing with his friends*? So that's how they found the pictures. After I did all that work and agreed to be his school slave in exchange for him keeping the photos private, he did it anyway. My mind raced. Jaxon was exactly where he was supposed to be. He really had it coming.

"I heard about the pictures," I said with a straight face. "I didn't believe it, and when none surfaced after Jaxon . . . I didn't hear anything else about it."

There was no emotion left in me for Jaxon and no need to pretend. But when you're a woman, and you don't pretend to be afraid of a man, it makes them curious about you—and Jamison was curious. The look in his eye and the way he feverishly scratched in his book, told me he was going to fully do his job. Maybe Mom and I would have to discuss him later.

"I thank you for talking with me." Jamison placed his notebook back in his pocket. "I'll see you soon."

"Will you?"

"You will." Jamison gave a small smile. He played the cop role well because I couldn't read anything behind his eyes.

"Did you come here just for me?" I questioned him now.

Jamison touched his chin and narrowed his eyes before responding. "Yes, I did Ms. Lewis. Yes, I did."

CHAPTER 6

"**AND THIS IS** your room?" Ms. Arletha glanced around. She threw her shawl over her shoulder and gasped. Ms. Arletha was tall for a woman and towered over Dad who looked equally perplexed as they shared a look.

"Uh, yes." I cleared my throat.

"And it's just y'all two? No one else?"

"It's just us," I said, biting my lip.

"I like your room, Indy." Sidney bounced from my desk, to my bed, and behind the dresser, peering out of the window.

"How do you open the windows, girl? These legos they call rooms don't even let no air in, girl. Not that you would want this kind of air," Ez boomed. I swear my giant of a grandfather crouched, while standing in my dorm room. I didn't realize how low the ceilings were before. "Can I sit here? Is this clean?"

Blinking rapidly, I couldn't believe my ears. Ez's house looked like an episode straight out of the tv show, *Hoarders*, but he was concerned my dorm room wasn't clean.

"Honey, we were just expecting, I don't know, at least a straight path through from one end of the room to the other?"

SOMEONE MORE LIKE MYSELF

Dad glanced around; his eyebrows furrowed together deep in thought. "And you drank all of this wine?"

I eyeballed my area, taking in everything with a new perspective.

Neither Theodora's nor my bed were made. We lined up the empty wine bottles against the windowsill. I moved them and cracked the window, letting in the cool November air, that Ez didn't want. On the floor sat a few empty chip bags, and lots of Kanekalon hair. Funny with a room full of people with prying eyes and the daylight—the mess illuminated. If it couldn't get any worse, my Meg Thee Stallion poster fell and slammed to the floor with a loud *thwack!* Sidney jumped and grabbed onto Ez. "Let's go, it's spirits in here, ya'll!" Ez yelped. Dad, Ms. Arletha, Sidney, and Ez scurried out of the room.

"We'll wait in the hallway," Ms. Arletha said. "Give you your privacy." She clutched her purse and slammed my door behind her.

"Uh—okay. I'll only be five minutes."

I raced back into my room and grabbed leftover hair off the floor as fast as I could. I made my bed and Theodora's, and emptied the trash, tossing the crinkled chip bags in too. I grabbed some mousse and pressed the lever down as I patted it into my braids, I palmed it until it got that wet and wavy color that I liked. Glimpsing myself in the mirror, I inhaled deeply.

'You got this, Indy!' Mom cheered in my head.

Me and the voices were ready to go.

Moments later, Ez, Dad, Ms. Arletha, and Sidney stood beside me at the campus center, buzzing with activities for homecoming. All the sororities and fraternities were out, stepping and putting on displays for us. There was a marching band playing the school fight song, and I felt the drums deep in my chest, pounding away.

"Yeah, ya'll hear that bass now?" Ms. Arletha swayed. "Come on, baby, dance with me." She grabbed Dad's arm. He tilted his head and smirked at her, letting her lead him as they two-stepped back and forth.

Crowds of people formed a circle around someone break dancing in the center, and all around us were vendor tables, selling everything from life insurance to discounted OnlyFans accounts. More food was grilled, and I watched Ez dart off in the direction of where the smells were wafting from.

"Ez, wait!" I shouted, as Sidney and I chased behind him.

He stopped dead in his tracks and loomed down at us. "SidRock, don't be following me now! You know I don't like people walking up on me, girl. You want me to thump you right between your eyes like this?" Ez put his fingers together and plucked Sidney on her forehead.

Her mouthed formed a surprised O, and she yanked at the back of Ez's jacket and giggled.

"Come on, girl, let's find something to eat." Ez and Sidney walked off together, not even looking back for me. Dad and Ms. Arletha were still two-stepping a few feet away, and I stood there, unsure of what to do or which way to go. People were milling around me, but where was my place? Who was I amongst these people? Had anyone else taken a life? Probably not, but I wondered anyway.

'Indy, do what you want to do, don't overthink everything, my oldest girl. Just walk, put one foot in front of the other. All you need is one percent, every day,' Mom's voice whispered to me. I pulled at my jacket and looked around. Mom's voice was soulful and mixed with love. When she wasn't out of her mind and talking crazy, she had the right words.

Doing what she instructed, I found a nearby table and sat down with a bottle of water I grabbed. I turned around and shared a glance with a familiar face.

SOMEONE MORE LIKE MYSELF

Chaquille Fox.

I sucked my teeth.

"Ayo, what's really good? Seriously. We got started on the wrong foot and I don't know how that happened. I really don't mean you no harm, miss," Chaquille talked with his hands. He dabbed them together after every word while he sat down across from me.

"That's the best you got?"

Chaquille laughed, and his white teeth shined against the sun. He placed his hands in his pockets and leaned in closer. "Word up—my bad. I mean, I'm sorry. I didn't mean to run into you. I don't want you giving me that mean face anymore and making work even more awkward," he giggled, and his shoulders shook. "Actually, let me make it up to you. My guys are having a party this weekend. You and your girls come through if you want. All the drinks on us. Here's my number. I stay in the dorms right next to yours."

"How do you know where my dorm is?"

"Um, all the freshmen stay in the same dorm." Chaquille frowned.

"Oh . . ." I said with more embarrassment than I wished. When I looked closer at Chaquille, I noticed his deep cheek bones and burning eyes. I crossed my legs under the table and squeezed. "So how do you like the theater?" I blurted.

"It's cool. I mean, Rita is a little different. And June and Fredo are weird as hell. But it's quiet and I like that it's connected to the art center. It's pretty dope when no one is there."

I nodded. I did like all the art in the connected studio space. It reminded me of Mom's art gallery back home where some of her artwork was sold to this day. Mom might've been schizophrenic, but she was the most creative woman I know. "You're right about one thing. June and Fredo can be weird.

Last week I caught them in the back trying on some of the costumes making TikTok videos," I giggled.

"See what I mean!" he snickered. "I checked the schedule, looks like me and you are up next to run the practice sequence for the Libra Festival."

This would mean Chaquille, and I would be working alone all week together with no one else there. The thought shot electricity through my veins, and it was a feeling that made me notice how nice looking at his face was.

"What you mean all you got is chicken hotdogs? I don't eat no chicken hotdogs!" I heard Ez say a few tables over.

"I'm sorry, sir, not everyone eats pork or beef so we thought we would meet in the middle with chicken," the boy behind the grill said.

I peeked over Chaquille's shoulder and saw Ez and Sidney. Sidney was eating a cheeseburger and Ez was hovering over an open flame, searching the grill with quizzical eyes.

"I gotta go." I moved around Chaquille and scampered off. "I'll let you know about the party!" I shouted over my shoulder.

"Word up, shorty." Chaquille nodded. When I turned around, he was gazing at me. I bit my lip as I studied his face once more before hustling to Ez.

"Ez!" I yelled. "Over here."

I smelled Booker's BBQ from the next section, and I knew Ez could get himself an old fashion Titus University, Booker made, pork hotdog. At a table across from Booker's, I saw Mr. Chestnut and a girl who ran track. They wore *Titus U* jackets and moved around each other in a connected and relaxed way. Mr. Chestnut placed his hand on the small of the girl's back, and she didn't flinch away. She giggled while checking her phone. Mr. Chestnut's phone dinged, and he took it out of his pocket, smirked, and looked at her.

SOMEONE MORE LIKE MYSELF

They were having a silent flirt party and only they were invited.

A vein twitched in my head, and I balled my fists. Mr. Chestnut was up to his old tricks. When Joya decided to abort his baby in high school, he didn't go with her, nor did he experience the cold, barren room filled with scared teenagers. It was me who sat with her and held her while she cried. Shit, he didn't even stop his behavior. He was doing the same thing I was doing; moving away to start over where no one knew him. I shuddered in disgust and hustled back to Ez, stealing one last glance in their direction. I had to tell Theodora.

When I sent my family back to their hotel later that night and trotted to our dorm, I was met with Theodora's family—and damn, there was a lot of them just like she said there would be. It seemed like they lined us up against the wall and fired shots at us. At least that's what their word assaults felt like. If I thought my family was bad, Theodora's family flamed us as they walked into the dorm and their thick, Nigerian accents demanded answers.

"Why is this floor dirty?"

"Who else sleep here? No girl sleep in this mess."

"Who drink that liquor, Theo? You drink that liquor?"

"What is that smell?"

"Hello, Mr. and Mrs. Nkosi, nice to meet you. I'm Indigo." I extended my hand to Theodora's mom.

She swallowed, looked at my hand, and turned to her husband. "John?"

Mr. Nkosi stepped forward. He was tall and balding at the top where the harsh, yellow dorm lighting bounced off his head. He wore slacks creased all the way down and cuffed at his shoe, and a large watch on his wrist. "Hello, where is it you are from, young lady?" Mr. Nkosi raised an eyebrow.

"About three hours from here, Sir. Tunica Rivers."

"And it's my understanding that Theodora is to spend some time with you and your family during the winter break?"

"Yes, that is the plan. . ." I nodded and flashed a nervous smile. His questions felt more like an interview than a meet and greet.

"And what will you and my daughter partake in? She has an affinity for smooth, fast-tail friends like yourself."

"Dad!" Theodora shrieked.

I took in a sharp breath and mulled Mr. Nkosi's words. This was my first time meeting him; what did he see in me that made him see me as a *fast-tail friend?* Shit, Theodora drank way more than I did.

"Theo, we will wait outside, honey. I can't wait to see your medical laboratory. *'Dr. Nkosi coming soon.'"* Mrs. Nkosi clicked her heels together and waited outside with the rest of the family, who had already traipsed into the hallway in search of more space. Theodora and I shared a knowing glance. For the second time, people had left our dorm room with their faces turned up. We had to clean better and lay off the liquor.

CHAPTER 7

CITATION NOTICE, the sign attached to the door read. It was printed on bright yellow paper, and anyone could walk by and see our business. I snatched it down and scanned it. It was from Mr. Chestnut and the Director of Dormitory Services. Someone reported underage drinking taking place in our room and because they were permitted to enter any establishment when there was suspicion of illegal activities, they invaded our room and executed a search while we weren't there.

"Theodora, wake up!" I shouted, storming to her bedside.

She was asleep with her head under the pillow and her voice was thick with afternoon naptime gravy only a college student could understand. "What?"

"Have you seen this?" I shoved the paper in her face.

"Oh yeah, I saw it when I got home from practice, but I didn't know what it meant. I was dog tired." Theodora yawned and wiped her eyes.

"Mr. Chestnut and some director came into our room and searched it. On suspicion of drinking."

Theodora's eyes bugged out of her head. "Did they find anything?" she whispered.

Theodora knew full well what finding alcohol in a dorm room could do to her track scholarship.

I paused for a second, thinking about my own college career. "I don't think so. I cleaned everything after your parents left, and besides, I'm sure we would've heard something by now, right?"

It had been weeks since homecoming and if someone reported us, we would've already known, right? I sat on my bed and looked around the room, thanking myself for doing a deep clean after our families threw major shade when they came to visit. When her father left out of the room, I heard him walking down the hallway screeching to Theodora's mom, *"But they're females, females!"*

"How can they just come into our room? That has to be illegal?" I fumed. I was not happy Mr. Chestnut was my dorm rep. Now he was trying to flex his muscles and show me that he could do whatever he wanted. I bet no one reported anything and he made the whole thing up.

"They were just doing their jobs, Indy."

My neck almost broke from whipping around so fast. "You really believe that, Theodora?" I gasped. "These people came into our room! Our safe space."

Theodora rubbed her eyes. "It's not personal. A few of the track girls just got busted for pot. They want to make sure the rest of the team isn't under the influence too."

"And what does that have to do with them searching our room?" I challenged.

"Nothing...everything, Indy. I don't know. I'm so tired!" Theodora yawned and fell back onto her pillow, pulling her eye mask back down.

I sighed. It was time to tell her about the real him. "Theodora. I haven't told you about Mr. Chestnut. He's a predator. Remember I told you he used to work at my high school? He used to mess with some of the girls there. He even got one of my friends pregnant. You can't trust him," I fussed.

Theodora lifted her eye mask off her face and her eyes bugged out of her head. She propped herself up on her elbows. "Damn. That's deep. He hasn't come on to me . . . Indy, if you were an older, white man, would you come on to me?" she asked with a serious face.

I stared at her incredulously. "Are you serious right now?" I was trying to protect her, and she was mad her hot, older coach hadn't made a move.

When she giggled and laid back down, putting the blanket over her head, I grabbed my textbooks and stomped my way to the campus computer lab. I needed a moment to myself to figure this thing out.

Just because he tried to move his location didn't mean he was a changed man.

Just because I moved didn't make me a changed girl.

I was still a killer.

When my cell phone buzzed, I saw Will's face. I smiled.

"Indy," he sang into the phone.

I beamed before I even said a word and I could hear him smiling through the phone too.

"Hey Will," I responded.

"Oh, we too good for a talk with our old best friend now, huh?" I snorted into the phone and glanced around, mindful of where I was. I grabbed my purse and tiptoed to the outside of the computer lab. The room spilled into an empty foyer. Conversations with Will could get boisterous.

"What's up?" Will asked, still smiling through the phone.

"I miss you," I admitted. I toyed with my locket. Will understood me better than most people and I didn't need to mince words with him.

"No, you don't because if you did, you would invite me to your new spot to see you."

"It's three hours away. Will you come this far? Can your car make the trip?" Will had an old hoopty that would break down on us at the worst times. It surely wouldn't make a road trip.

"Try again. How about you let me worry about if my car can make it, and yes—I will come visit you. You still didn't extend an invitation."

"Well, there's no point in an invitation right now. Winter break is in a few weeks and I'll be coming home with some friends. How about we get together then?"

"That'll work. And remember that cabin my family owns in Tennessee? We're going down for New Year's Eve. I figured we could try skiing like the white people do and just celebrate life. How about you and your friends tag along?"

A cabin in Tennessee? Snow and skiing? I had visions of us hitting the slopes and me wearing a fly ass ski-suit. I've never been skiing, but I wanted to try. I was sure Naomi and Theodora did as well.

"You can put us down, we'll be there." I beamed into the phone.

I hung up with Will and spent the next hour in the computer lab catching up on Freshman Seminar work and thinking about him. We had been best friends practically our whole lives and last year was the first time I looked at him as more than a friend. *She say he just a friend, she say he just a friend* . . . well I did, and then I didn't. Somewhere in our senior year he started looking so manly and I wanted to smell him, touch him. But it happened at the wrong time because Mom and the voices wanted to touch me too. It also didn't help I was dating

Malachi, who was now my ex-boyfriend. I wasn't sure who I was, not when the voices could take over at any moment. I had to keep myself and others safe. I wasn't ready to date anyone right now. Not if it might cost them their life.

Still, I loved to hear from Will. His voice sounded like home.

"Rita is in a mood," Harper said. She leaned forward and rolled her eyes from side to side.

I had yet to meet Rita, even though I had been coming regularly and on time the past few weeks. She was usually away on some big out of town, costume purchase. "I would just stay out of her way. The cast is back there, and they will need a few things fetched. You're with Chaquille today."

I paused. Knowing it was almost our turn to run the practice sequence for the Libra Festival together, I was still nervous. I found myself staring at Chaquille when he was lifting the stage sets behind the scenes.

Harper said each duo had to work in pairs, so we knew each and every part of the sequence. No one was responsible for one part, we were responsible for every part. Titus Theater was the school's money maker, and the walk from the main campus parking lot to the theater was a straight line. They wanted to make it as easy as possible for the rich people dressed in suits and heels to park and easily make their entrance. The inside of the theater was ornate, with orchestra style seating, and a spot for a full band set up. A large screen rolled up and down when needed, and there was even a balcony section. The large, deep gold curtains were thick and held the stage's secrets until it was time. Rita was a fan of cosplay, and she often had the actors work overtime to dress up as characters from the plays throughout the campus. A character could plop

down next to somebody while in the library or walked by in the hall while in class.

The marketing was genius and kept the seats packed.

The real action went down behind the curtains though. It was us: me, Chaquille, Fredo, and June, who kept everything going. We made sure the costumes were on the racks, in order, and tagged with the correct scenes. I steamed the costumes and took them for dry cleaning. We collected the tickets and even created the graphics.

"Hey," Chaquille said when I entered the breakroom in the back.

"Hey," I breathed back.

"Hi, Indigo, nice to see you again. I'm from Brooklyn, and I also dj sometimes, and you didn't come to my party after I invited you, but it's okay. Now you go." Chaquille was smirking. He slapped his hands together as he talked and pointed at me and himself.

Watching Chaquille hop around; he looked like he was rapping, and it made me chuckle. "I'm Indigo, I'm from Tunica Rivers in Louisiana. I write sometimes, and I forgot about your party. Sorry." I was putting my things in the locker and Chaquille was across from me, opening his. He turned around and shot me the widest grin for no reason.

"Boy, you are crazy," I snickered. I couldn't help myself.

"No seriously, I don't like bad vibes. We cool?" His eyes were different this time around. Apologetic and sincere.

I nodded. "We're cool. Let's get out there before they look for us."

"So, you're a writer, huh?" Chaquille asked as we strolled to the center aisle and began collecting fake tickets for the practice sequence.

"Yeah, I wrote a lot in high school and I'm trying to do it here too. And you're a dj?"

Chaquille beamed, and that wide grin flashed again. My stomach fluttered, but I hoped it was gas.

"Yeah man, that's why I told you to come to the party. I'm kind of a big man on campus," he laughed when he said it, but his voice didn't waver.

"Is that right? And what's your major?"

Chaquille tore off the tickets faster when I asked that. "Finance. My mom wants me to be a businessman, but in the words of Jay-Z, 'I want to be a business,—man.'"

"So, what's stopping you?" The fake patrons were really Titus students who were told they would get free food if they stood in line. The line was picking up and Harper was peeking her head from the front vestibule area to see about the holdup.

"I don't know. Does anyone know why anything stands in their way? It just does."

"Can you guys yap less and pick up the pace more," Harper charged. She wore red, cat shaped eyeglasses and a full kimono, complete with chopsticks in her hair. She wore all of this even though this for a practice run.

I hurried my pace while Harper glided to the front of the line; her long cape flowing in the wind behind her.

"If you are still interested, I'll be spinning tonight on the ninth floor."

"I may be able to swing that." I nodded and continued taking tickets. I would check with Naomi and Theodora. Another party before buckling down for the end of the semester wouldn't hurt anyone. We decided that for winter break, Naomi and Theodora would drive home together, with Naomi dropping off Theodora in Maryland before heading to New Jersey. Soon, we would all be in Tunica Rivers for a day before heading to Will's cabin in Tennessee.

Later that night after work, Theodora, Naomi, and I made our way to the ninth floor. The elevator dinged and there were

a few students with red cups spilling out of the apartment. We called the ninth floor the penthouse because it was the largest apartment in the dormitory and reserved for upperclassmen. Tonight was a scaled down version of what the dorm parties typically looked like because some students were knee deep in finals. I didn't plan to stay long myself, I wanted to get in some studying too. I was looking forward to a month off. I tried so hard to get away from home, but I was clambering to go back.

I finished my first college semester and while it was not my best, I was able to pull up my grades enough to pass. The extra credit Mrs. Winifred allowed me to submit really saved me by the skin of my teeth. I would get my shit together and come back in the spring ready to really tackle college now that I knew what was expected of me. I wouldn't let my thoughts of Jaxon stopped me from what I came here to do. I would do better.

But tonight, I was getting faded.

I glanced around the apartment looking for Chaquille. I thought he would be spinning like he said, but there was no dj, only a small speaker in the room's corner, playing music from the radio. By the way Chaquille described it, I thought this would be a crazy party, but there seemed to only be a dozen or so people lounging around, talking, and laughing.

Chaquille swooped in behind me. "Theodora tells me you're a wine drinker and nothing heavier."

"Theodora is always somewhere snitching!" I was defensive. Chaquille handed me a small cup, which looked like it could only hold teaspoons of alcohol. I gazed around and everyone else had a large, red cup.

"I wasn't snitching, I just said my girl doesn't like the hard stuff." Theodora's eyes were wide, and she looked like she was caught in a lie.

"She's right, I don't like the hard stuff. Is that why you gave me this medicine cup of ... what is this? Juice?"

SOMEONE MORE LIKE MYSELF

"Nah, shorty, chill. You amp so fast, do you know that? I was just making sure that's what you wanted. No disrespect."

Naomi and Theodora giggled, and I relaxed slightly. I don't know why I thought everyone was out to get me. I questioned everyone's intent since Jaxon's death. If someone came and told me the sky was blue, I would still go outside just to check it out for myself. Trust was something I didn't have these days, but I was trying. I *don't* like the hard stuff, but I also don't like Theodora telling people. They would think I was weak, and I couldn't handle my liquor. The only time I had an issue was last year at Spring Fling... but that was a different Indigo. This Indigo was mindful of alcohol these days.

"And why aren't you spinning anyway, DJ Khaled?"

It was now Chaquille who looked surprised, and he chuckled. "Change of plans. My mans took home some of my equipment, so we're having an old-fashioned radio party. Don't judge me by what you see here now. I can do better than this," he said, waving his arms around. He seemed embarrassed by the few people and the fact the speakers weren't blaring out something loud and fast.

"This is fine," I looked around. "Sometimes quieter is better."

"You two are a snooze fest," Theodora cut in. She and Naomi were sitting on top of the kitchen counter. She hopped off and said, "we've got the next month off from school and I don't have track practice. Anyone in the back have any bud? Never mind, come on Naomi. Let's see what we find."

"I'm forever down for the bud," Naomi grinned. I shook my head and watched them disappear down the hallway. That girl loved getting high.

"You smoke, Indy?" Chaquille asked.

"Every now and then. You?"

"Na. Ya'll won't catch me slipping." Chaquille leaned against the counter where I was sitting, and his hand lightly rapped

my leg. I jumped a little under his touch. He caught my jolt and moved his hand away. I wasn't afraid of Chaquille, and I cursed myself for being so jumpy. Jaxon had my ass traumatized. Chaquille's touch felt electric. I examined his face. He was dark-skinned with the deepest waves. He was fine as fine could be, so I slid closer.

"Catch you slipping how?" I laughed off the moment, hoping he would too.

"I'm just saying. I'm not a prude or anything, but I don't get how people put their mouth on the same little strip of rolling paper and just puff, puff, pass. It skeeves me out. Keep it up. Puff, puff pass something you can't get rid of," he said with wide eyes.

I laughed a big hearty laugh I felt down to my toes and up through my braids. Chaquille's face registered surprise, and before I knew it, we laughed together until people looked at us to see what all the fuss was about.

"Tell me about home?" Chaquille gulped from his cup.

I took a deep breath and welcomed Chaquille into my world of Tunica Rivers. I told him about nothing and then about everything. It felt good laughing and joking like this. Chaquille was cool, and when I thought I was talking too much, I searched his eyes for boredom, but he was hanging onto my words. I talked on.

CHAPTER 8

I DUMPED MY STUFF at Dad's house and took the thirty-minute drive to Ez's side of the river. Sidney was never one to miss a moment with her beloved Ez, and she happily rolled out with me for a visit. Ez still used the canoes as transportation; he didn't go anywhere that required a car, and if he did, Dad or Ms. Arletha took him. When we got to the house, I looked up and inhaled. It had been close to three months since I was here, and it still smelled of pine trees and saltwater reminding me I was home. My Tunica Rivers. Before Mama Jackie died, it was vibrant with a lush garden, the grass was cut low, and the house smelled of something sweet, even if Mama Jackie wasn't cooking. The roof was partially caved in where those sweet smells used to waft from.

Eyeing the damage, I noticed missing shutters and the attic crawl space window broken. When I walked inside, a foul stench hit my nostrils and I covered my mouth. My stomach churned and threatened to empty. Ez's kitchen was piled high with old newspapers, jugs of gasoline, and candles. Ez had candles of all sizes: the small chunky ones, tall pillar candles, and candles in mason jars. They were all lit at varying lengths and their

smoked billowed in the air, making the ceiling stained from soot. The candles simmered from burning so long, and the hot wax dripped onto the floor over the jugs of gasoline. In the living and dining room, Ez had stock-piled flushable toilet wipes. Ez made himself a pallet with a sleeping bag and a flat pillow right under the ledge with pictures of Mama Jackie.

The cats had multiplied since the last time I was here.

He was still feeding them, and large sacks of cat food and real food scattered throughout the house. Even though it was a chilly December night, Ez still kept the window open so the cats could come and go as they pleased.

'*My God, Ez. My God . . .* ' Mom whispered in my mind.

My thoughts exactly, Mom.

"Ez, what's going on here?" I glanced around. I peered at Sidney and she looked away. I asked her many times about Ez, knowing he struggled to keep it clean, but she said he was fine. Ez was not okay.

"What you mean, girl?" Ez wiped his hands on a dirty dish towel and took a swig of water from a small jug in the kitchen.

"I thought we talked about this. About keeping the house clean. Remember when Sidney and I came over, and we showed you how to use the stove and clean up after yourself?"

"Oh, this ain't nothing but a little dishes, girl. Ya'll always messing with me, especially your dad. Don't come here with them coolas, Titus girl, and boss me around. Mind your business you'll live longer," Ez spewed. His fat head blocked the kitchen light above him and a piece of panel from the kitchen touched Ez's dome where he stood. His enormous stomach was protruding from his overalls, and his work boots were worn down and exposed his big toe. He wore no socks.

"We're not messing with you, Ez," Sidney's voice was softer than mine, then she went and stood beside him. "Tell Indy how we cleaned the entire basement," she urged. "But then the pipes burst. But we did clean it."

My eyes widened. "The pipes burst?"

"Yes, girl you heard her right." This time Ez's voice wasn't loud, and he shifted his weight on his feet. "I don't know what happened. SidRock and I was cleaning the attic. Cleaned the whole damn thing; you should see it, Indy." Ez smiled bright. "So, then SidRock said, *'well let's clean the basement too.'* And I said, *'I reckon we do.'* So, we goes on down there, and we got all of my bikes, and your mom's old stuff organized. We heard a loud noise, and I said, *'SidRock, you better run, girl!'* and the next thing I knew, the water was to my ankles. It's been like that for a few weeks now." Ez took a bite of a leftover slice of pizza from the refrigerator. The broken-down refrigerator door was taped up on the sides and Ez's pizza was already chewed, like he or something had already been nibbling.

Ez's house was one of the few homes on the island that had a basement. I stomped across the living room, pried open the small door, and flicked on the light. From the top of the steps, I could see the glimmer of water. I shut the door behind me and closed my eyes, resting my head on the door. "You can't live like this, Ez; the house isn't safe. Has the city come back?"

Ez shifted again and avoided my eyes. "I told them city people they can try to come here and take my land if they want to. This land got our family blood on it and I'm not leaving," Ez rambled while he searched through a mound of papers on the table before finding the one he wanted and thrust it in my face.

I examined it, and my stomach sank. It read: **Notice to vacate.**

Hours later, I needed an explanation and now. "And you knew this, Dad? You knew Ez's house looked like that?" Dad and Ms. Arletha stole glances at each other. Ms. Arletha was baking her famous lemon pound cake for Christmas and the house smelled heavenly from the citrusy scent. Dad stood next to her helping, but in man fashion—not really helping. He was tickling Ms. Arletha and whispering into her ear before I stormed in with questions.

Dad sighed. "Yes, I knew about the basement." He didn't look at me.

"And you let him live there? And you, Sidney! You never told me?"

"Indy, what were we supposed to do? Ez is autistic. He has... quirks. I tried to get him to move in with us, and he refused. We tried to get someone in there to clean and patch the basement. I sent three plumbers over there and he chased them out of the house and said the cats didn't like them."

"It's true, Indy. Ez wouldn't let anyone in the house. We tried to clean a couple times, and he completely refuses anyone inside. Today was the first time I had been inside in weeks because you were there." Sidney nodded her head. Her voice was soft. She was never one to speak against Ez and she wouldn't now.

I sank at the kitchen table and my head was pounding.

"Honey, we're doing the best we can with Ez. But he needs help." Ms. Arletha placed the cake in the oven and wiped the countertops. I smelled the bleach in the dish rag and I studied the large birthmark that covered her forehead and eye. She saw the bigger picture. Not that I didn't believe my dad and Sidney; they loved Ez too, but my dad didn't have the patience for Ez, and Sidney had *too* much patience for him. If Ms. Arletha said they were doing their best, then I believed her. The reality hit me that Ez and his autism was becoming too much for my family to manage and it was worse now since I was away at college.

After my disagreement with Dad about Ez, I stomped to the bathroom and turned on the shower. Glancing at myself in the mirror, something raged to be let out. I gripped the sides of the sink and closed my eyes. I leaned forward and took in deep breaths, trying to settle my nerves. I was home from school a few hours and already I felt like I was spiraling.

My phone buzzed beside me, and with shaky hands, I unlocked it and read the email. Titus University Wellness Center had one opening for tomorrow at 3:00 p.m. I called the center weeks after my fateful appointment with Jill, and requested a new therapist. If I could make it back to school and confirm my appointment for tomorrow, I could meet with someone new. Without a thought, I hit confirm on the screen.

Less than twenty-four hours later, I shuffled into the office of Angela Carlton, a middle-aged Black woman. She skimmed me over from above her glasses which sat on her nose.

"I'm so glad you could make it in. We had a cancellation at the last minute and you were first on the waitlist. Just a reminder, Titus University and the center deem anything you say violent in nature toward yourself or anyone else as a reportable offense to crisis. I just wanted to let you know, but otherwise you have my full confidentiality."

I rubbed my hands against my jeans and stared down at my sneakers. "Yea, uh, thanks."

"So, what brings you in?" Angela grabbed a clipboard and clicked her pen.

I gulped. I came all this way and now I didn't know what to say. During the ride, I was talking to myself in the car. It was

the voices, but nonetheless—*we* agreed I would be honest and tell someone what was going on with me. Angela was ogling me, and she was feverishly writing away on her clipboard. I hadn't even said anything yet, and she was already writing. What the heck could she have on me that fast? "What are you writing?" I squinted.

"Oh, nothing, just making some notes about our session. Does that bother you?"

"No, no, it doesn't. I was just curious." I leaned back in the chair and folded my arms.

"So, you're a freshmen it says here. Your file from your previous therapist says this is your first time in counseling, your major is Liberal Arts, and you have a hard time expressing yourself, and you may shut down through the session and turn inward."

What the fuck? Where did that come from? "Who said that?" I sat up in the chair. I know Jill didn't say that about me. After just one session?

Angela removed her glasses, and they hung from around her neck. "Full disclosure, Ms. Lewis." She stole a glance from her clipboard. "I like to read from the previous therapist's notes and discuss them with new patients. It's a good starting point to hear what you agree or disagree with regarding yourself."

Patient she called me. I was a patient. My mom was a patient.

"I'm not a patient. Just call me, Indigo—actually Indy. You can call me Indy."

Angela said nothing and scribbled in her notebook.

"What are you writing?" I couldn't help but ask again. We still barely said anything, and she was squiggling away.

I was tripping.

"I'm not writing much of anything, Indigo. Does me writing bother you?"

"No." I sucked my teeth.

"Okay then." Angela smiled. Her lips were pursed, and her eyes flashed. "Let's move on. Tell me about your time here at Titus University." Angela sat her clipboard down and scooted around in the chair like she was waiting for me to tell her a delightful story.

I snooped around in her office. She had two different couches next to each other and odd pieces of furniture that didn't match. There were pictures of her and her sorority sisters; they were all older in the picture. They looked like the type of women who wore slips to church on Sunday and made the repass tea extra sweet.

Leaning back in the chair just like Angela, I felt my heart beating out of my chest. I said, "my time here at Titus has been different. I hear things ... I hear things." There, I said it out loud. I didn't realize I was holding my breath until I felt a deep sigh escape my mouth.

"What do you hear? Is it someone you know?"

"It's ... my mom. Mainly my mom."

"Have you thought about hurting yourself or hurting anyone else? *Have* you hurt yourself or anyone else?" Angela picked up her clipboard and began scribbling again. She wasn't looking at me but said, "keep talking, Indigo."

Had I hurt someone? Yes? But Jaxon didn't count. I was starting a new life, and he was in my past. If I kept repeating it long enough, I would eventually start to believe it. Jaxon wasn't my fault, and therefore, I could move forward. Had I hurt myself? No, not really, but again, yes—yes, I did. It was so confusing to keep everything straight in my mind. My palms were wet, and I wiped them against my jeans.

"Indigo, we have about fifteen minutes left in the session. Have you hurt anyone else, or hurt yourself?" Angela pressed. She stopped scribbling but held the pen tight in her fingers.

Running my fingers through my braids, I thought about Angela's words. Anything deemed violent in nature would have to be reported. A murder was certainly violent. I stared back at Angela. "No, no, I have not had any of those thoughts." I said without a crack in my voice.

She leaned back in her chair, her eyes full of relief. "Good, let's move on. Have you guys been drinking or doing any drugs in your dorm? You know that could cause some delusions."

"No," I sighed. I was already lying. Why quit now?

The rest of the session was more yes or no questions, and I think Angela preferred it that way.

With a card in my hand for a follow-up session with Angela, I walked out of the Wellness Center, grumbling. What a waste of time this was. Why did I ever think anyone could help me? I was on my own.

'You have me honey, don't forget, we're here with you too.'

"I know, Mom," I said out loud to no one—but everyone. "I know."

"Indigo?" I heard while pressing the elevator button.

I turned around with an attitude, unsure if I heard that one for real or in my mind this time.

Chaquille.

"Chaquille. What are you doing here? It's winter break?"

He got into the elevator and zipped his jacket. "Chill, Indy, I was going to ask you the same thing," he shifted his weight. I squinted behind him and noticed he was walking from the Titus Medical Clinic.

"I had an appointment that I couldn't miss," I mumbled.

"Yeah, me too." He put his hand in his pocket and avoided my eyes as the elevator dinged and opened into the lobby.

"Well, I'll see you —"

"Do you want to grab something to eat from the dining-hall?" he interrupted.

'Go ahead Indy, you need something fun after that mess up there,' a voice in my head countered.

'Yes, go, Indy!' another one cheered.

I swallowed and said, "sure."

We walked to the dining-hall from the Wellness Center, and if there was such a thing as a Titus University winter wonderland, this was our version. The campus was empty with mostly everyone already home. The buildings were lit up and had prickly pines in the windows. The twinkling lights shone bright and small speakers were hidden, while they played holiday music on low. On a normal day, I was pushed and hoarded to one destination. I tried to keep my head down and get to where I was going. There were always so many people around me during the day, I never really got a chance to look up and around. The campus was slow, and I took in the sleek and shiny buildings and the tall skyscraper outline of Titus University Hospital a few miles away. The trees and yards were manicured—even in December. The outside areas were beautiful, other than the eyesore we called home at the dorm halls. They almost didn't match, but somehow melted perfectly together. Like me in a way. Beautiful on the outside, and yet to be renovated on the inside.

The dining-hall was quiet, and I glanced around to make sure they were open. We were the only ones there. "Are we allowed to be in here?" I looked over my shoulder.

"Booker is working the grill tonight. He volunteered to work so everyone else could have off. Then they're closing up shop for a few weeks," he pointed. Sure enough, Booker was in the far-right corner of the dining-hall, flipping beef patties over a hot grill. His long apron and tall white chef's hat were clean and shiny, like they hadn't seen much action all day.

"Finally, someone comes to eat," Booker fussed. He and Chaquille dapped each other up and grinned.

"Wait, so you're here too? Don't you guys go home for winter break?" I looked between Chaquille and Booker.

"What them young, sensitive boys say, Indigo? Home is where the heart is," Booker chuckled, and his eyes squinted until they were closed. He tickled himself with his comment, and Chaquille stifled a laugh too. "So, what can I get you guys?" he asked.

"Cheeseburger with the special sauce," I said; my mouth now watering.

"Do I hear two?" Booker looked at Chaquille.

"Two." Chaquille smiled.

While Chaquille and Booker talked, I grabbed a table and saw a text from Will.

> **WILL:** Can't wait to see you on the slopes this week!

I pressed a heart into Will's text. I was looking forward to his Tennessee cabin. I was looking forward to seeing him and what our friendship could turn into. It was never the right time for us. Either he was dating someone, or I was. Now we, could be a *we*. The idea excited me.

"Here you go," Chaquille said, placing down two trays full of food for us.

I bit into my burger, and Booker's special sauce seeped out of the sides and ran down my cheeks. I moaned and wiped my mouth with napkins. "My goodness, this is so good. I think this makes up for you trampling me all of those times." I took another bite.

With a mouthful of his own burger, Chaquille coughed a little and sipped his soda. "How many times can I apologize. Booker ate me up about it anyway. *'Don't run off the Freshman girls'* he said, with the damn chef's hat on." Chaquille motioned with his hands and made a hat over his head.

I snorted and covered my mouth. Booker and that hat was a sight to see. He propped it up on his head every time it leaned over, and he never took it off. I'm glad someone besides me, Theodora, and Naomi teased him about it.

"That's your frat brother. You gotta love him," I giggled.

Chaquille took a long glance at me before stuffing French fries in his mouth and wiping his hands. "So really, why are you here, on Christmas Eve, in this fine establishment," Chaquille waved his hands around.

"I had an appointment at the counseling clinic," I admitted.

'No girl! You shouldn't tell him that,' a voice countered.

'I think I may agree on this one, Indy. Too much information honey,' Mom said in my head.

It was too late because the words already slipped. I inhaled and waited for Chaquille's eyes to bug out of his head.

They didn't.

"Oh okay. How did it go?"

"What do you mean? People usually freak out when you say you're going to counseling." I gave a nervous laugh.

"Yo, I don't know. I mean, I'm from New York. People go to counseling and shit all the time. But sometimes when people go, they are expecting something. So, was it what you were expecting?" He gaped at me. I had fries in my hands but didn't bring them to my mouth as it was hanging open at Chaquille's words. What was I expecting from counseling? What were my intentions? I knew I wanted someone to help with the voices, but did I want someone to help with the thoughts of murder too? The excitement I felt when I thought about Jaxon's demise? I didn't want help with that—just yet. I wanted to see where that would take me. And if it took me to places that scared me, what did that say about me?

"That was rhetorical, shorty. You don't have to give me an answer," he chuckled.

"Shut up," I smirked, snapping out of my thoughts. "I don't know. I don't know what I was expecting..." I admitted again.

Maybe fixed. I wanted to be fixed. I wanted to be someone more like myself. The magazine owner, living in a penthouse suite, living life, type of girl.

Chaquille shrugged and took a bite of his burger.

"And you! What are you doing here on Christmas Eve?" I rolled my eyes at him.

"Like Booker said, sometimes home is where the heart is."

"He said that's for the sensitive guys," I reminded.

"I know what he says. Booker is my frat brother, but he don't speak for me." Chaquille leaned back in his chair and put his hands in his jacket pocket.

"Do you have family?" I asked.

"My mom and sisters still live in Brooklyn. I'm the youngest."

"The youngest. Did they go to college? I bet they taught you all the ins and outs," I babbled. "I didn't even know college didn't have bells. One day I was waiting for the bell to ring to be dismissed from class. An older lady said to me, *'baby, if you don't get your things and go. This college, honey—ain't no bells!'*"

Chaquille threw his head back and slapped his Timberland boots against the carpet in laughter. "Yes, they went to college, and they taught me a little something, something... It's just not my thing though."

"Meaning?" I gave a look.

"The waking up early, writing papers, the dumb-ass remedial classes that don't even count toward your degree. What's the purpose, really? And it takes too much time away from my music, anyway. That's really what I want to do." He leaned back and sighed.

"Please tell me you're not trying to be a rapper?" I turned up my nose and sat my burger down.

"Nah," he said. "I told you. I dj. You still have yet to come to one of my parties."

"Not true! I came to the last one before I left."

"That doesn't count. I didn't have my equipment or anything," he mumbled.

"I know, I know. I'll be at the next one, I promise."

"I got something. I really do. And I know what I have, it won't be found here, in college."

"Mmm, that's deep, James Baldwin." I nodded.

Chaquille chuckled again. "And what are you here for? I've seen *Girl, Interrupted*."

"What!" I gasped, and pink lemonade shot from my mouth. I choked for a few seconds and giggled behind Chaquille's words. "I am nothing like *Girl, Interrupted*!"

"And I'm nothing like James Baldwin." Chaquille shrugged with a smirk.

"Touché, touché."

"Okay. This will tell me everything I need to know. Do you put sugar or salt in your grits?" Chaquille quipped.

"Tell you everything you need to know, huh? Ummm, I'm a sugar girl," I said with conviction.

"And you're a serial killer. Only serial killers put sugar in their grits!" Chaquille tried to keep a straight face as the words came out, but his shoulders shook while he chuckled anyway.

My throat tightened as I mulled over his words . . . *and you're a serial killer*. He must've been psychic too.

"What? You put salt in your grits? I think you are the serial killer!" I said through bites of my burger.

Chaquille and I spent the next hour talking over cold French fries. He didn't talk about his family, even when I asked. I wondered if he had anywhere to go. Why was that my concern? I hoped he had someone close to him for the holiday and wasn't spending it alone. I didn't want our time to end, and

when Booker came to us and said it was lights out, Chaquille walked me to the parking lot. Light and airy drops of snow fell and landed on my hot head and shoulders. Snow in Louisiana was a rarity, and the moment made butterflies dance in my belly. Chaquille walked on the outside of me.

Someone had taught him well and I noticed.

I noticed a lot of things about him, and I wanted to notice more. We exchanged numbers and promised to talk during the break. A lot of it sounded like lip service, the type of things you say to people when you want to end the conversation. Promises to meet up and spend time. Chaquille managed to run me down at least twice on campus and I still wanted to get to know him better. I found myself wondering what he would think about Jaxon...

On my drive home, I pored over Chaquille's words about his dj skills. He said, *'I got something. I really do. And I know what I have, it won't be found here.'* As I gripped the steering wheel, I wondered what talents did I have? And would any be found at Titus?

CHAPTER 9

TUNICA RIVERS WAS in full Christmas mode, complete with fake snow and a white Santa Claus down at the strip mall in town. It made the little snow on Christmas Eve with Chaquille more beautiful. I remember the first time I saw snow. Ez and Mama Jackie took Sidney and me to Ohio to visit one of her distant cousins. The day we arrived, and stepped foot outside of the car, it seemed like the skies opened and little bits of cold heaven fell onto my lashes. I stuck out my tongue and let the few seconds simmer while I squeezed my eyes shut and did it again. There was extra pep in my step when I beamed and gave the *black* nod when I passed someone in the streets who looked like me. I was home. Tunica Rivers was home. Fake snow and all.

Ez, Sidney, and I spent our gift cards and Christmas money on new clothes and new hair. Sidney bought a long, sleek ponytail from the beauty supply store. I bought a bad ass pair of sunglasses since I didn't like people to look me in my eyes these days. I also picked up a few packs of braiding hair so Ms. Arletha could wash my mane, clip my ends, and braid it right back up. Me and my box braids were a packaged deal,

and we could add hair braiding to the list of things Ms. Arletha was good at. She was becoming worth her weight in gold in this family. With the help of me and Sidney, Ez purchased a few shirts but not before he huffed and puffed, complaining it was too hot in the dressing room.

"How much longer ya'll girls reckon you got?" Ez raised his eyebrows. Everything he wore was oversized, and his camouflaged jacket and straw hat were no different. It looked like it could fit three Ez's.

Sidney and I finished shopping, but after Ez tried on a couple shirts; he decided the mall was too busy for him and he would rather wait in the car. Clothes shopping was fun, and we were excited when Ez said he would tag along, but now he was antsy.

"Ez, are you sure you don't want to get anything else?" I questioned.

"It's too many bodies moving around in there, girl. No, Ez is just fine." He removed a straw from his hat and cleaned his teeth. He sang Smokey Robinson from the old cassette player in the car and tapped on the dashboard. His baritone voice sounded perfect against Smokey's smooth notes. "And you be careful, SidRock, don't you get none of that pink stuff on my car," Ez growled at Sidney chewing bubblegum.

I giggled, watching Ez squint at Sidney. His long frame was crouched down in the front seat.

"Your car? Ez, this is my car, remember? You gave it to me last year before graduation and you said, *'Indy, now you take care of my baby,'* and you handed me the keys. You don't remember?" I smirked at Ez and forced back a smile, knowing the fire storm that would come.

Ez's head whipped around. "You telling a lie and the truth ain't in you, college girl!"

Sidney and I giggled while Ez fumbled to get the car started. "Talking about I gave her the car. I said you could use her.

Don't be going and hitting them mens either like your mama. Are ya'll done yet? This is a lot for my Bentley." Ez patted the top of the dashboard.

I was not like my mom. I cringed in the back seat.

"Bentley?" Sidney made a face. She let him skate right by the comment about Mom, but I heard him.

"Yea, this is a lot of back and forth for my Bentley. He's not used to these long rides."

"Ez, I drive Bentley to and from college. Bentley is just fine," I dragged out the last part. To him it was Bentley, but to me it was *The Bus*, and The Bus would not be hitting anyone.

"When ya'll going to see your mama?" Ez eyed me from the rearview mirror, and I tensed up. I wanted to see Mom while I was home, but I was leaving for Tennessee with Will for New Years and I also made plans with Joya, my friend from high school.

"I want to see Mom too." Sidney nodded.

"I don't know if I'll have time, Ez, I have to —"

"Oh, phony bologna Indy, go see your mama. Them letters is nice and all but ain't nothing like the real thing."

"Are you coming too?" I questioned.

"You know, I really don't like Trochesse. An old buddy of mine, who I was in the war with . . . well when he came home, they made him go to Trochesse. He said he could speak to the dead. You know that's the old wives tale about that place. If you stay long enough, you start to know things. Yeah, that's what they say." Ez let out a hearty laugh, but I found nothing funny. My stomach was swirling like a storm. He said, "I'll go with you girls. I'll do that. For you all."

I glanced at Ez from the back, and I watched Sidney side eye him from the passenger's seat. "We love you too, Ez," she said with a nod.

I grinned and gazed out of the back window to help Ez pull out. My eyes connected with a familiar grey Altima. A car I

couldn't quite place even though I stared harder, trying to will myself to remember. My face flushed red, and my fists balled when the owner of the car walked up. Mr. Chestnut was there, holding shopping bags, with a girl who looked like a teenager. She wore a Tunica Rivers Technical High School softball uniform. They were walking from a uniform shop. Buying new uniforms, I guess he could say. Or whatever it was we were calling statutory rape these days.

No amount of real or fake snow could match the fury building inside of me and I was disgusted that fast. I grinded my teeth. He was at it again. How was no one seeing this? Did he have that much pull in Tunica Rivers and at Titus that he could freely roam around doing what he wanted? The mall was about thirty minutes away from Tunica Rivers and he skipped the uniform shop in town that all the teams used on McTaugh Road. Why would he drive all this way? Unless he was trying to be unseen and unheard.

I saw him and I heard him.

'He's not going to stop, Indy. You should have handled it last year when he hurt Joya.' Mom said.

I scowled and looked away.

While I had no more direct run-ins with Mr. Chestnut, I knew he was picking on us. Theodora and I came home a few weeks ago to find that we had two more room citations for stupid things.

"Come on, Theodora," I urged. She had to see it. *"Two citations, really? Every college student I know has alcohol in their dorm rooms."*

"It's not you, Indy. He just wants to make sure no one on the team is drinking. He's just doing his job as coach."

"Fine," I grumbled. *For as smart as Theodora was, she was blind as a bat, and you might as well call her John—because she ain't Cena thing.*

Too many secrets floated in the wind, and I felt trapped. I

turned down The Bus' old school roll-down window to let in some cool air. I was sweating too.

"Hey guys, how about I take the car and drop you off back at the house? I need to go back out and search for a snowsuit, and remember, I still have to go to Will's house for dinner?" Tunica Rivers seemed to teeter between three phases: jacket weather, sweater weather, and hoodie season. Finding a snowsuit for Tennessee was proving harder than I thought, and besides, I needed a moment to think about what I just saw.

'He's still up to his tricks, Indy,' Mom seethed on the ride home. I pushed her out of my mind when we pulled up at Ez's house.

Ez said, "reckon it's getting dark, college girl. Don't be out too late." He topped over the car, holding all of Sidney's bags from the mall, staring at me. His large arms protruded from his flannel sweater because he refused to wear a coat. He said, "real men don't wear no Parkas, except for ya daddy," with a chuckle. I never told Dad that one—and I don't believe Sidney did either. I peeked at Ez in the rearview mirror and I drove off; he didn't go in the house and he stood there watching me until I turned out of his circular, rocky driveway.

Will lived on the other side of town and whenever I went there, I had to slow down and make sure I made complete stops at all the corners. The cops here were ruthless and people were pulled over for walking in the wrong direction down the street. I had experienced it many times with my ex-boyfriend, Malachi. When he used to pick me up, we made sure we had all identification needed close by so we didn't have to reach anywhere in the car for anything. Whenever I asked Dad why things were so different in sections of the city he talked about

funding and taxes. I didn't know what any of that meant or what it even mattered, but I knew I had to be careful.

When I pulled up to his house, my brakes screeched to a halt in the old clunker, and Will's front door swung open. He didn't wait for me to get out when he yanked the door open, lifted me to my feet, and knocked the breath out of me. "Indy," he breathed. I was smothered in the crook of his neck, and I inhaled. I didn't realize I was tense, but my arms relaxed into his and I let him hold me a second longer.

Will put me down, and I looked up at him and grinned.

He grinned back.

"You mean to tell me that I have to cuss you out in order for you to come see me?" Will leaned forward and placed his hands to his chest and winced. His eyes danced as he stifled a smile.

"Whatever Will! I didn't know if you're hooptie would make it," I shot back. I was still pressed against him in front of The Bus. He smelled like honeysuckle.

"That's true. I'll give you that one. But you should've asked again. You should've insisted," Will said with a straight face. My insides swirled at the way he looked at me. His eyes were strong and intense, catching mine whenever I stole glances at his peck chest no more. Will had filled up and out. Plumbing school was doing him well and he had picked up a few pounds. His arms and chest were broad and even the veins in his neck popped in some weird, masculine way. I studied every curve in his face and freckle across his nose as if it was my first time seeing him, really seeing him.

Okay, Will.

"Indy, get on in here, girl!" I heard Mr. and Mrs. Simms behind Will in the house, and his older sister, Dominique, was there too.

Will's parents were married his entire life. It was an old school, high school sweethearts, love tale. Will even had the standard issued, rancher style house, white picket fence, and the dog sitting in the backyard. Mr. Simms did something with big banks and normally fell asleep in front of CNN when all those ticker numbers were flashing at the bottom of the screen. Mrs. Simms didn't work because she used to design Barbie dolls for Mattel and well—they were loaded, and she didn't have to work. She reminded me of Ms. Arletha in some ways. Being most comfortable in the kitchen. That was what a good mom did, right?

Mrs. Simms' dining room was a smorgasbord of food. Fried chicken, red beans and rice, ham, macaroni and cheese, collard greens, mashed potatoes, iced tea, sweet tea, hot tea, hot toddies, lemonade, and coffee for the elder Mrs. Simms, Will's grandmother.

I looked around the table and smiled. Tunica Rivers had some of the best damn cooks this side of Louisiana had ever seen, and I almost jumped up and down at all the yummy things I was about to partake in.

"Indy, tell us about your school. Any fine men up that way? You know I'm bagging and tagging?" Dominique didn't flinch and looked interested despite her outburst.

"Don't talk like that at the table, you ol' hot tamale self," Mrs. Simms swatted Dominique's arm. Dominique giggled and shrugged her shoulders at her mom. They both had chubby, round, chocolate faces, looking so much alike.

"Indy, please excuse my child, who won't move out." Mr. Simms cut his eyes at Dominique.

Will cleared his throat.

"Indy, please continue," Mrs. Simms instructed in a motherly, almost demanding way.

Now it was my turn to clear my throat. "It's okay. I mean, the dorms could be a little nicer, and the professors more helpful, but I think it's a learning experience."

'*Good answer, Indy! Our girl nailed that one. Okay, get ready team—they're gearing up for more,*' the voices said in my head.

Shit, I thought. It was quiet the past few days, and the only voice I heard was Mom's. I . . . I was caught off guard. Not here, not with the Simms family gaping at me, hanging on to my every word.

"A learning experience, huh? Well, maybe you can show this genius some learning experiences. Uber can't pay all the bills, lil bro." Dominique chewed at the same time and food shot out of her mouth.

"Hey, I am finding myself," Will said. His eyes were wide and mouth full of food.

"Well, I'll agree with Dominique there. You can do better than Uber, son," Mr. Simms gave Will apologetic, but stern eyes.

"Whoa, when did this turn around on me? And I *am* still in plumbing and heating school. I can't help it if the apprenticeship is unpaid," Will huffed.

"Don't jump all over him. He still has time to figure out what he wants to do. Rich, when you were his age you and me were married and pregnant so you had to get a job. Had to. Will doesn't have kids, or a wife and we should be thankful. I don't want to hear no more talk about who won't get a job and who won't move out. We can stay together as long as ya'll want. Our doors are eternally open. Now pass me down them mashed potatoes, they look like they stiffening up with all of ya'lls 'yappin." Mrs. Simms pointed with a kitchen spoon.

Mr. Simms snorted into his juice and wiped at the corner of his eye. The room was quiet for a second before Will said, "really Ma?" and the room erupted with laughter.

"Indy, how is your mama, girl? You know she and I went to high school together," Mrs. Simms asked, changing the subject.

I bit down on the inside of my cheek, and Will cut his eyes at his mom. Will knew me well, and talking about my mom wasn't my favorite thing, but I didn't shy away from it either. "I believe she's okay. I'm going to go see her before we head off to Tennessee." I sipped my soda.

"Oh, yes, we are ready for some fun. You know the lodge has been in our family for decades now, right Rich? They say Black people don't ski, but we get out there and show them how it's done." Mrs. Simms beamed at her husband. He nodded like she handed him the baton to take over the conversation. My heart lurched as I looked over at Will. I was in a better place, right? Would Will be a part of my penthouse dream? My foot bounced under the table at the thought. Looking at his parents, I wanted to pass the baton to someone. I wanted someone to look at me to fill the gaps in conversations and remember my own life better than even I did. Someone there for everything.

When I snapped out of my thoughts, Will was staring at me with a quizzical look.

'He really is so handsome,' a voice in my head said.

And he was, he really was.

He wore a navy-blue zip up hoodie, jeans, and a fresh pair of Nike's. He leaned back in the chair when I looked at him but sat up straight when his mom barged in with questions. His hazel-colored skin reminded me of coffee with extra cream.

'Will is in love,' one of the voices sang.

"Shh!" I hissed out loud.

"Indy, are you okay?" Will leaned in.

"I'm good, just have a little headache, that's all." I poked at my temples and feigned pain.

After helping Mrs. Simms clean the dishes, Will and I sat in the living room watching football. We giggled and I placed my legs overtop of his while his chilly fingers crept up my ankles and shins.

"Have you talked to Malachi or Mila?" Will asked.

I shook my head. "I was just thinking about him! I haven't heard from them at all. I texted him and Mila a few times but didn't get a response," I said pensively. How did you go from being best friends and spending so much time together, to not knowing them or their lives anymore? My friendship with Malachi and Mila seemed to be at a standstill. We weren't friends but we weren't *not* friends. Even though they knew nothing about Jaxon, the shame someone would find out, weighed me down like bricks. For some reason, Malachi and Mila reminded me of how far I had descended and let Jaxon take me out of character. Or put me into character... even a little bit of both. They were tied to my past, and that was a past in which I was hard pressed for money and almost willing to do anything for it. Did that mean the friendship wasn't real? If it can't withstand the distance?

Mr. and Mrs. Simms spent the next hour giving each other googly eyes while me, Will, and Dominique rolled our eyes at them. Will's grandmom was asleep in the living room and Wheel of Fortune screamed in the background.

The Simms were easy and uncomplicated while I had two different therapists.

We were not the same.

CHAPTER 10

MY DEAREST INDY,
When are you coming to see me? I marked off your college breaks on my men of Omega Psi Phi calendar.
Thanks for that, by the way.

I love looking at those men. They can put their shoes under my bed any day. When it came in the mail, I had to fight off Ruth-Ann and Cordelia. Them skeezers was trying to rip out pages, especially Mr. March. I could tell where he was marching to, but anyway!

Indy, you know I worry. Sidney and Ez are best friends . . . and I just thought, her dad, King, isn't really around. And yes, your dad cares for her like she's his own, but Ez really is her own, you know?

Her real grandfather.

Besides, it really made little a difference what they say Ez has. Who's to say this autism thing doesn't make him smarter or more in tune with spirit than the average bear? What if he's the lucky one? He was the best daddy he knew how to be to me. I keep having these dreams, Indy. About Ez. That he needs help. Make sure someone is checking in with him. You are the oldest and you have to be there for him.

JANAY HARDEN

Anyway, this letter won't be long. I just wanted to say when are you coming to see me? I love my calendar and go check on your grandfather, Indy. You know I be having my dreams and they never lie.

Love,
Mom.

I shoved Mom's letter underneath my seat and flipped the driver's mirror down. I applied more gloss to my lips and ran my fingers down my braids. As I primped my hair in the mirror, and mulled over Mom's words, I caught a reflection of myself and stared.

When we found out Ez was autistic, Sidney and I were the last to know. Dad thought he was protecting us by not telling, but he inadvertently taught me how to protect. I was protecting him from my own mental health issues, and my silence had far more consequences. I had my dad's heart, but Sonia Lewis was always in my mind.

Two hours later, Joya and I sat across from each other in the diner, giggling. We talked a few times during the semester, and I promised her I would catch up with her when I got home.

I smelled fresh lemon tarts. They smelled like Ms. Arletha's famous tarts, but she made hers with love and displayed them on our kitchen table in a glass container. Here, they made the tarts fast, and men in steel toe boots and tan work jackets pointed and demanded a piece with anxious tones and expectant faces.

Our table was covered with food. Each of us ordered at least three appetizers, one entrée, soups, salad, bread, and dessert. I unbuttoned my jeans so my stomach could spread

like it bust out of a can. Joya Ranks was now a senior at TRHS, and she had my old position, editor of the school's newspaper.

"Nice car." I motioned outside toward Joya's sleek, white Audi.

Joya shook her keys on the table next to us, and chuckled. "Getting knocked up by a teacher has its benefits."

I coughed on a piece of a roll lodged in my throat. I grabbed my neck and slurped down a swig of my orange juice. Joya was motionless and waited for me to respond.

"Excuse me?"

"You heard me." Joya looked away and stared out of the window.

A woman sitting behind us in the diner peered over her shoulder. I lowered my tone, mindful of where we were. When Joya popped up with a brand-new ride around the time she was dealing with Mr. Chestnut, I assumed it was some sort of payment from her parents or even a hush gift from Mr. Chestnut himself. Joya was laying down nothing but full houses on the table.

"What does the car have to do with that?"

Joya sighed. "My parents bought me the car if I got the abortion. You know that. I'm sure you wondered, or people made up all sorts of things."

I froze, remembering her abortion all too well. It was a scene I would never forget. I seethed. Girls only had themselves and each other. "Do you and your parents talk about it at all?" I pressed.

Joya shrugged. "No, my mom was just happy I agreed to get the procedure done, and my dad still acts as if nothing happened."

The waitress stopped in front of Joya and me and we both jumped back. "Coffee?" she pointed.

Joya shook her head and watched her as she walked away. "And Gregg..."

Gregg. She called him by his first name. I shuddered.

"He's back."

"What do you mean 'he's back?'" I made a face.

"He's home for winter break too. He says he wants to see me."

"And?" I shoved pancakes into my mouth to settle my stomach. I knew he was home when I peeped him at the mall, but I needed to see how much she knew, and if she knew what I knew. I knew nothing at all.

"I don't know. I'm thinking about it . . . While he's home."

My mind ran at warp speed. I couldn't have Joya wrapped up into Mr. Chestnut all over again. I had to protect her. He had her under his spell just like he did with Theodora and so many other people.

"Say, uh. I'm going to Tennessee with Will and some of my college friends. How about you tag along? Will's family has a mansion so I'm sure there will be room," I lied. I had no clue what the house looked like or if they had room. I prayed they did. I needed Joya away from Tunica Rivers and *away* from Mr. Chestnut.

Joya scrunched her face. "Are you sure they wouldn't mind? I mean . . . I don't have anything else to do, and my parents love you, so I'm sure they wouldn't have a problem with it," Joya spoke like she was trying to convince herself first and me second.

"I was just at Will's house last night, they said they have tons of room," I lied again.

"I don't know, though. I won't be able to see Gregg if I go, he's not staying all month," Joya deliberated.

"Do you love him or something? Is that it?" I questioned. I didn't mean for it to come out so sharp, but I was confused. What was the benefit of Mr. Gregg Chestnut? What made him so great that he could bypass everyone's common sense and bullshit detectors except mine?

SOMEONE MORE LIKE MYSELF

"It's been two years, Indy. I can't just walk away. We have to at least talk it out." She slumped her shoulders in the booth.

'Oh, now Indy, this is bad. We have to take care of this,' a voice in my head mumbled. *'Two years!'*

'He's a fucking Chester the Molester,' another voice screamed.

I know, I grumbled in my mind. This had been going on even longer than I thought.

I tried to blink away the voices, and my eye twitched. With every whisper, Joya reignited a flame in me that simmered. I was trying to find some other reason to convince Joya to come with me when she nodded. "You know what. You're right. You're right. Let's go to Tennessee!" she said with a smile.

I exhaled. I wouldn't let Joya sit around waiting for Mr. Gregg Chestnut. I pulled my phone from my pocket and shot Will a quick text message.

> **ME:** Hey, do we have room for one more for New Years?

> **WILL:** Sure, I don't think my parents will mind. Who is it?

> **ME:** Joya

> **WILL:** You invited Joya and both of your girls from college. I hope you still have time for me.

> ☹

> **ME:** Of course, crazy, lol.

JANAY HARDEN

I wolfed down another pancake as Joya discussed all the new high school happenings. I listened as best as I could, but my mind was thinking about so many things. Hiding in plain sight was cumbersome.

CHAPTER 11

"**Wow, you didn't** say Will and his family were loaded." Theodora's eyes were wide.

"Word, Indy—you could've prepared me; I would've brought my fur coat or something," Naomi huffed.

"Your fur coat?" I smirked.

Joya and I gazed up at Will's family cabin but calling it a cabin was an understatement. The large house looked completely wooden from the outside and on the corner of the property sat logs. With windows large enough to be the eyes to your soul, they lined the bottom to the tops of the house. Smoke billowed from the chimney, and Mr. Simms was on the side, chopping more wood. He waved and said, "ya'll head on in and get out of this cold. I know you Louisiana girls ain't used to this Tennessee freeze."

He was right about that, and I hustled to the house, shivering. I settled on one snowsuit after having it rush shipped online and I hoped it was warm enough. I pulled my scarf tighter around my neck and took in the trees heavy and full of bright snow through the windows.

Joya strolled through the house lightly touching the textured wallpaper with her mouth gaped open. "All of this is Will's?"

"I guess, he's been holding out this whole time." I nodded.

"No one has been holding out." Will came out of nowhere and he nudged my shoulder. I leaned into him and smiled.

"Thanks for letting me tag along at the last minute, Will. This is amazing." Joya looked around with wide eyes.

"Well, I for one, am going to enjoy these next two days. I bought a new snowsuit. I've never been skiing." Naomi did a happy dance and shimmied in the living room with Theodora. They were gawking at the massive stone fireplace and built-in bookshelves behind it.

Will took my hand and led me into the kitchen.

"I was thinking, do you want to go out to a movie tonight? We can leave everyone here and find somewhere in town," Will asked. His eyes were hesitant.

"Like a date?"

Will leaned back onto the counter and crossed his arms. "I mean, yes . . . no . . . It's whatever you want to call it."

"I'd like to call it a date," I said with a half-smile.

The skepticism left from Will's face. He transformed, flashing a grin, and uncrossing his arms. "Okay, it's a date."

"Where is your mom? And Dominique?" I looked around. I hadn't heard Dominique's loud voice yet and I knew she would be around here somewhere starting trouble.

"They're on the other side of the house preparing for dinner."

"The other side of the house?" I repeated. My cubbyhole back home didn't have another side. The whole house *was* the front, back, and side. I gazed at Will and wondered if this was what having two parents, and living the Black American dream, looked like. Could I have that? Instead of the penthouse, could I have the house . . . and with Will? "I'm going to grab the girls and we'll go help," I took Will's hand and palmed it. This would be a good weekend.

Joya, Naomi, Theodora, and I spent the next few hours helping Mrs. Simms prepare dinner. We moved around the kitchen, laughing, and sampling everything on the long, white, marble counters. "You dragging all that wagon, Ms. Naomi," Mrs. Simms said and motioned with her eyes down to Naomi's large rear-end. She nodded at her in approval, and we giggled as Naomi's face reddened.

Will was at the breakfast nook eating chips while Dominique was flipping through a magazine, paying little attention to us. She helped cook, but once Mrs. Simms realized Theodora could make authentic Jollof rice and pepper soup, we were all banished from the kitchen as she and Theodora worked their magic. I was worried Joya and my college friends wouldn't get along and it gave me a headache thinking about sleeping arrangements. I didn't have to worry at all because everyone vibed.

"Theodora, you should probably model. You ever heard of Naomi? Not your friend. The other one. You remind me of Naomi Campbell." Mrs. Simms swayed her hips like she was walking down a runway and sashayed with a serving spoon in her hand.

Theodora giggled and flipped her hair. She was used to people telling her she should model because of her height. Her brown skin, and deep cat eyes caught the attention of many at school, but Theodora preferred to stay to herself. I remembered a comment Theodora's mom said when they came for homecoming. *"No meat, Theo. No skin on these bones,"* she said, as she jiggled Theodora's waist. *"How we find you a husband with no meat?"* I wonder if she would tell them she wasn't interested in husbands right now, or her waistline.

"Woman, if you don't leave the girls alone," Mr. Simms said, setting the table. "Anything in here I can help with?"

"You want to cut them potatoes over there?" Mrs. Simms pointed with the knife.

"Uh... not particularly."

"Then what did you ask for, crazy?"

"I'll help you, Mr. Simms." Joya grabbed some plates and followed Mr. Simms around the table while Teena Marie blared from the speakers.

"It's snowing again," Will said, glancing up from his chips. "We can go skiing tomorrow morning."

"Have you been before?" I leaned into him over the counter.

"Yes, a few times. It's not really my thing." He gave a shrug.

"Well, me and my lady are heading out. We're staying at the casino in town tonight. You guys are on your own after dinner. My lady is dessert."

"Old man!" Mrs. Simms shushed her husband and grabbed potholders as she and Theodora scooped food and piled our plates high. The house smelled of cinnamon and cloves, with a dash of something spicy from Theodora's soup, which tickled my nose. Mrs. Simms began running down the rules of the house and how to set the alarms as she scooped the simmering brew over the stove.

"Honey, the kids will be fine. They're not even kids," Mr. Simms fussed.

"Oh, hush. I just want them to know where we'll be. Ain't nothing wrong with being safe."

"You're right, my love." Mr. Simms trotted over to his wife, placed his hands around her waist, and kissed her cheek.

Mr. and Mrs. Simms laughed, and she swatted him with her oven mitt. They moved throughout the kitchen one behind the other, opening the fridge, holding the cutting board in place, and cleaning up after each other. They moved in synchronicity, and they stood in front of the kitchen window over the sink in a dance of familiarity, which existed only between them. Without words, they anticipated each other's moves because they knew each other better than they knew themselves. Just beyond them, I made out the fluffy snow falling outside.

'*We're here for you, Indy,*' a voice in my head whispered.

'*Yes, we'll never leave you,*" another corner of my mind mumbled.

A tear trickled down my cheek, but I wiped it away before anyone noticed. I wanted synchronicity and familiarity too.

CHAPTER 12

After dinner, I retreated to my room I was sharing with Naomi. We had our clothes spread out on the bed. Joya and Theodora shared a room because they both wanted to get up early and hit the gym at the far end of the house. Naomi and I couldn't care less about the gym and were looking forward to sleeping in without setting an alarm.

Joya shouted from her room across the hall, "ya'll? Did you see the hot tub?"

"I saw it." I shrugged, shoving clothes into the dresser.

"Ummm, hello, I think we should try it out?" Joya complained. With Theodora and Joya in agreement, they didn't wait for me to respond, and pulled their bathing suits out of their bags. Naomi and I followed.

Twenty minutes later, five women surrounded Will. He stared at me across the hot tub as the water bubbled up and the steam covered his face. Theodora Facetimed someone. I looked closer; it was the same boy I had seen her with around campus recently. Dylan was his name. I recognized him because he was the Resident Assistant for our floor. Why would she be Facetiming him?

Naomi was taking selfies with her defined cheekbones pursed into duck lips. She sat her breasts on the edge of the hot tub, so they were perched up while she tilted her camera and posed. She was fly for a white girl, and she knew it.

Dominique was on the other side of the hot tub, pouring herself a drink. Whatever it was, made Dominique hiss and place two fingers to her neck.

Will's focus was steady. The way he studied my face slowed my breathing. While everyone around us was in their world, Will and I were in ours. It was a world that met in elementary school and demanded the same time and attention as any relationship—only it never was a relationship.

Outside was quiet and calm. Twinkling lights lit up the patio space, and all I could make out was white as far as the eye could see. No wind stirred and the night stars glistened above us. Stella dendrites they were called, those are perfectly shaped snowflakes. I learned about it in my Intro to Chemistry class. Funny, I couldn't remember it then when I took the test, and I pulled a low D on the assignment, but I remembered the answer clearly now. Stellar dendrites fell and melted like warm butter against Will's arm resting on the ledge.

Could I, Indigo Lewis, even dare something would work out for me, and he could... be mine? Even though it wasn't cold in the water, I shivered. Holidays at the family's cabin... us moving through the kitchen in best friend intimacy. But could it be? Through this hazy winter wonderland, with the softest snowflakes falling around us? This time, not even the voices interrupted. We shared energy. We spoke the same conversation, just without words. I melted under Will's smolder as my stomach did all sorts of flips. Tonight, would be the night, I decided.

And I was ready.

"Drink this, Indy." Dominique handed me a red cup. She was sweating profusely, and I couldn't tell if it was from the

alcohol or the hot tub. Her large breasts were spilling out of her bikini top.

Naomi, Theodora, and Joya gulped their drinks, while ever so cool Will sipped his. He rested his other arm on the ledge, and his chest pecked out. He never took his eyes off me.

I took a large gulp of the dark liquid, and it burned my chest going down like I knew it would. My nose cleared and my eyes watered.

"My girl can do better than that, ya'll have to see her knock them back on the fifth floor," Naomi said, holding up four fingers.

We all burst out laughing, and we took another sip of the flaming dark liquid. Joya coughed on hers and took a swig of water she had sitting on the edge.

"Theodora, have you guys seen the women's advocates on campus?" Naomi asked. She leaned forward and splashed water in Theodora's direction.

"Oh, you playing?" Theodora pushed water back. "Yeah, I saw them go through campus one day last week, it was powerful."

"What was this? And where was I?" I slurred my words. Things were looking a little hazy and my stomach was starting to turn. Saliva collected in my mouth.

"I think you were sleeping. It was the day you forgot to set your alarm and woke up late."

"Oh..." I grumbled.

Sometimes college seemed like a setup and designed for students to fail. On the other hand, I really had to kick it into high gear when we got back to school. I had to show Sidney what I could become and make Dad proud. All his hard work wouldn't be in vain. I had to get out of my own way.

My phone buzzed.

> **CHAQUILLE:** What it do?

I smiled at his text, and I saw Will flinch from the corner of my eye.

> **ME:** I'm actually in a hot tub, lol.

> **CHAQUILLE:** Oh aight, well I just wanted to check on you, make sure you made it home okay. You never texted me the other night.

Chaquille sent a crying emoji with his text and a flyer for his next event. I didn't text him back the other night after everything with Ez and Jill. I tapped my phone and enlarged the photo to get a better look. He wore large headphones and a hoodie with his hat over his head. He played the starving dj artist look very well. He was cute. More than cute. I would give him that.

As Will still stared at me, I texted Chaquille.

> **ME:** My bad! A lot has been going on. We'll definitely make it to your next spin session. Hopefully, you'll be spinning lol.

> **CHAQUILLE:** Haha you got jokes, huh? Yeah, I'll be spinning the next time for sure. I'll be looking for you...

I was trying to text Chaquille, but my hands kept wetting my screen. I wiped them on the towel next to the hot tub and Dominique swooped in and placed another drink in my hand, despite my objections from my already churning stomach. I

gulped this one down too. I nursed what I thought was my third drink, but Naomi reminded me that I already had a lot of drinks. This realization hit my stomach first. Tonight, something was threatening to spew in front of people.

This time it was from the ass end up.

Within a few minutes, I was out of the hot tub, racing to the bathroom. The girls and Will were giggling as water splashed everywhere. When I ran out, clutching my butt, they were hushed. No one dared to say a word, not even the voices in my head. I raced to the house, flinging the patio door open. It jammed, and I remembered Mr. Simms telling me earlier the door got stuck sometimes. I had to lean my weight and apply a little pressure onto the glass. It was damn near frozen. I felt my stomach knot, then pop, preparing to rumble. I banged and scratched at the door like a helpless animal. My stomach exploded and the loudest, longest fart escaped my behind and I saw the whites of my eyes in the glass door. I tried desperately to pry it open, but the sliding glass wouldn't budge. I contemplated breaking the glass.

My eyes turned darker. I glanced around, looking for something sharp to open the door with, when feet paddled to me, taking wide and quick steps. Walking face first into my fart air was Mrs. Simms, and she came from the other side of the door and unlocked it. It slid open with perfect ease like I hadn't been ready to smash it to smithereens seconds earlier.

"Hey, baby, are you okay? Ya'll don't be out here drinking. Rich, I told you we shouldn't leave the kids! They already out here sipping and giggling, and we haven't even made it to the casino! And what's that smell? Oh my! Is there a dead racoon out here? Rich, grab the rat poison from under the sink. I think there's a racoon hiding under the patio again!" she yelled behind her into the cabin. Naomi, Joya, and Dominique were standing up in the hot tub with their hands covering their mouths in shock by all the things taking place. Their mouths were hanging open because of me.

"Excuse me!" I rushed past Mrs. Simms and Mr. Simms, now coming outside with rat poison and a flashlight in his hand.

"Oh no, oh no." Dominique grabbed her butt and screamed. She and Joya slapped each other's padded snowsuits and burst in hysterical laughter. Strangers crinkled their faces in our direction as they guffawed and reenacted me running for my life last night before my stomach unleashed sounds and smells reminiscent of a zoo. Their ski helmets covered their faces, and their goggles were foggy from the tears coming to their eyes.

Under my navy-blue ski suit, long johns, and headgear, my face was a deep shade of red hidden behind dark, black sunglasses.

'I told you not to drink. Now look at you. All hungover,' Mom said in my head with a deep sigh.

Naomi and Theodora were trying not to laugh, and I could see them pursing their lips together, stifling their giggles. They checked on me throughout the night to make sure I was okay with genuine concern, but now they were having a tough time holding in their amusement. Especially with Dominique going for an Oscar award winning performance at my expense.

"You too, huh?" I shook my head between them.

Naomi let out a deep grunt before she cackled. I spread my legs and knees inward like the ski instructor showed us. Using my ski stick, I stepped away from them and searched for Will. My stomach was not cooperating this morning and was still shaky from last night. When Mrs. Simms returned from the casino, she and Theodora made a large breakfast spread,

complete with thick slices of French toast with strawberries. I took one bite, and I was back in the bathroom within minutes. Now it was coming out of both ends.

"Do you think it's something you ate?" Naomi had asked. She held my braids as I heaved and cried into the toilet.

"We all ate the same thing. No one else is sick," I coughed.

Naomi said, "girl, you just cannot hold your liquor," and shook her head, while dabbing my forehead with a wet towel. I tasted bitter alcohol on my tongue, and the aftertaste in my throat was chalky against my teeth.

I slid to Will, but I wasn't moving too fast on this hill. Every move made my head pound harder, and I was slower than the rest of the girls. Joya skied like she did this for a living. She looked like a professional, gliding across the snow in her bright, pink snowsuit. We started at the green hills, which they say are easier. The girls were ready to move up to the next level, and I was searching for a tree to hurl behind. I refused to stay at the house. I paid good money for this snowsuit, and I was going to be seen one way or another.

'Always worried about the wrong things, my dear,' Mom said with another sigh.

"Leave me alone," I grumbled out loud.

When I made my way to Will, he was fumbling with his ski poles with his brows furrowed together.

"Are you okay?" I questioned.

"I should be asking you that. You passed out last night, and this morning you were at the breakfast table, silent with sunglasses on."

Yikes. He was right. My eyes were bloodshot red, and I didn't want Will's parents to see me that way, so the glasses went on and stayed on.

"I just can't get this to fit right," Will grunted. He stepped off his snowboard, lifted it above his head, and yanked on the shoelaces.

"Will. Our date. We never got to —" and before I could say another word, Will's snowboard hit me square in my head and my eyes rolled back then I blacked out.

CHAPTER 13

"MAMA JACKIE?" I said, sitting up.

"Hi, my Indy Lindy." She patted my leg and smiled. My grandmother, Mama Jackie, had cocoa brown skin and soft gray hair that shined against the moonlight. Her deep laugh lines creased her face, and they reminded me of the rings around tree trunks. They were smooth and ingrained into her face from years of jokes and love for us.

Wait. Why was it night-time? I was just skiing with Will and the girls?

"You've hurt yourself pretty good," Mama Jackie read my thoughts. "You needed a time-out of sorts, so they sent you here."

"They?"

Mama Jackie smiled and ignored my question. "Stand up my, girl, let me look at you."

As the family jewel gone too soon rose to her feet, so did the memories. Mama Jackie on the lake with Grandpa Ez. Grandpa Ez... He let us call him that when Mama Jackie was still alive. That was before the cancer stole her away. Against the moonlight, she wore a baby-blue, frilly dress that looked like doilies. She had a white shawl wrapped around her body. She was barefoot and smelled like heaven. If heaven had a smell, it was Mama Jackie. She was a lady.

SOMEONE MORE LIKE MYSELF

I saw a younger Sidney and Ez on the lake, rowing back and forth. She screamed, "faster Grandpa, faster!" As she clapped and squealed. He grunted and kicked into second gear and cut through the water, willing to go that extra mile for his Sidney. Mom and Dad watched from the edge of the water. He built our house for her.

"Oh, dear, she's up," Mom sang, in a fake English accent.

Sonia Lewis took my breath away. It had been so long since I had seen her dressed up. I looked her up and down, taking brain pictures of every inch of her. She wore a floor length, white boho dress. It was frayed at the ends. Her hair was curly and unruly on her head. Black ringlets formed at her scalp, and her moisturized mane glistened against the stars.

Indigo stars.

Every time I had seen my mom in the past three years, she wore a blue and white scrub set. Standard issued Trochesse: Home for the Criminally Insane attire. "Mom, I-I..."

"Indy Lindy, cat got your tongue," Mom cackled.

Her eyes danced and roamed my body. Maybe she was taking brain pictures too. I spent so much time trying to escape my mind, but now I was trapped inside and having visions. How was that even possible? Mama Jackie was clearly dead—we buried her years ago and Ez hadn't been the same since. But Mom? For someone who was in an insane asylum for purposely hitting a man with her car, she sure was happy.

And I was happy to see her.

"Took her long enough, right, Ms. Sonia?" Chaquille rapped.

Chaquille.

What was he doing here? I mean, it sounded like he rapped it. His New York accent was heavy here, wherever here was. His words sounded melodious, like if he had a mic, he could flow right into a set.

"What are you guys doing?" I stood up and lost my balance again. My head was pounding already from the alcohol, but now it was pounding from where Will hit me with his snowboard. That memory flashed in my

mind when I looked around and realized I was back in Tunica Rivers. Will wasn't here, but Chaquille was. I had to be dreaming.

Chaquille caught me before I tripped, and when I bumped into him, his chest played music. It was like that game we used to play as kids, Operation. As my body touched his, he illuminated into what looked like neon music symbols. He looked down at himself and smiled.

"What the—"

"You stop all that drinking." Mama Jackie stood in front of me, wagging her finger.

Chaquille held me up and as my knees buckled from my stomach pain, he whispered, "I got you."

"Half the time I'm falling because of you," I mumbled.

"Na, I don't think I was given a fair shake," Chaquille whispered in my ear. "But I'm here now."

"Why are you here? I don't need anyone."

"The girl thinks she doesn't need anyone. But you needed someone last year with Jaxon, right?" Mom giggled and shoved her hand over her mouth. "Did I tell you I had a dream you did it, Indy? Yup. I was laying in my bed, and it came to me. I was just grinning away, just like Morgan Freeman in the prison cell, in that movie, Lean on Me. I was smiling just like that. What a moment. My dreams don't lie. I know'd what you did," she giggled and danced with Chaquille.

I sucked in humid air and felt nauseous.

Mama Jackie placed her hand on my stomach and shut her eyes.

"Mom— I saw you..." I started.

Mama Jackie rocked me, and she hummed a low tune I couldn't decipher. She moved her hands and fingers over my belly, tracing a pattern. I looked down, and one by one, colors lit up my body starting from my thighs up to my head. The colors changed from red, orange, and yellow. When it stopped at my head, the color became a bright purple. Mama Jackie whispered and closed her eyes again. She rubbed and rubbed until my stomach aches and nausea were gone.

"Wow," I said, standing up straighter. I arched my back, and it cracked from hunching over.

"That should do it," Mama Jackie said and took a step back. "Your turn," she said to Mom. "And hush all that fussing. It's over now, and that boy is somewhere far away from our girl."

"My Indy Lindy," Mom's English accent was just above a hush after being scolded by Mama Jackie. "My, how you've grown. Got these little boys right where you want them." She motioned to Chaquille. "Remember, they go out with you—you don't go out with them," she snickered. Mom danced in place and waved her hand to the skies. "You look just like your mama, girl—good for you. You'll catch a big fish with that face. As many as you want, girl. But you are the biggest fish. Now Indy. What are we going to do about this, Mr. Chestnut? He just cannot go on like this." Mom stared into my eyes, and my knees felt like they would buckle again. My stomach felt fine, but it was the weight of a parent giving their child an assignment that felt heavy.

"Sonia!" Mama Jackie scolded. 'That child just don't stop." Mama Jackie's thin hair blew in the wind. "We're not even talking about that man!"

"I know Mama, but Chestnut must be dealt with, just like Jaxon. She's gotta do this. She knows it too."

Mama Jackie whipped around and stared at me for a long time. Her eyes roamed my face, hair, and finally my chest. It was like she was seeing me for the first time as a teenager. Not the young adolescent I was when she passed away. But a woman. Her granddaughter, who had to make some tough choices. Survival was the name of the game in this family, and we took people out for less.

"My Indy—all grown up and making her own decisions," she fluttered. Tears glistened in her eyes.

"I'm here to give you your superpower." Mom swung her hips and pressed her fingers together. She shimmied like she was dancing with maracas. She didn't notice Mama Jackie's disdain—but I did.

"My superpower?"

Mom nodded with a mischievous grin.

"And what's my superpower?" I leaned in. The voices? It was that. How do I get rid of them? Surely, she knew. There had to be something to rid myself of them since therapy wasn't panning out.

"You Indy. You are your superpower. You have to listen to your dreams. We have dreams in this family. I like to call us Moon Maidens." Mom grinned.

"What kind of cockamamie crap is that?" Chaquille challenged.

"Oh, you hush, boy. I don't even see you over there—how's that for cockamamie?" Mom stuck her finger in Chaquille's face and crossed her arms at her chest. When she did, she lost her footing and tripped under her feet. Mama Jackie, who I would consider the Black Mother Teresa, giggled.

Heat surged through my body. It had been so long since I heard my grandmother's laugh. Within seconds, tears pooled in my eyes. Grandpa Ez still had an old-school house phone, with a press and click voicemail box. Mama Jackie's voice was still all over it when she thanked people for calling and recited Galatians 5:22-23. I knew that scripture through and through, as it was one of her favorites. When it spoke of forgiveness and self-control, Mama Jackie recited that part with fervor and added in a little giggle at the end that made us snort listening to it. She used to get so worked up talking about the Bible, and her love for the Lord, that she preached, even in a voicemail message. They were leftover family gems and we hung on to them with everything we had. I hoped she would forgive me with that same intensity for the things I had done. Even in my dreams and now, even knocked out, the ladies in my life were with me.

Mom and Chaquille shared a glance, then a smile, and then a laugh. Mom's tone was aggressive. She talked at men—directing them to do what she wanted. She said it was the Aries in her. To anyone else in the south, they would've found her tactless, and she was in some ways. But Chaquille found her amusing. That was the New York in him.

"Anyway, yes, you are your superpower, Indy. My girl, you put so much effort and energy into the negative. Worrying about so many things. The only person you have to listen to is you. You got those bad nerves from your father, girl. You're in college now, and Mama Jackie and I want you to have fun. Take control of the driver's seat."

"Take control how, Mom? How? I have to worry about things," I hissed, trying to keep my voice low so Chaquille didn't hear. He was standing at the edge of the water now, laughing with Ez and Sidney.

"Nonsense. No one is worried about that boy, chile. We have to focus on Chestnut now." Mom waved her hand at me and turned her nose up as if I had said aliens landed.

"Indy Lindy. I don't condone nothing ya'll thinking 'bout doing, but I know that he is a nasty old man and well—women have to do what they have to do. Protect yourself at all times. Okay, my girl?"

"Okay, Mama Jackie." I nodded. And I meant it.

"It's time for you to go back now, my girl." Mama Jackie rubbed my braids, and Mom clasped my hands.

"Do I have to?"

"Yes, you have work to do," Mom said. She cupped my face with her hands, and her smooth skin was cold against my face. Tears sprang to my eyes again as I felt myself come to. I blinked away stars, and different eyes looked at me as I adjusted to the bright whiteness of the snow.

"Indy . . . Indy, are you okay?" Will questioned, his eyebrows pinched together.

"I'm fine," I wheezed. My voice strained, and my head was on fire. Joya, Naomi, Dominique, and Theodora stood off to the side. Their eyes were wide with concern.

I sat up on my elbows, sinking into the snow.

I was taking L's all weekend.

CHAPTER 14

TROCHESSE: HOME FOR THE CRIMINALLY INSANE soared in front of me and Sidney. I looked up at the building that still wore a sign on the east wing which read: **the colored side.** Last year, Trochesse's board of directors voted to have it removed, but they decided against it because some stuffy white guys said it was historic.

Mom was still on this side.

The line moved fast and I was thankful. My back and head still pained from our fateful ski trip with Will and the girls. I was the laughing stock for days. By the time we got back to Tunica Rivers, I was ready to see my mom. Ez was in front of Trochesse, standing guard and making sure the line moved according to his standards. He gawked to his left and right, frowning at anyone gazing at us too long. To them, he was a giant of a man. To us, he was our protector, and he would protect us from his own daughter if he had to.

Last week made four years Mom was locked away. After she ran that old man over with her car and laughed about it; she was as good as gone. I wondered how it looked to them. A dark-skinned, heavyset, round-faced woman purposely hitting a decorated war veteran. She didn't know that's what he was, but that's how the news liked to spin it. They constantly mentioned she was a Black woman with mental health issues, as if it were a double negative of some sort. Not only was being a woman hard enough but dammit, you just had to go and be a Black one too.

Four long years. She missed junior and senior prom, getting my driver's license, and then crashing Ez's car the same day. Not a big crash, but enough to get him riled up. Graduation. She missed Sidney's heart and her become this amazing person. My courage to do things I never thought I would have to—and most importantly of all, that I enjoyed doing those things. I couldn't forget that part. The thoughts in my head were still living rent free. If it lived in me, I must enjoy hurting people, right? I mean, I only technically hurt one person, but murder was a biggie.

Once inside, we found a metal table and waited for the patients to come out of their rooms. The hall was buzzing with activity and a lot of families were visiting their loved ones after the holidays. Nurse Meanface raised an eyebrow over her glasses. Her pale skin turned deep red as she leaned over to the other nurse and pointed to Mom. We had problems with this nurse. She had it out for Mom, and she wasn't fond of her performances with her band, *The Band-aids*. This was according to Mom, so who knew how true it was.

Nurse Meanface nodded to Ez, and he gave a weak smile and pursed his lips. His eyes lit up when he spotted Mom coming down the spiral staircase, but it quickly faded when he realized she was wearing a full Chinese kimono. Her face was painted white, her lips were bright red, and she wore what looked like chopsticks in her hair. From where I stood, they were really toothbrushes.

"Flowers for the lady?" A stocky, Black man leaned in. His sweater and even his shoes resembled Mom's dress. When I

snooped closer, I realized it was the same material. They had made costumes for the visit.

Mom often wrote letters about her band. She gathered everyone in Trochesse with an ounce of musical talent and she whipped them into shape, naming herself their manager. She was the only one who could sing, and the others tried to keep up with Mom. Her right-hand man was Minister because he could play the drums and she said when he did, he moved everyone in the room.

He handed me and Sidney one rose. Sidney smelled hers. I brought mine to my lips, letting it tickle my nose. The smell reminded me of Mama Jackie's perfume.

I turned to Ez and placed the flower to his nostrils. When he inhaled, I watched his breathing quicken and his eyes sparkled. He smelled it too. Mama Jackie. Just as quick, his eyes saddened and his brows furrowed.

"Get that out my face, girl," Ez said, swatting the rose away. He plopped down at a table and the whole thing sank under his weight. I thought I saw a tear in his eye.

"Minister, tell the people I'm on my way," Mom said from the top of the steps.

She kicked her leg out of the kimono and her long, shapely brown stems glistened from the shea butter I'm sure she slathered on before we got here. The kimono stopped right above her knee, and she wore her Trochesse issued unisex Crocs. The other visitors in the hall cried out and clapped with love for the antics. Minister, who was indeed the rose pusher, threw more roses at Mom's feet.

"Ruth-Ann!" Sidney squealed.

"Who, chile?" Ez stumbled to his feet and raised his fists into a defensive stance.

"Ruth-Ann is in the band, Ez! And Cordelia and Gordy too!" Sidney slapped her hands against her cheeks and said, "go, Mom!"

She stood on the metal table and cheered while Mom strutted her way down the spiral staircase with Gordy, Cordelia, and Ruth-Ann in tow, wearing their own kimono print sweaters and matching belts.

An all-Black band in a mental hospital, putting on concerts during visiting hours. Life was wild.

"You get down off of that table now," Nurse Meanface hissed.

This was the first time I saw her down from her little bubble in the center of the room. It was the hub of activity where visitors went to check on their loved one's medical concerns. I had seen her take a cuss out more than once during a visit. Her face told how she felt, but she never said a word to the patients' families, which was more than I can say for the other nurses.

During our last visit, Ez, Sidney, and I were in line while another nurse was on break. She sat under a weeping willow tree on a picnic table on the phone, interviewing for another job. Ez was tickled by that.

"She over there begging for a new job, at her job," Ez laughed. It was a rare occasion when he didn't glower at someone else. He just laughed. It was funny how people saw things differently. What type of person hated their job so much they held an interview during their lunch break? And what did that mean for Mom's care?

"I'm sorry." Sidney's lip quivered. She looked so much younger than thirteen. Ez's head whipped around in a flash, and he scowled at Nurse Meanface, and what a mean face it was. She didn't look much older than Mom who was in her forties, but for some reason she *looked* old. She wore heavy make-up caked on and I saw her pores, the size of little needles, littering her face. The make-up sat in the specks and made her face shine. She lined her eyebrows with brown liner, and I could see where she didn't take her foundation all the way up into her hairline.

Baby girl didn't know how to blend.

"Who are you, lady? Don't be talking to SidRock like that." Ez hovered in front of Nurse Meanface.

"I'm sorry, Mr. Campbell. Ms. Lewis' daughter cannot stand on the tables in this facility."

Ms. Lewis' daughter, she said. Like Sidney didn't have a name or wasn't important enough for her to learn. We had been coming here for four years and she didn't even know our names.

"What seems to be the problem here?" Mom sauntered to us and swept a rose under her lip.

"Ms. Lewis, how are you today? Your daughter here cannot stand on the tables. I know she is excited to see you, but these are the rules." Nurse Meanface nodded over her glasses.

"You hear that, ya'll? Nursie nurse nurse, here says that my Sidney can't sing to her mama. She says that children can't be children. What do ya'll think about that?"

Mom's friends, and some of the visitors, nodded and clapped. An old man in the back, sitting in his wheelchair, rose and screamed, "come on now, Sonia!"

"Mom, it's okay," Sidney said, getting down from the table. She tugged at the back of Mom's kimono and eyed Nurse Meanface, who was staring at Mom with her arms folded.

"Now, Ms. Lewis, we go through this all the time, and you continue to break the rules. You know what happened last time."

"What happened last time, girl?" Ez slid between Sidney and Mom, while he demanded answers from Nurse Meanface.

Mom glared at Nurse Meanface. Even though she was at a clear disadvantage, she would never back down from a fight and would rumble with the beast. "And who made the rules? More white people who don't know nothing about us little people down here," Mom's voice echoed through the hall. "We can't wear our hair bonnets out of our rooms, we can't play Spades, we can't listen to the radio too loud because our music is irritating. Why don't you just say it, ya'll don't like Black people up in here, up in here," Mom's voice bellowed through the hall. Ruth-Ann, Cordelia, and Minister stood off to the side of Mom, clutching each other, looking on. They made me smile. They took great care to match their costumes, and now they were upstaged by whatever this was. And what was this? What was happening?

"Ms. Lewis, I did not mean to upset you. Can you please lower your aggressive tone so you can resume your visits and everyone else's?" Nurse Meanface's shoulders were tight, and she straightened her tiny lips into a flat line.

"You hear that now, ya'll? I'm aggressive. I'm aggressive!" Mom shouted. "Always the angry Black woman story, right? You know I went to a place like this when I was younger. They talk any which way they want to you; they withhold food when they feel like it, and then they start to tell you how to think, how to feel. My own daddy put me there. Well, no more. No more will anyone tell us how to think or feel, Nurse!" Mom pointed at Nurse Meanface, but I watched Mom command attention in the room. The old man in his wheelchair stood up. Albeit leaning against a wall and clearly pained—but he stood. Others and their families watched and embraced. Everyone listened to Mom's words as she infected every part of them that wanted to rage against the machine.

It was days like this I didn't understand how I felt or why. My mom was powerful. When she talked, people listened. They trusted her. How she managed to get dozens of people with mental problems to listen to her spoke volumes. Then again, I had mental problems and I listened to her in my head and in real life.

She affected everyone she encountered, and while I was proud of her, I just wanted my mom. I wanted to sit in her

arms and cry. Let her tell me everything would be okay. I wanted to tell her about Will, and Mr. Chestnut, and Ez, and if she thought I could have it too; the sickness. I wanted us to figure it out together; I wanted help. I needed help. If I told someone about Jaxon, it would have to be Mom and only Mom. Only she would understand. But *would* she understand? She wasn't the most reliable storyteller or secret keeper, nor did she remember what she said and to whom. A good story was a performance, and she lived for the performance.

"Cut that talk out now, Sonia!" Ez screeched. His voice echoed through the hall, which was now quiet except for a few phones chiming. Someone from the back of the room had their cell phone out.

They were recording us.

My family was funny to them.

I cringed. "Mom, it's okay," I said through clinched teeth. I moved closer and breathed into her ear. "Everyone is okay."

Mom didn't look at me, but her eyes bore a hole into Ez. "You tell me to cut it out. You and Mama Jackie did this to me."

"You wasn't right, Sonia! You needed help. You was saying all that crazy stuff. You was cutting up them cats and talking to the walls. What were we supposed to do?" Ez faced his daughter. They shared the same syrupy skin. The horizontal lines in their foreheads matched and they had the same dimple on the same cheek.

"Code 7, we have a code 7 in the rec hall," Nurse Meanface pressed into her radio.

"You see how they do us!" someone screamed from the back of the room.

"This is our time!" another screamed, banging her hands on the table.

"Allie, is everything okay?" a voice said behind Nurse Meanface.

She turned around. I peeked around her shoulder and my mouth dropped open.

Mr. Chestnut stood there with a fruit salad and a bag of food. His wedding ring shined brighter than ever, and I never noticed it before. "Allie—baby, what's going on?" Mr. Chestnut looked confused between Nurse Meanface, and what seemed like the rest of the rec hall.

"Honey, I'm okay. What are you doing here?" Nurse Meanface softened her face. It melted into daydreamy reverie, and the corners of her nasty mouth turned into a smile.

Mom kicked her leg out to expose the deep slit in her dress, but Nurse Meanface flinched anyway.

"Let's go, Allie," Mr. Chestnut assessed the crowd and grabbed her arm.

"Mr. Chestnut?" I whispered. I couldn't help myself.

"Yeah, I remember you too, Mr. Chestnut," Mom said, giving herself a deep, baritone voice. The way she could switch characters and voices so quickly was quite admirable. I looked at her partly with amazement and fear. Who was this woman? She was someone new each time I saw her.

"Indigo, right?" He pointed at me and closed one eye.

This asshole knew exactly who I was.

The Band-aids moved from next to Mom, stood behind Nurse Meanface and Mr. Chestnut. Ez, Sidney, and I closed out the other end of this haphazard circle with Mom. Nurse Meanface, and Mr. Chestnut were in the center. Eager eyes filled in the gaps on each side.

"Gregg, what is this?" Nurse Meanface or Allie said.

"This is one of my previous students, honey."

"And did you tell her about me? Ohhh Mr. Chestnut," Mom said. Her voice was still in a deep baritone.

"I will not stand for this," Mr. Chestnut said, clutching the bag of food he brought for . . . for who, really? I eyed Nurse

Meanface's ID badge by her waist and sure enough, it said Allie Chestnut.

His wife. Nurse Meanface was Mr. Chestnut's wife.

My blood ran cold when I made the connection. Nurse Meanface didn't seem so big and bad anymore. She had to know who or what her husband was. I mean, he got Joya pregnant last year!

"Cordelia, baby—come forth." Mom motioned, now switching to her best and my personal favorite—an English accent. "Remember when we were in group, and they made us make a list of all the people we hold grudges against?"

"Sure do, boss lady." Cordelia nodded. "That was a good one." Her kimono poked more from the front than the back.

"Would you believe I had Ms. Nurse Allie here on my grudge list. And I was thinking of taking her off, because well, maybe it's not her fault that they treat us like this here . . . but I changed my mind."

"And why is that, boss lady?" Cordelia mused.

"Because I didn't know she was entangled with the infamous Gregg Chestnut of Tunica Rivers. You know where I'm from, Cordelia?"

"Where you from, boss lady?"

"I'm from Tunica Rivers too. And I know what it smells like in the morning when the world still sleeps; it smells fresh. Like laundry. And by the time people like Chestnut here muddy it up with their lies and bullshit, it smells like something I don't like."

"Gregg, what is she talking about?" Nurse Meanface pressed. She looked between Mom and Mr. Chestnut now.

A patient howled and banged his hands on the table. His neck bulged as he shouted at the sky and laughed crazily. A trail of spit cascaded out of his mouth. In unison, each table behind and around us banged on their tables and shouted like they were howling at the moon.

Out of the corner of my eye, I saw Sidney take a seat. Her eyes were wide, and she cowered. I bit my lip, hating she had to see this. However, I didn't want to stop it. My pulse intensified, and I felt jolts through my body. The back of my neck tingled under my braids. I watched every face in the crowd in slow motion. They were eager for more. This was action to them and standing beside my mom, I itched to feel her need to perform. To help her. What did this do for her? And if I was like her—what would this do for me?

"Ya'll stop that right now!" Nurse Meanface yelled. The hall erupted into howls and shrieks from the patients and their visitors. The circle closed until Mr. and Mrs. Gregg Chestnut, the colonizers—were in the center with nowhere to go.

"Nothing, honey, she used to be one of my students too. Another nobody doing nothing with her life. Now move," he demanded.

The last syllable didn't make it into the air before Ez stormed to the front, slinging me and Mom out of the way. "Say it again to me, pretty boy! I'm beef, you chicken sausage!" Ez roared. He paced back and forth, and he ripped the buttons from his shirt and flung it open. Sidney just bought that shirt earlier, especially for this visit. I balled my fists and my temples throbbed. I didn't need voices to know what to do here. I took a few steps, stood next to Ez on his left side, and Mom stood on his right. Not a weak side in sight.

I glanced back at Sidney. What were we about to do in front of her? Ez was quirky and had his ways. Dad blamed it on his autism, but he said it like it was a negative thing. I didn't see a negative side to Ez, only how much more I loved him. And Mom... So much of me was her—and so much of her—was me. I wanted to talk. I wanted to learn as much as I could and figure out how to manage life with this thing living inside of me, straight from the horse's mouth.

Before anyone made a move, a large siren screeched through the hall, and the water sprinklers went off from above.

"Oh no, my hair, darling!" Mom cried in her English accent.

"SidRock, you okay?" Ez rumbled.

She nodded but said nothing.

People ran in different directions in and out of the building. Nurse Meanface stood there with her make-up and mascara running down her face.

"Come on, woman," Mr. Chestnut tapped her shoulder and turned away before she could respond. He whipped around and glared at me and Mom before he stalked off.

"Indy, let's go!"

Ez grabbed my arm and pulled me out with the other herds of people making a beeline for the door to get away from the water and screeching alarm. Ez's powerful arms pulled me from behind while Sidney held his hand in the front and led the way. I turned around and saw my mom; people were patting her on her back and congratulating her.

She waved to me.

CHAPTER 15

"MILA. I'VE BEEN texting you... how are you?" I asked. I glanced her up and down. I leaned in to give my high school best friend a hug. When she backed away, I almost fell into her.

She didn't want to hug me back.

'Now, what's this about?' Mom hissed in my head.

Yea, what was *this*?

"Indy, hey... It's been a long time."

"It's been a few months. I thought you were going to come to Titus to visit like we talked about?" I whined. Mila and I were thick as thieves and the fact she dropped off the face of the earth, while I was amid the toughest year with starting college and everything else going on didn't sit right with me.

"Oh, I uhh... I've been busy working at the office."

"Busy working at the office?" I repeated and sucked my teeth. That was a lame excuse. Bullshit and she knew it. Why was she acting like this?

Tunica Rivers only had a few gas stations, and I always went to the same one right in the center of town. I was up early this

morning, running a few errands. As fate would have it— we made our way to our old haunt at the same time.

"Indigo... hey," I heard his voice.

Malachi.

I swung around from my side of the pump and watched him fumble with a bag full of snacks and treats. He was still eating anything he could get his hands on. Normally, it was funny, but I needed to know what the fuck was going on with my two former best friends.

They awkwardly stood next to each other while Mila pumped. "Guys... what is this?" I asked straight up. They were standing next to each other. Their eyes darted in every direction except mine.

Malachi cleared his throat. "Indy... Mila, and I are... are... hanging out."

"Hanging out?" Mila repeated.

"Mila is my girl, Indy..." Malachi corrected with unnecessary bass in his voice.

"Is this why I haven't heard from both of you? I've called and texted."

"Sorry you had to find out this way, Indy. I wanted to tell you face to face. *We* wanted to tell you face to face," Mila said.

Malachi cut his eyes at me, and I gazed between my ex-boyfriend and my best-friend. They both shared parts of my heart I thought would be cemented forever. Only they had wedged me out and found something between the two of them that didn't require my presence or even consent. Not that they needed my consent, but damn.

"How about I come over later, and we can talk?" Malachi asked with earnest eyes.

"Go over? Malachi—no," Mila stepped in.

"She's right, there's no need to come over and talk about anything. I see you two found everything you needed. Thanks for the heads up though, I appreciate you letting me know . . . you know, friend to friend," I spewed.

"Indy, stop. You're a college, career woman now, right? You've texted a few times; yes, I'll give you that. But where were you when my grandmom passed away? I never heard from you, and you knew how close we were. Malachi was here. We . . . we were there for each other. And besides . . . why is it any different than you and Will? I dated him first. And now he barely talks to me and Malachi because he's hung up on you. You made your choice and so did Will. You guys pushed us out. You went away and forgot about us little people. We made our choice too. Come on, Malachi." Mila motioned for Malachi to follow her. Malachi looked between me and Mila, his yin and yang. He got into Mila's Dodge Neon and drove off without looking in my direction.

'The nerve of that, hussy! After everything you've done for her!' Mom shouted in my head.

"Stop, Mom!" I flared.

Another patron looked at me from behind the pump next to mine. I held back angry tears as I shoved the nozzle back. It was only 8:30 a.m. and I felt enraged. How dare the two of them think they could date or keep something like this from me! The last time Will and I talked about them, he said they were dodging his calls and since he was knee deep in plumbing school, he didn't press the issue. I wondered if he knew they were dating. I wondered how he felt . . . knowing he and Mila used to date. Would he care? Would he care that I cared? Why did I care? I rested my head on the headrest and thought about Mila's grandmom with whom she was close to. How could I miss that? Was I a bad friend? And why didn't my dad tell me? I banged my hand on the steering wheel in frustration. I couldn't hold back the tears any longer and they fell down my cheeks.

I started The Bus with the weight of lies and deceit spilling from all directions. I drove down the road with my hands tight around the steering wheel intent on my original destination before I spotted Mila and Malachi. I was going to turn Mr. Chestnut in; that was my next mission. After spotting him at the mall and then at Trochesse, something had to be done. Only I didn't want the blowback to catch up to me.

Searching online the night before had me racoon eyed and crazy looking the next morning. I needed to find something to help Ez and a way to take out Mr. Chestnut that didn't leave me having to explain about Jaxon. I wiped my wet face and pressed my way to the Tunica Rivers Social Services building per Google. I needed to find people to help with Ez, and they had this legal advocacy program where I could file an anonymous complaint about school employees.

He couldn't keep getting away with this. I had two weeks left of winter break and I wanted him handled before I returned. Titus was too small for the both of us. Shit, Tunica Rivers was too small for the both of us, and that was more reason he had to go. Chaquille texted me this morning and I had left it on read. He wanted to get together for lunch when I returned. I was living a whole different life right now in Tunica Rivers. Titus, lunch dates, and even Chaquille, were not at the top of that list.

The worry about what or who Chestnut would do next kept me up at all hours. Since I saw him at the mall with that girl, it was on replay in my brain. Surely, he wasn't untouchable. Would we stop being overlooked? Would we stop ignoring what men did to us, to save face for them?

When I got to the building, I checked the directory and made my way to a corner office down a short corridor. A middle-aged male receptionist looked me up and down as I walked toward him. He didn't hide his eyes while he roamed my body, taking in each curve with a slow head nod.

"How may I help you?" he asked, licking his lips.

I wanted to say *yes, which floor handles rich old men who take advantage of teen girls?*

"Yes, uh, is this the legal advocacy group?"

"Indeed, it is."

"I'd like to file a complaint, about ah...ah...man..."

"Is this about a party?"

"Well—sort of, I guess..."

He shook his head and sat his pen down. "Honey, you have to stay away from those parties. Have you tried talking to the guy first?"

"Excuse me?"

"The man. You said a man, right? Sweetheart?"

'I told you go home, Indy—these people crazy!'

'Did he just say...'

The voices rang out and I felt nauseous. I grasped the sides of the counter to steady myself and bit my bottom lip. I took in a deep breath. "No, that's not what it's about. Well, it is—I'd like to report something, for someone else."

"Oh, honey, you can't report something for someone else." The man sat back in his chair and scratched his beard. He winked at me like we shared a secret, and I was supposed to know the answer already.

"Why not?"

"Well, honey, if the woman —"

"Please don't call me honey." I sucked my teeth and looked at him straight away.

"My apologies." The man held up his hands and slid back in his rolling chair. "If the woman is not alleging anything happened, what are we supposed to do with that? I'll tell you what? You bring this person in, and I'll see what I can do. If we get enough women to come forward, we might even get them to give a presentation or something."

"A presentation?" I repeated.

He nodded. "You know last year was terrible, just terrible. All they did was hand out condoms and offer STD testing during the lunch hour rush at the high-school. You young kids have to be careful." He gave me one last glance over.

My hands went limp. "Fine. Where can I find, uh—human services?"

"That's on the fourth floor. Take the elevator—actually, no. The elevator is broken. You're going to have to take the stairs. Sorry," he shrugged.

Climbing the steps one by one, my breathing became more ragged with each landing. By the time I reached the fourth floor, my underarms were perspiring, and my toes were wet and clammy inside my socks. I swung the door open and burst into the human services office. Two ladies waiting jumped in their seats and clutched their purses. My braids swung wildly and I could feel the little foundation I had on my face sweating. Damn, Theodora told me I had to stop wearing that drug-store shit and get something more high-end. My light make-up pooled in an oily mess on my skin.

"Hi, uh, I would like some information about the day program for older adults?" I said to the receptionist. This one was younger, and she looked about my mom's age.

"What is this for?"

"Uh, a family member."

"Is he on drugs?"

"No."

"Is he a person living with HIV?"

"Uh, I don't think so."

"Is he a domestic violence survivor or perpetrator?"

I crinkled my nose and shook my head.

"Is he diagnosed with anything?

"Autism."

"Who diagnosed him and when?"

"I'm not sure."

She looked at me and cleared her throat. "And you are?"

"I'm his granddaughter, Indigo Lewis. Look." I leaned in so no one else could hear. "I don't know when he was diagnosed or anything like that. I know my dad says they diagnosed him as autistic, and I believe he is. He needs help."

"I understand that, Ms. Lewis. But are you listed as his emergency contact?"

"I don't think so."

"And you said autism. That is the developmental disabilities department."

"Where is that?"

"On the seventh floor. But they go to lunch at 1 p.m." She pointed to the clock. It was 12:53 p.m.

Sighing, I pulled at the bottom of my coat and tried to calm down. "Do you have any pamphlets or anything?"

The woman turned around and rummaged through a file cabinet. She fished out a few crinkled flyers. "Here," she pointed. "Call these people. They have some day programs, but again, you're going to have to talk to the developmental services department."

"Thank you." I crumpled them in my hand. I left the fourth-floor office and trekked back down four flights of stairs.

The elevator was my life.

I barreled out of the building and fired up The Bus. Why did everything have to be so hard? This college student with schizophrenia—and a family that would rival the Gallagher's—thing was getting old.

I made a quick left onto McTaugh Road when I saw the red and blue lights flashing behind me.

"Fuck!" I grumbled, pounding my hands on the steering wheel.

JANAY HARDEN

The pamphlets I had begrudgingly taken from the social services building fell to the floor when I slammed on the brakes and pulled over. I reached over to the glove compartment and hesitated. *Wait. Should I reach anywhere?* I was a Black girl, and things happened to Black girls at the hands of police too. Sandra Bland, Korryn Gaines and of course, Breonna Taylor. I sat back in my seat and rubbed my fingertips together. They were cold.

I watched the boots walk up in my driver's side mirror. They were quick steps, like a younger officer, which could be good and bad depending on what type of day he was having.

My heart beat out of my chest.

"Good evening, Ms. Lewis." He was familiar, but no kin to me. "License and registration," K. Jamison said.

I sucked my teeth a little louder than I typically would for an officer. *"Don't be making them shifty, Indy."* Ez taught me and Sidney. I steadied my breathing and my chest rattled. "May I reach into my glove compartment?"

"You may."

I rummaged through my things until I found it. I handed my identification out of the window slowly and carefully, but I was sure he knew all my information already, just like I was sure this wasn't a random cop stop. Was Jamison following me?

He wanted to fuck with me. He strolled back to the car to run my tags and license. I took deep breaths and banged my head against my seat as I waited for him to return.

"Ms. Lewis, you've been in town for some weeks now. Do you plan on returning to college?" K. Jamison coolly asked as he rapped on the window again. I knew this wasn't a regular stop.

"Umm yes. I'm still on winter break and I'll be back soon. Why, plan on meeting me there again?"

"Ms. Lewis, I'm going to be honest with you. I think you know something about Mr. Green's disappearance. I don't know what, I just have a feeling. If you know something, I suggest you tell me now before I come back and it's not a choice."

"I don't know what you feel. I know nothing about Jaxon."

K. Jamison looked at me curiously for a long time and searched my face for lies, in that intent and serious way that cops do. He tapped on the hood of my car and gave back my ID. "You have a good night, now. I'll be keeping an eye on you."

When he got in his car, I felt hot liquid pool beneath me as my greatest shame was threatening to be discovered.

CHAPTER 16

I SPLASHED WATER ON my face and wiped the sweat away from the mirror.

"Indy, you ready?" Ms. Arletha tapped on the door. "Your phone was ringing."

"Just a minute," I called out.

I was up early. We were visiting Ez again to help clean. By the looks of the house when I visited weeks ago, he was getting worse at keeping up with the maintenance. Ez needed us. The brochures I picked up from the social services building were still sitting in my glove compartment in The Bus, along with spray cleaner and some bleach I used to clean the seat after I peed on myself.

Ez. I was more worried than ever. I noticed his twitches had increased, and sometimes when he spoke, he fumbled his words, and repeated himself. His heart was still the same; he was loud and broodish. But something about him was different.

Will was coming with us. When I grabbed my phone, I was sure it was him calling to say he was outside. Good, I wanted to quiz him about what he knew about Mila and Malachi and when he found out. I hated to be the last to know something.

When I put my passcode in, I had one missed Facetime call from Chaquille.

I smiled and pressed the green button as I laid on my bed.

"Indigo Lewis," he said with his thick New York accent. I watched his eyes roam the screen, studying every inch of my face, then broke into a grin. When the receptionist at the social services roamed my face and body, it felt wrong. When Chaquille did it just now, it felt... magnetic. I cursed myself for forgetting to text him back.

"I just called to check you out. Let you know your girl, Harper, is still crazy."

"I heard," I giggled. The theater was still open during winter break, and they were running on a skeleton crew. Harper texted me and said she cussed out Rita for taking the coffee machine out of the break room. I didn't know Chaquille was still working though.

"When you, June, and Fredo get back we really should start practicing for the Libra Festival as a unit. You know, get our hand, eye coordination down pact." He gave a sly wink.

I burst out laughing. "I guess you're right. Harper would love that."

"She was the one who told me to put the word out, so I'm doing my part."

"Oh, so you aren't calling to see my pretty face?" I teased.

"I mean, now that I'm looking at you, I see your left lash is on lean a little bit. Otherwise, looking good." He gave a thumbs up.

I giggled again and realized... I missed Chaquille. I wasn't sure exactly what I missed. But when I got back to school, he would be one of the first people I *had* to see. We chatted for a few minutes before he got quiet. "Listen, Indigo... when we get back—"

"Indigo?"

When I heard Will, I jumped up off my bed. I had a handful of braids in my hand I was toying with, and I was smiling into the phone.

"Oh hey," I said, my cheeks flushed.

"I'll see you when I get back to school. I gotta go," I breathed into the phone before hanging up.

"Am I interrupting?" Will shifted in the doorway. He wore a nervous smile.

"No, no." I shook my head, but for some reason, I felt guilty. "I'm ready." I rushed around and grabbed my bag.

Ez's house used to be an easy drive, but there seemed to be extra debris and branches in the road. The Bus bounced up and over every pothole. Ms. Arletha's shiny, black wig hit the top of the inside of the car as Dad drove. Sidney was in the middle of me and Will, and she bounced the highest and cackled.

Before we turned into Ez's driveway, he met us at the front of the property and guarded it with a large shotgun.

"Benjamin!" Ms. Arletha exclaimed.

"What are ya'll doing here?" Ez's eyes rolled. He wore a white t-shirt. It was ripped and dirty. His work boots were untied, and the tongues flapped around with each step he took. His gun was shiny and blinded me as it caught sunlight under the trees. "What ya'll doing here?" Ez repeated. I could see his neck bulging.

Will's eyes were wide as saucers, and he clutched his seatbelt.

"Let me talk to him." Sidney climbed over me.

"Sidney no!" Ms. Arletha grabbed Sidney's arm, but she was already jumping out of the car.

"Ez. It's just us," she called out to him.

His eyes softened. "SidRock, if you and them savages are here to tear up my place, I'm not in the mood now, you hear? I'm not in the mood."

"Ez, you know we have to do this. You need some help."

"I don't need no help, girl." Ez stumped his foot and the butt of his gun hit the ground. Dad gripped the steering wheel. I held my breath watching their interaction.

"I know you're hungry. Let us come and make you some food?"

Ez's eyes softened again. "Well, I did just buy me some deer meat. You know how to fry it up with some eggs?"

"Ms. Arletha does."

"Oh no, she cooks with all that butter. It's not good for you." He waved his hand and tightened his grip on the gun.

Before I could stop Will, he jumped out of the car and walked up behind Sidney, placing his hand on her shoulder.

"Hi, Mr. Ez. Remember me? I'm Indigo's friend—Will."

"I know who you is, boy. Don't you think it's high time to cast the rod or go catch another fish?"

I gasped.

"Um, anyway, Mr. Ez. I have to be somewhere at four this afternoon, so we can't even stay long. How about we make you breakfast, and we'll see what happens from there?"

My eyes darted between Will, Sidney, Ez, and the gleaming gun resting between them. Dad still clutched the steering wheel, frozen. Ms. Arletha placed her hand on his knee, and he jumped under her touch.

Ez was quiet while he worked a piece of honeysuckle between his teeth. He spit it to the side before bringing his gaze to Will. "You reckon about an hour or so?"

"Yes, Mr. Ez." Will turned to Dad for confirmation, and Dad quickly nodded. He still hadn't said a word.

"Fine. And not a minute longer. You buggers stay moving my stuff." Ez turned and pulled a bike from a tree stump next to him. I didn't see the bike, but it must've been there the entire time. He hopped on, unsteady at first, but soon flew into the brush and disappeared into the woods down a trail.

He looked like a crazy old man.

Once Will and Sidney hopped back in the car, no one said a word. Will looked over at me and placed his hand on my shoulder.

He nodded.

I nodded back.

The bumpy ride into Ez's long driveway was an unfamiliar landscape. What was once thick brush with dense trees had turned into the Little Shop of Horrors. Ez was collecting furniture. Old toilets and couches lined the long driveway, while tables, chairs, and a front car bumper sat off to the side of the house.

"My God," Ms. Arletha placed her hands to her mouth.

I surveyed the scene and my mouth fell open. I saw a gaping hole in the roof. Cats roamed the property and as we parked, I heard them meowing around the tires. Ez zoomed out of the woods from somewhere I couldn't see, and his bike screeched to a halt in front of the car. He glared at us and shouted he changed his mind, and we better not go into his house. Where most people held water bottles under their bike, he had rigged it to hold his gun in place and it gleamed back at us, ready to defend him and his property if necessary.

Ez was not okay.

CHAPTER 17

JOYA AND I were on a stakeout. I had on my dark shades and Joya wore a ball cap over her head. She checked her lipstick in the mirror, and I observed Mr. Chestnut over my sunglasses. I wore a black beanie over my head and my braids were warm underneath.

In the words of Lil Kim, we were both dressed in all-black like an omen.

We sat across from Tunica Rivers High School hidden behind the bushes. I glanced around; it looked so different from when I was a student not long ago. Everything looked smaller; the parking lots, the building.

Convincing her to come along to spy on Mr. Chestnut was easy. When I lied and told her I was writing an article for the Titus Tribune about Theodora and the track team, she didn't question it. She wanted to catch a glimpse of him anyway. After Mom and 'em in my head went over the pros and the cons, it seemed like a win-win. Joya said his Saturday's schedule was the same and he never deviated from it. An early morning run at the school, and an afternoon stop to a bakery. He had a sweet tooth.

The *real* reason to tail him—now that was more difficult to put into words.

"I just want to put it all behind me, Indy. Things with my parents just got back to normal. I'm over it," her voice cracked while checking out Mr. Chestnut from afar.

I cocked my eye at her. "We're not doing anything, Joya. We're just watching him."

The sun was shining on this bright January day, and the rays illuminated her worried expression. She shifted in her seat and searched through her purse. She pulled her sunglasses onto her worried face, trying to block me from seeing her.

I saw her. I saw her fear. And I saw that he did this to her. When would men stop making us feel this type of fear? Fear of being chosen, left, or forgotten? This was even more reason I was here. Someone had to do something about this predator, and since so much of his dirt had fallen into my lap and we shared the same air at Titus—I volunteered as tribute.

It was up to me.

Mr. Chestnut had been a track coach since my mom was a teenager. During that time, he had relationships with high-school girls. Those were the facts. So why did he get away with it so easily? And flaunt as if he was untouchable? The girls never reported him so no one ever knew. This made no sense to me, but I wasn't surprised. He was white and a man with money. He was already at an advantage I knew nothing about.

'But he is touchable, Indy,' a dark voice in my head whispered. *'Touch him like Jaxon . . .'*

No, Indy! Don't think like that . . . I shushed myself. I glanced over at Joya, and she was sitting cross armed, staring out of the window. We were in The Bus, and the seats sat low and far back. I crouched up slightly, so I could get a better angle of Mr. Chestnut and whoever the girl he was with. Right now, they were sitting in the car but I was sure Mr. Chestnut had better things to do than hang out in a high school parking lot with cameras everywhere.

No, he didn't have better things to do—he had the audacity. That's what he had, the audacity.

I gritted my teeth and watched him place an arm around his companion and lean in. I couldn't see well, and Joya was no help, refusing to look my way. That was at least three women I saw him linked to in a few months, but how many other women was he running and ruining? I thought about Allie, or Nurse Meanface, or whatever I should call her these days. I wasn't sure anymore. She was siding with her husband and laying down the law on Mom and other Trochesse's patients. It was the first time I saw grumblings of descent in Trochesse. The way Mom used to describe Trochesse made it sound like *she* was the one away at college. How could Nurse Meanface be married to someone like him? Didn't she see what kind of man he was? Hell, didn't anyone see what kind of man he was?

Telling Dad about Mr. Chestnut was my next move, and I was planning to do it tonight. Dad and Ms. Arletha said they had a big announcement anyway, so I guess we all had announcements.

"Indy, I want to leave," Joya interrupted my thoughts, sounding annoyed.

'Take the girl home, Indy Lindy, she's not built for this,' Mom fussed in my head.

I studied Joya's face before my phone buzzed, and I saw a text from Will telling me to come over. I fired up The Bus, and it roared to life louder than ever. I saw Mr. Chestnut peer into his rearview mirror and frown the same time I ducked. "Oh, shit." I tugged at Joya's arm so she could duck too. Thankfully, the seats were so low, he could only make out my braids. Even so, I had to be careful. Who knew how this might end?

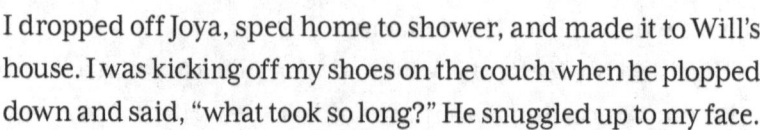

I dropped off Joya, sped home to shower, and made it to Will's house. I was kicking off my shoes on the couch when he plopped down and said, "what took so long?" He snuggled up to my face.

"I was running a few errands and then had to grab something from home."

A little white lie never hurt.

I hadn't showered in two days. I was up the past couple of nights, planning and plotting what to do about Mr. Chestnut, and time escaped me. He and Nurse Meanface challenged what I thought I knew. They left stains on my skin where Ez had grabbed my wrists and ushered me out to safety when things got crazy that day at Trochesse. I ruminated about Joya's sadness while watching him be something to someone else.

Shifting to thoughts of Ez, my stomach flopped. I called one of those developmental places on the pamphlet. I left messages for two different places, but no one called back. I googled the address to a day program in town, and they accepted Ez's insurance. When I got there, they told me they only accepted applications online. I raced home to do the application. When I finished the online form and hit the submit button, the website crashed. After spewing enough curse words that would make Mama Jackie roll over in her grave, I slammed the laptop closed and paced my room for a few hours.

At this point, I was looking forward to returning to Titus tomorrow. I could breathe there.

I tried to stop thinking about all the things that went wrong during winter break at home. I shifted my gaze back to Will. Hanging out at his house was a welcomed and quiet treat as I laid on his couch. His parents were in the kitchen singing and dancing. Mr. Simms was cooking his one go-to meal. Chicken Parmesan. I smelled the garlic from the couch. I buried my feet into the Simms' thick, plush carpet.

"I want to talk to you about something. I forgot to ask you at Ez's house the other day."

"Oh?" Will perked up.

"I saw Mila and Malachi at the gas station. Did you know they were dating?"

Will's jaws tightened. "Malachi did tell me, but we haven't really talked since. Same with Mila."

"And you didn't tell me?"

"Indy, I didn't know how you would feel. Let's be real, the whole situation is a mess. You and Malachi... me and Mila... now you and me... hopefully... Shit, it might be you and Mila next," he chuckled.

"I'm serious, Will," I punched him in the arm. "They are our best friends. In a matter of months everything changed."

"Indy, things can't stay the way they always were. Everyone is doing their own thing. I guess they found something in each other, like I found in you. Give it some time."

I sank into the couch and thought about Will's words. It wasn't silent for long before Will changed the subject.

"Now I want to talk to you about something."

Did he know? Could he know what I did? Who I was? I sat up as slowly without looking pressed, wondering what he wanted.

"Listen, I was thinking about... us... maybe... seeing where things go." Will instinctively pulled for his hairbrush he kept in his pocket. He kept it there to make sure his waves were spinning, but he ran it across his head when he was nervous. He stood in front of me, peering down.

I looked up at him, giving him heart eyes. "Seeing where things go, huh? You sure that's what you want to do? I mean, you think you know me, but you have no idea."

"Indy, stop it. I know you better than you know yourself," Will chuckled. He threw his head back, showing all his teeth like I said something so ridiculous he couldn't help but laugh.

Now I was the one to chuckle. Men thought they knew it all.

Ron Isley was crooning from the kitchen while the onion popped and sizzled over the too high flames on the stove. Mrs. Simms slid in behind Mr. Simms. She saw me watching, and she winked, turned down the flame just a bit, and moved before Mr. Simms noticed.

I noticed.

Will leaned in closer, and now we were face to face. He and I had been best friends for so long. So many things happened between us, and he was there for my every, everything. We've never kissed, let alone thought about going further. I exhaled as I looked up into his eyes. So familiar and yet so new. His lips. So pink and inviting. I licked my own, wanting to get a taste and wondering how it would change our friendship like it changed Mila and Malachi's friendship. I closed my eyes and when his lips touched mine, it wasn't filled with fireworks or horns blasting. It was quiet and easy. I smiled up at him and stroked his chin.

CHAPTER 18

WHEN I HOPPED in the car that night to head home, my hands landed on a picture of Mama Jackie caught between the middle console and seat. Mama Jackie's round, mocha face looked so much like Mom's. She coiffed hair into a neat press and curl, stopping at her chin. The curls were damn near perfect. I remembered Mama Jackie's pink, foam rollers she swore by. Her strands were shiny and moisturized. She spent long days in the kitchen, whipping together an egg and mayo concoction she claimed was good for the hair. *"Eggs are protein baby; they keep your mane healthy and strong."* She slathered it onto me and Sidney's hair in the kitchen while we sat with plastic grocery bags wrapped around our napes just in case the mixture slid down onto our clothes. It always did, and I hated it. Sidney and I smelled like potato salad for the rest of the day. The hair food didn't seem to work for my hair. It never really grew no matter how much holy water, juices, and berries Mama Jackie basted it in. She eventually said, "you have your father's hair!" and threw up her arms.

"Well, whose hair does Sidney have?" I turned my nose up to Mama Jackie a tad too high in the air for her liking. She said

I was smelling myself and popped me in the lip with the comb. I turned around, folded my arms, and seethed on the inside. Mama Jackie's hair grew like a weed and every three months, she would have inches, and I mean inches cut off. She said, *"ladies wear their hair short and neat, Indy Lindy. And it wouldn't kill you to wear stockings now and then too."* Mama Jackie didn't take no mess. She would bake cookies, sing to Ez, and watch Jeopardy every night at 6 p.m. When she was disrespected—man her Texas sized fire came out, and she didn't back down.

When we buried Mama Jackie; Mom, Sidney, and I stood shoulder to shoulder, oldest to youngest, wearing stockings. Mine itched, but I kept them on for her, anyway. After that I stuck to my braids, no kitchen combinations for me. If Mama Jackie were here, would I be able to tell her what was going on with me?

My hands shook on the ride home, and I gripped the steering wheel tighter. When I pulled up to the house, the lights were on. I could see Ms. Arletha through the curtains, stirring batter for a cake. I knew it was a pound cake because Sidney sat next to her, grating lemons, and measuring flour. Dad was in the living room, sitting in his favorite chair in the corner in front of the tv. He was sprawled out, and I giggled when I saw his work boots outside on the front porch. Those things reeked whenever he took them off, and Ms. Arletha vomited last week when he peeled his toes out of his socks, and I do mean peeled.

When I walked inside, they greeted me with another face; one I hadn't spotted from outside when I observed them.

K. Jamison.

"Hey there, Ms. Indigo." Jamison leaned in and gave a cocked smile. "Can I call you Indy?"

"No, you may not!" I blurted. But I didn't mean to blurt it—someone somewhere deep inside of me did. Or did they?

"Uh, okay. Ms. Indigo," K. Jamison cleared his throat.

Ms. Arletha gave me a confused frown.

"How did you get here?" I peeked outside. I didn't see a car.

"We're patrolling some neighborhoods by foot these days. Can't be too sure what's going on, you know, with Jaxon still missing." Jamison let that last part linger, like it was meant for two different audiences.

Me and them.

I swallowed.

"I really came by to talk about Ezra. The city has exhausted all their citations. They won't be issuing any more."

"What does that mean?" Dad stood. He wore a bright, white, fresh pair of socks and had it not been for K. Jamison standing in my home, threatening to add it to the list of things burning around me, I would have laughed.

Jamison shifted his weight. "It means they will be filing a motion to formally condemn the home. Ezra will have to move."

"Have mercy!" Ms. Arletha put her hand to her stomach.

"Dad, you knew this?" I looked between Dad and Jamison.

"I certainly did not." Dad's jaw was tight, and his nose was high in the air now, just like Mama Jackie hated. Dad's eyes pierced into Jamison's with anger.

Ms. Arletha walked to where K. Jamison was sitting, and she removed the glass of water she placed on a coaster in front of him. She did this for all our visitors, but today she trotted to the sink and tossed it.

"You told me you came over here to talk about helping Ez. Helping! You ain't say nothing about no condemning!"

"I'm sorry, Mr. Lewis. I should have led with that. I also wanted to talk to Indigo."

K. Jamison didn't break a sweat as he turned to me and fired off questions.

"Did you know Jaxon had a bike? And if so, did he ever ride it to—"

"That is enough, sir. What is your badge number?" Ms. Arletha roared to life. "You will not con your way into our

lives. You may leave, and if Indy isn't under arrest, you are not welcome back into this home." Her eyes were dark. She reminded me of Mama Jackie on the rare occasions when she lost her cool. She was a disrespected and disillusioned Black woman.

Dad's eyes were wide with surprise while Sidney's danced with wonder at Ms. Arletha. Ms. Arletha was the mom figure she needed, while her real mom was the Nelson Mandela of the coo-coo house.

My eyes held more tears. Tears from being tired. So emotionally tired. Could I get one normal day without something from Tunica Rivers chasing me in some way? A fat one fell from my eyes, melted down my face, and settled into the corner of my mouth where I tasted its salt.

"Don't cry, Indy." Sidney locked arms with me.

Dad's eyes widened when he saw my tears, and I'm sure he was racking his brain trying to remember the last time he saw me cry. "Get out of my house!" Dad demanded. His voice was even but rough. He didn't need to raise it for us to feel its presence.

"I apologize family. I'm the bearer of bad news. I'm just doing my job. I have a teenage daughter myself, and if something happened to her, I'd never stop asking her friends. Never."

"Out," Dad repeated. His face and voice didn't change.

"Ms. Lewis, I'll be seeing you around. I do have more questions, so be on the lookout for me." He nodded in my direction.

Ms. Arletha shut and locked the front door behind him. We closed the windows and blinds so no one could see in or out—not anymore.

"Well, this is certainly one way to spend the last night of your winter break, Indy," Ms. Arletha declared.

So much had happened this past month. I was looking forward to Theodora, Naomi, and Harper, and even... even

Chaquille. "What did you guys want to talk about?" I sat down on the couch, far away from the side K. Jamison sat on. I would let them go first before I shared my own news about Mr. Chestnut. Ms. Arletha cleared her throat and looked between Dad, Sidney, and me.

"Benjamin?" She went and stood behind him, placing her hands on his shoulders. He looked like a child, and she the parent.

Right now, they both looked nervous.

"Well, uh. 'Letha and I wanted to tell you guys... we are expecting. Surprise."

"Expecting what?" Sidney asked. Her naivete was usually amusing, but today it gave me a headache.

Ms. Arletha rubbed her stomach, and Sidney's eyes danced again.

'What the hell?'

'Houston—we have a problem.'

'How cute, we need some new faces around here,' the voices swirled in my mind and rambled at once.

The events of the day played in my mind like they were on a reel. Joya, Mr. Chestnut, Will, K Jamison, Ez, and now a baby. I wanted to talk about Mr. Chestnut. I wanted him exposed. There was no room for him. Not here, and not right now.

I swallowed and smiled at Dad and Ms. Arletha. I couldn't ruin their moment. I knew what needed to be done by my own hands. Tunica Rivers and Titus University was not big enough for me and Mr. Chestnut.

"That's great, guys." My face lit up and I grinned away my own truths.

PART 2
FOES

CHAPTER 19

THE BULLSHIT STARTED when I got back to Titus. I read the letter twice, just to make sure I was understanding correctly. Financial aid package revision. Titus University was revising my scholarship package and for some reason, I had a balance when the school year was paid in full since I received an endowment from the pottery studio where I worked last year. I made a mental note to call Ms. Montague from the studio to see what was going on. This was the last thing I needed.

With only a few days into the spring semester, I was fortunate to not have any run-ins with Mr. Chestnut. That was difficult, considering how much Theodora spoke of him these days now that track season was in full swing. He started creeping into my thoughts after our run-in with Nurse Meanface. I hoped whoever she was, and whoever she thought we were to her husband, wouldn't affect Mom. By the dwindling number of letters coming from Trochesse, I wasn't so sure. Patiently waiting for the next one to arrive in the mail, I made up horror stories in my mind about how Nurse Meanface was treating Mom after her brief show of strength. I checked my calendar,

and one should have made its way to my student mailbox in the city center at least four days ago. I watched those prison movies where they tortured people for fun. Even though she technically wasn't in prison, her mind bounded her with mental chains, and that was the same thing.

I called and texted Ez, Dad, and Ms. Arletha a few times checking in. I felt more like a case manager than anything. *Did you check on Ez? Did you take your meds, Ez? Ms. Arletha, how do you feel? Sidney, did your dad pick you up this weekend?*

I crumbled the paper and tossed it into the trashcan next to Theodora's bed. I noticed it was made already, and she was gone for the morning. Where did she go so fast without saying anything? Since we'd been back, she and I had hardly talked and now that I thought about it—she'd been out of the room for the past few nights studying with Dylan. The only excitement I had these days was thinking about Ms. Arletha and the new baby. It was a bombshell she dropped, and I remembered how she looked at me with expectant eyes.

I was the oldest child and according to family rules, I was in charge. If she wanted our blessing, it would have to go through me. I was ecstatic for them, and she made my dad happy in a way Mom never could. She was the stability and loving housewife, who baked cakes and washed windows for fun. Mom would never submit.

I turned on some music through my Bluetooth speaker and let the beats wake me up this morning. *Shit . . .* I thought. I was out of hair oil to grease my scalp and my braids. I looked through Theodora's things briefly; I knew she kept argan oil around here somewhere. I didn't find any oil, but I did find pictures of Theodora and her family. They stood together in their African attire; the elders in the back and the younger generations in the front. Theodora smiled, but to me it looked forced. Her eyes didn't match her pinched grin. Right under the picture was another small Polaroid photo from when Naomi and her friends: Ivelisse, Dylan, Theodora, and I went to a go-karting range. Theodora's face was different in this picture. She wore bright red lipstick, and she was smiling so hard, her eyes were shut with Dylan's arm flung over her shoulder, grinning too with his head in the crook of her neck. We were all cheesing. I put the picture back, slipped into my Crocs, and trekked to Naomi's room in search of hair oil.

"Hey, girl, what's up?" Naomi said after I knocked on her door. She had it cracked and stood tall and unmoving. I stood close to her, waiting for my invitation in like she typically did, but she didn't move.

"Do you have any hair oil I can use? I don't have anything, and I haven't gone to the store yet."

Naomi looked at my long-braided mane and I knew how crazy I sounded, asking my white bestie for hair products, but I was desperate. I cracked a smile and waited for Naomi to giggle too.

"Yeah, hold on one second." She shut the door behind her without so much as a second glance.

'Hmmm. I'm drawing a blank, guys. Is she mad?' Mom mulled in my mind.

"So, it's not just me? She is being weird?" I said out loud. I glanced around suspiciously, making sure no one saw me. I heard voices behind her door and some shuffling sounds. Who did she have in there? And why was she being so shady?

The door cracked, and Naomi poked her head out. "This is all I have. I have to make my store run soon too," she pushed a small container of coconut oil toward me. She moved so quickly I almost dropped the greasy container and caught it before slipping through my arms and hitting the floor.

"Naomi, wait. What's going on? Did I do something?"

Her eyes softened, and she tilted her head toward me. "No, Indy, you didn't do anything. I'm just tired, that's all."

"Do you need anything?"

She hesitated and I saw her neck twitch. It was like she wanted to say something but was holding back. "No, I'm fine," she nodded. "Just need to get some rest."

"Okay." I slowly backed away.

I tried to peer over her shoulder to peek into her room. Naomi was one of the lucky ones who wasn't assigned a roommate; she had the entire dorm room to herself. She pushed the two twin beds together, hung some string lights, and had Bluetooth speakers mounted into each corner of the room. She also had small houseplants sitting by the window and a guitar she played only when she was tipsy. So again, who was behind the door?

"I'll catch up with you Thursday night. You're going to Chaquille's party, right?" Naomi leaned in closer, making the space tighter between me and whoever was on the other side of the door.

"I'll be there. I have to work this afternoon, so see you for S'mores?" I asked. I searched Naomi's eyes for something, anything. She loved S'mores and believed they should be listed on menus in every restaurant—even the fine dining ones like Bahama Breeze.

She nodded, and quietly shut the door behind her. It wasn't a slam, but it was definite and final. It was enough to make me walk away from the door without knocking again. I felt a sharp pain in my stomach, knowing I wasn't wanted and there wouldn't be any S'mores.

'Well, that was rude. Add her to the list guys,' a voice in my head said.

"No, not Naomi," I fussed. The words came out of my mouth as real as the ones saying it in my mind. I walked away from

Naomi's door and went back to my room, but this time with a door slam.

I oiled my fingers and rubbed them into my scalp, working my way down my braids until most strands were coated. I flipped my head and made a messy bun on top of my head. Slipping a band around my edges, I pulled it down and tucked my ears. My edges looked a mess and were not cooperating, so I hid them away until I got my hair re-done. I searched through my basket of clean and dirty clothes. I sniffed through them until I found an acceptable long sleeve Titus University jersey shirt, sweatpants, and my Nikes.

I checked my phone, and I was right on time for work.

'You go, Indy, way to be on time this semester,' Mom jeered.

I gave a sheepish grin. Harper would surely have a field day and tease me for being on time. My goal this semester was to make sure I got to class and work with minutes to spare. Last semester, I passed with all C's. I didn't tell anyone when they asked, and Dad proudly told people I was acing my way through college. I thought it would be that way too; easy classes, friendships that would last a lifetime, and even a college sweetheart or two. What I got so far was different, and I didn't know it if was by my own design. These days, C's got degrees, friendships were sketchy with a door slam, and college sweetheart? That was a joke too. But I would do better. I just had to take the first step and make sure I was more consistent every day.

Once I was ready, I opened my door to head to work and there Mr. Chestnut stood with his hand up, ready to knock.

Again.

"Ms. Lewis." His smile was big, bright, and condescending. There was a hint of sarcasm behind his words, and my stomach turned as he got right to the point. "You and your family leave my wife out of this. Okay?" Putting both hands in his pockets, I could tell they were balled. I was glad he didn't beat

around the bush; at least I knew what to expect this time. I knew I wasn't wrong. I was on to his game.

I opened my mouth to respond, but no sounds came out. The words caught in my throat, begging to let loose, but something trapped them. Mom interrupted my mind with so much never-ending chatter about my life. When I needed her to speak for me like right now, I was on my own. My throat was parched, and I felt my underarms moisten.

I was clenching my legs together, trying not to pee on myself. His unwelcomed presence jarred me. I looked around and realized how exposed I was. It was ten in the morning and most people were in class or still asleep. This was one of the quietest times in the dorm, and he chose this moment to show up. That said something and he knew it. He had access to me. I didn't like it and it proved I wasn't safe.

"Are you threatening me?" I managed to croak. The words sounded stronger than I felt, and I was thankful.

Mr. Chestnut removed his hands from his pockets, and he used one hand to palm his salt and pepper beard. His brown and gold Titus U jacket was zipped all the way to his neck and his collar was popped out of the sides. He looked like a car salesman. "Woah woah, don't get hysterical. That's a strong word to throw around. I just want to make sure we don't have any more misunderstandings about what you think you saw at the school and anything anyone has told you. Leave my family alone and I'll leave yours alone. Understood?" He took a step closer and placed his hands on my door. He was so close; I smelled his breath. He breathed deep and looked me in my eyes and didn't blink. "Understood?" he repeated.

"Understood," I uttered. Hot liquid ran down my legs and wet the front of my sweatpants. He glanced down at the damp spots and his lips curled into a smirk. Slowly, he backed away from the door and walked down the stairs without a glance back.

I closed the door behind me and fumbled with the locks. He saw me at the school watching him with Joya. My hands were shaking, and my breathing was shallow. My pants, underwear, and socks were wet. I was trembling. I glanced around my room, and it closed in on me as I gasped for air. Light crept in through the metal standard issued dorm blinds, and I hurried across the room and snapped them shut. I peeled off my wet clothes and wiped tears from my eyes, pacing the room.

Work would have to wait today.

"I just don't want to go."

"But why?" Chaquille narrowed his eyes. Naomi and Theodora said nothing. They both stood in the doorway with their arms folded.

Chaquille was the guest dj tonight, and we'd been looking forward to this party since last semester, but since Mr. Chestnut's visit, I wasn't up to going.

The voices screamed in my head about what to do. I watched the doorframe where Mr. Chestnut stood days before and I got up, checked the lock on the door, laid back down, got back up to check the door, laid back down. I did this repeatedly until I exhausted myself. Tonight was officially my third night without sleep and by the time the sun cut through our blinds this morning, the voices settled down and my body collapsed onto my bed. My days reversed, and I slept when the sun was out and watched guard when the moon was high. I slept through my classes and two days of work. Harper called every day, but I had yet to return her calls. Chaquille reached out too, but he was the type to call my roommates when I didn't answer, which was what he did today. I hid in my bed through it all, not wanting to move and face a world where women weren't

safe. What did that mean for me? For Sidney? College was supposed to be my big break, and I was messing it up. What was I doing here anyway?

Chaquille and I had been hanging out since I returned from home, but right now he was getting on my nerves. "Chaquille, I can't. I have too much work to do," I whined. I was sitting on my bed in my robe. My braids were matted under my bonnet and my clothes piled up in the hamper.

"You haven't been to class or work, what work do you have to do?" Theodora sucked her teeth. She had some nerve. She had been disappearing in the mornings for weeks. Although I never asked her where she went, I also didn't sell her out. I cut my eyes at her and crossed my arms.

"Indy, we're just worried about you. That's all." Naomi sat on the corner of my bed.

I cut my eyes at her too. Naomi and Theodora were acting funny these days, and how ironic they were concerned about me. "I don't know what the big deal is, I'm fine," my voice cracked as I spoke; I hoped they believed me.

They didn't.

"Indy, you're not fine. You haven't left this room!" Theodora's voice rose, and she shook her head.

How could I tell them that Mr. Chestnut was outside? How could I tell them he came to my door? My door! How could I tell them about the voices, or about the things I thought about doing, and had already done? I was shackled to Jaxon, and even though he burned away in that incinerator, I still worried. K. Jamison was on some real life *I Know What You Did Last Summer*, shit, and now the voices were happy Mr. Chestnut was on his way to becoming a part of the freshman fifteen weight I would unwillingly carry.

Only he would be dead weight.

The voices begged me to let them have at him, and he was a heavy load. It was better to stay in this room where it was safe and no one, including me, got hurt. "I'm just tired. I'm sorry, guys. Maybe I'll catch up later," I lied. I had no intention of leaving this room. I had a date with *BET*, butter pecan ice cream in our dorm fridge, and my bed. Theodora asked once this morning if I had showered as she stood over my bed and sniffed. I lied and told her yes, but it had been three days since water had touched this behind. My heart felt heavy, my mind even heavier, and nothing in me wanted to let anything—let alone water— touch me.

"Fine." Chaquille frowned and stomped to the door.

Naomi and Theodora quietly followed behind him. Naomi hung back in the doorway and paused, looking at me strangely. "Please come by the party. It'll do you some good to get out of the room for a while. Please."

I sighed. "Okay, Naomi, we'll see."

Hours later, I was licking a spoonful of ice cream. I had the carton positioned in my lap while watching tv. I did take a shower which felt great. I was ready for a comfy and safe night in.

'Indigo, honey. You are not using that brain of yours.'

I turned the tv up louder, trying to ignore Mom's voice.

'Child, you hear me talking to you. What is it you think you are doing?'

"Mom! He's out there, and I just don't want to go anywhere for right now."

'The girl is scared to death, Sonia! Won't even leave the boom boom room,' another voice cracked.

"Well, what am I supposed to do!" I screamed out loud. I felt silly, and I was glad Theodora was gone so she didn't have to hear me like this.

'You came to college to learn. To change. You came here to grow. Not hide in your room eating ice cream.'

Fat tears rolled down my face as I took another large scoop of ice cream and shoved it into my mouth. *BET* was showing old reruns of award ceremonies, but I couldn't focus on. "Maybe I shouldn't have come to college. I could've stayed home and went to City College in Tunica Rivers."

'And what would that do? Indigo, sometimes we have to stand up, honey. Don't let anyone back you into a corner. You came to college looking for something. So go find it.'

'Yeah, go find it, Indy, we're bored! We don't want to stay here another night,' two voices came through at the same time, but they were more childlike. I had never heard them before. How many were there inside of me?

"What did I come here to find?" My grades were going to tank and my job was surely in danger too; I was rarely there. I had called to make another appointment at the Wellness Center, and they hadn't responded yet. I had yet to follow up with the letter from the financial aid office. It didn't seem like I fit here at all. I griped, shoving another large spoonful in my mouth. My phone rang and it was Joya. I let it ring and licked the spoon.

'Girl, if I have to tell you to get your ass out of that bed one more time...' Mom's voice trailed off.

I muted the tv, and in the distance I heard music bumping and people laughing. It seemed like the world was out having fun and making memories, but I hid in a room, desperate to forget my memories. What did I come here to find? I wasn't sure, but I know I didn't come here to let the voices keep me holed up in my dorm room. Nor Mr. Chestnut. He was the problem... not me... Right? This week I would tell someone about Mr. Chestnut. I tried before, but I would try again. But tonight, what would I do tonight?

'You'll get up and go be a college student, Indigo Lewis.'

I hopped off my bed and the ice cream carton fell over. I grabbed it before it spilled onto my bed. I rummaged through my closet until I found a pair of jeans that hugged my hips right. I found a clean t-shirt that said *Ready to Rumble,* and I was. Pulling my bonnet off my head I checked out my hair in the mirror. Even though my new growth was coming in strong, it wasn't as bad as I thought. I grabbed some of Theodora's gel and sculpted my edges down until they were shiny and laying smooth. I twisted some braids in the front and around my head until it was pulled back into a simple, rolled French braid. I rummaged through my top drawer until I found Mom's old hair clip. It was really a broach in the shape of a moon. Mom used to wear it when she performed with *The Fat Cats.* She loved that group, and she loved this broach. She said it was her lucky charm, and it kept her safe. I fastened it into my hair. I slipped into an oversized jean jacket and headed toward the bumping noise.

Minutes later, I was surrounded by a mob scene, or so it felt like. My breathing quickened, and I bit the inside of my cheek nervously as I entered the hall where the party was in full swing. Scores of students lined the walls and floors. Couples were dropping it low, grinding, and some kissing in the middle, as a mashup of R&B and rap music sizzled from the speakers. A dank haze wafted in the air and there were many giggles and red eyes throughout the room. I spotted Chaquille; he had headphones up to his ears and fiddling with two laptops. Two girls I never seen before stood on both sides of him in tube tops and tight jeans. Their red cups were lined with lipstick around the rim, and they bobbed their heads as Chaquille pressed one button and the beat dropped. He said he was a dj, but I was expecting a few old speakers and a rickety laptop. Chaquille had a whole setup, complete with groupies; he was in his element. I watched him in amazement. He moved around the stage, tending to various gadgets and instruments, knowing exactly what to do and which buttons to press.

JANAY HARDEN

The music thumped through the speakers and for a moment; I felt the beat in my chest and the energy of the room. I squinted and searched for Naomi and Theodora. When my eyes landed on Theodora, she was in a corner whispering with Dylan, sipping from red cups. Dylan's face was flushed pink from whatever he was drinking. Although Black people surrounded him, he leaned against the wall and swayed to the music. He dapped up a few of the guys making their way through the crowds. He didn't look afraid. Not that he was supposed to be afraid, but still. Before I made my way to them, Joya, Naomi, and Naomi's friend, Ivelisse, popped up from behind the stage.

I paused. What was Joya doing here? I knew she and Naomi had become friends since the fateful ski trip they still wouldn't let me live down, but did she drive all this way and not tell me? Heat washed over me as I watched them giggle and dance together. They became friends and had pushed me out. I didn't know that for sure but balling my fists and heading toward them, that's how it felt.

Naomi was the first to spot me, and her eyes widened in surprise when she saw me making my way toward them. "Indy!" she yelled and threw her arms around me. I hugged her back and Joya stood behind her, smiling.

Chaquille scratched the record and switched songs to a slower Jamaican beat. Partygoers shouted in approval and before long, Theodora and Dylan were full on grinding up against the wall next to us. I shouted over Naomi's shoulder. "Don't hurt him, girl!"

"You can handle all that, White boy?" someone chuckled. Dylan did what he could behind Theodora, but he was no match for her. Titus was a smorgasbord of different races, but this party was Black AF tonight. Theodora wined her hips, slinging her long braids over her shoulder. Her red cup never left her hands, and she didn't lose a beat as she dipped it low and twerked her way into Dylan's heart. His face was redder now, and he held onto her waist, trying to match her speed. Theodora gave that man something he could feel.

The hairs on the back of my neck stood. I felt someone looking at me. I glanced up at Chaquille on the stage, and he was full on gawking. He studied my face, and he paused so long; the girls standing next to him leaned over to see what he was looking at. I held his gaze and for a second, I didn't hear the music; I didn't see any of my girls around me. I saw nothing but Chaquille up there. He interacted with the crowd and paid special attention to people dancing while our eyes darted back and forth at each other. When it seemed like people were slowing down, he switched gears and put on something with more bass to get the groove going again.

"Yours?" Joya said, motioning to Chaquille.

"Not mine." I shook my head, shooing her and that thought away. Chaquille looked good, and he was up there giving me all the local celebrity vibes, but he wasn't mine. Why would she say that? My stomach fluttered at the thought of being *his*. "What are you doing here, and why didn't you tell me you were coming?" I had to scream over the music into her ear.

"You know Naomi and I exchanged numbers. She invited me last minute. I called you a few hours ago!"

I nodded, remembering her name scrolling across my phone while I was shoveling ice-cream into my mouth.

"You know I've been dying to get to a college party anyway. This is lit!" She grinned.

I looked around, surveying the room. There were groups of people: dancing, laughing, drinking, or variations of all three. I had to give it to Chaquille; he was killing this party tonight. I don't know why, but I scanned the room once more, looking for Mr. Chestnut. He would never be at a college party.

He would be easy to spot being the only other white guy at the party besides Dylan. I looked around anyway, holding my breath. Surely Joya wouldn't tell Mr. Chestnut she was coming? They were finished—she said it herself.

"Are you staying tonight?"

"Well, I was going to ask you if it was okay for me to crash at your place. I told my parents I was staying at Desiree's house tonight so I'm free until tomorrow morning." She danced in place and shouted in my ear.

"Yeah, that's fine. Are you staying with me or with Naomi?" I asked with an eyeroll and full of sarcasm.

Joya tipped her head back and said, "aww, the evil step-sister from Tunica Rivers wants me all to herself, huh?"

I clutched at Joya's arm, and we cackled until tears streamed from our eyes. I grabbed Joya, and I hugged her tight around her neck. We had formed a spontaneous friendship and I was grateful for it.

Theodora had let Dylan up for air, and now Naomi and Ivelisse stood on the other side of me. Something told me to glance back to Chaquille, and when I did, he was no longer on stage. Someone had taken over for him and was doing their best to hold over the crowd until Chaquille returned. The music changed and the other dj opted for Chloe and Halle. Their soft voices were sensual, slow, and changed the mood to something flirty and sexy. I craned my neck looking for Chaquille in the dimly lit room and when I turned, he was standing behind me. The song echoed around us. His eyes bore into mine and in that moment, I was glad I forced myself out of my room. The look in his eye was one I didn't want to miss.

Damn, he really is fine.

Chaquille took my hand and led me to the dance floor. I resisted, not wanting to be in the center of attention. I mean, the middle? You had to have major confidence to dance in the center. I didn't have it, but I let Chaquille lead me there anyway.

I watched him part the crowd and people slapped his shoulders as we moved through. The same girls who stood beside the stage with their red cups were now rolling their eyes at me. I held my head high, not knowing why he chose me, but I felt like I chose him. I didn't care. I was at a college party with my friends. I had a conversation with my mom and others, and shit, this night was a personal success—and what they thought right now wasn't my problem.

The music was loud. Chaquille nodded to the new dj and he turned it down so we didn't have to scream to talk. We danced in place, and not only could Chaquille spin music, but he could dance. I mean, he wasn't winning any dance competitions and he couldn't touch Theodora, but his smile was bright. He grooved to the music, and he really felt it. I hadn't felt anything like this since I had the urge to kill Jaxon, and lately—Mr. Chestnut.

"You can do all of this, and you still want to stay a college student?"

Chaquille smirked. "Woman please. I tried to tell you I was dope. I had to beg you to come to a party to see for yourself."

"You're right. I'm sorry." I tilted my head closer and looked him in his eyes. Something about him and those damn brown eyes drew me in. I wanted to kick myself for not responding to his texts when I was home for winter break. Was there something here? I hadn't dated since last year, and although Will and I were talking, we weren't technically in a relationship. "How can I make it up to you?" I batted my eyes at Chaquille.

His mouth fell open, and he gave a dazed look. "Make it up to me, huh? Let me come up with something." He placed a hand to his chin and rubbed it with a dramatic effect.

I giggled and said, "so, are you going to tell me why you and I ended up walking out of the Wellness Center at the same time on a random, December day?"

Chaquille's smile faded, and he gawked around like someone was listening. He pondered for a second while my hands became clammy with nervous excitement. I wanted to kick myself once again for asking that question. "I have epilepsy. Sometimes my seizures get really bad. I stay on campus because it's just easier, with my doctor's and all. They're all here in town."

I pondered Chaquille's words. He was epileptic. I didn't know what else to say. Should I lighten the moment? "Is that why you keep bumping into me?" I joked.

"Hey, maybe," Chaquille chuckled. I watched him lick his lips and I wanted to kiss him right where his skin parted. I wanted to lean in and taste what he tasted.

"Now your turn. How is the counseling going?"

I gripped his shoulder harder. I hadn't told Dad or anyone why I needed to return to school for a few hours, and they were none the wiser. What would he think? That I was crazy and had issues? I side-eyed Chaquille and before I could change my mind, I said, "I don't know. I just don't think they get me." A chill ran up my spine as I beared my truth.

Chaquille nodded. "What were you expecting?" He searched my eyes.

"I don't know, maybe too much. To feel better, maybe..." I trailed off.

"And how do you feel?"

"Like no one understands. I'm sure that's how you feel about your epilepsy."

"I'm not ashamed of my epilepsy. I just don't tell people, so they don't treat me different. People like to look at you like you're a victim or something. I want to come up and make a name for myself with my music as a dj, not a dj with epilepsy."

"So, you don't think it's weird?" I was intrigued and stopped dancing. We stood in the middle talking, while people shimmied all around us.

Chaquille frowned. "Why would I think it's weird? People go to different doctors every day. Why not go to the head doctor too? Maybe if more people saw someone, the world wouldn't be so crazy. We all have a touch of something."

I tilted my head away from Chaquille, blinking away the tears forming in my eyes. I wiped my face before he noticed, but I was too late. "My bad, Indy." He pulled me closer then placed his hands around my waist. I welcomed his touch, and when he saw I wasn't pushing him away, he hugged me tighter. I don't know how I managed to cry in a room full of people, but I did. I laid my head on Chaquille's shoulder. I sniffled a few times, trying to get myself together.

I saw Naomi making her way toward me with fire in her eyes, darting between me and Chaquille. She probably thought he did something to me. I hated they thought I was so weak. Before she reached me, someone shoved me hard, and I fell into someone standing behind me.

"What the—" and before I could finish my sentence, someone came from behind and punched Chaquille in the back of the head. Naomi's eyes were wide as she pushed through the large crowd, trying to make her way to me. Within seconds, a melee had ensued, and Chaquille and I were at the center.

CHAPTER 20

"LET'S GO!" NAOMI tugged at my shoulder.

"Chaquille!" I shouted.

I grasped at his ankles as three bear-sized guys stomped him. Chaquille was doing his best to fight his way off the floor and people around us screamed and scattered. Joya was wide-eyed and frozen in a corner. Theodora searched the room for the exit signs. Naomi held me back as I tried to claw my way back to Chaquille. People scampered out of the hall and made enough room for Chaquille to roll once and hop to his feet. For a moment, his eyes met mine. I broke free from Naomi's grasp and with a mean growl, I jumped on one goon. I pummeled the back of his head and neck with the intensity of Mom and the speed of Grandpa Ez.

I scratched at his throat so hard, digging deep until I drew blood. His whimpers sounded like Jaxon Green when I used my strength to throw him into the incinerator. As fast as Jaxon danced into my memories, Mr. Chestnut was there too, in my mind. I could scratch out his eyes the same way I was doing this ogre. Taking care of myself would be my main priority and I wouldn't stay locked in my dorm room. I earned the right to enjoy my freshman year just like everyone else. Mr. Chestnut wouldn't stop my shine. Getting to him before he got to me would be my second main priority. I squeezed my arms around this dude's fat neck even tighter. He yelped and swung his arms around his back, trying to shake me off. I peeked over his shoulder. Chaquille stood for one millisecond with his mouth gaped staring at me. When he snapped out of it, he rushed us.

Before long, Naomi, Theodora, and anyone else tipsy enough to jump in, rushed the center of the room. It seemed like it was forever, but it was about three minutes before the hall lights flickered on and the police burst into the room. Joya was closest to the exit door, and she raced out with Theodora, a terrified Dylan, Ivelisse, and Naomi hot on her heels. I extended a hand to Chaquille while he had the big guy in a headlock. He released his grip around the man's neck, took my hand, and sprinted to the exit. We dashed from the back of the building and spilled into the alleyway. Running down the short, unpaved pathway, water from the earlier rain kicked up around my boots, clacking down the road.

"Damn, Indy, you down for me like that?" His words were short and strained as he gasped for air. I didn't respond. My throat was on fire and my legs cramped like a bitch. My body felt loose, it tingled like I was electrocuted.

I was tipsy without being tipsy.

High without being high.

Violence was my dopamine when things got to be too much. Jumping on that guy's back made me feel proud. I could take care of myself, and I would. If I had to. Chaquille asked if I was down for him like that? I liked him, but I was down for *me* like that.

Moments later, we burst into Naomi's room, and she slammed the door shut behind us. "Are you okay?" she screeched.

"Yo, that was crazy, man!" Dylan pumped his fist, real white boy style too, with a grunt at the end.

"Indy came through with the uppercuts and body shots. Girl, I didn't know you had it in you. Where did all that anger come from?" Theodora slapped her palm against her forehead and *phewed*.

There were so many sides to me, Theodora would never understand.

"What was that about?" I questioned Chaquille. He paced the room.

"Indy, come here," he finally said, motioning with his finger. He was the only one in the room who hadn't spoken on the events of the night. When he did, his first words were saved for my name.

I sauntered to Chaquille and we plopped down on a couch.

"Hey," he said, moving a braid out of my face with the brush of his finger.

"Hey," I breathed back.

"You really had my back, back there."

"Back, back there?" I chuckled.

He chuckled too. My body relaxed. We were so corny, but it was *kinda* nice.

"I did what I had to do; they were about to roll you out. What was that about anyway?"

Chaquille sighed and looked past me at something on the wall. He had this look on his face that told me that he was either remembering something or trying to forget. "I don't know, man. I try to stay lowkey. I only spin here and there, but some people don't like someone coming in from New York and spinning in their territory. First, they send someone to check out one of your parties. Then they send the girls. And the girls will do whatever they need to get information. And then they start showing up for themselves and trying to shut you down."

"So, you mean to tell me all this is about is a bunch of people fighting over who will be the dj for local parties?"

He nodded. "You would think we're talking about dope, right?"

I laughed.

So did he.

"You know, from what I heard, you're not bad. Not bad at all. Don't let them stop you, you got something good here."

"Don't think I forgot about what you said. You'll make it up to me. Mhhmm girl, I have a few things in mind." Chaquille looked me up and down with an exaggerated stare and wide eyes. He was so crazy, and I couldn't keep a straight face as I laughed at him.

I could be down for him, *like that.*

Chaquille tried to be serious but giggled. "Na, for real. I heard through the grapevine that you like the water, so I thought you and I could go fishing."

"What? You heard I like water? From whom? And do New York City boys go fishing? I thought they showered and did all their business in Timberland boots?"

Chaquille squeezed his eyes shut, laughed out loud, and held his stomach. "Yooo that was a good one. I will leave the boots at home for our fishing date. And I asked Naomi what you like to do, and she said you like to sleep, and you live on the water so anything water-related is fun to you."

Chaquille had consulted Naomi about what I liked. He liked me. The realization was like a gut-punch. Was I ready for him? Everything in me wanted to scream, *'if you know what's good for you, you'll run the other way, mister.'* Before I talked myself out of it, I cocked my head and squinted one eye, looking at him sideways. "We can do that ... go fishing, I mean."

Joya sat down across from me and snatched off her bucket hat she was wearing and dabbed away sweat. "Indy ... you

are so crazy." Her eyes were still wide with fear. She jumped when Dylan shouted his approval once more for the events of the night and did a fist pump. Naomi and Ivelisse sat in hushed voices in the corner. I felt bold now. I marched right up to Naomi. "And what's all the whispering over here? I recall you slamming a door in my face."

"No, she didn't mean to, we just—"

"We just nothing," Naomi interrupted. Ivelisse pursed her lips into a straight line and looked away.

My eyes widened. Could Naomi... and Ivelisse... Was it her who was in Naomi's room when I went there just days ago? And if so—why was she hiding it? I was one to talk, hiding my too-legit-to-quit crew in my head, but she felt safe enough to tell me... right? Theodora passed around a bag of chips and a small blunt, and Joya was cracking open a wine bottle now. Dylan was playing music from his speaker he randomly always kept with him.

"What do you guys want to listen to? Wait wait I got it." He waved his hands at us.

I stared at Naomi, ready to press her again, but she moved across the room and helped Theodora hand out snacks. She cut her eyes at me while she shuffled around. I glanced at Ivelisse and plopped down on the couch with a thump. Something was off.

I heard the sultry and sweet poetic sounds of Snoh Aalegra, making its way higher until it sat at a low rumble across the room. We all quieted and let her voice take us to a smoother place. "I knew you guys would dig Snoh," Dylan beamed.

Chaquille and I talked until the sun rose. Talked, smoked, and napped here and there. Well I puffed when Theodora passed it around. Chaquille just passed. I stared into his brown eyes and his deep waves. His Timberland boots scraped the floor under him until he took them off. He said he wanted to drop out of school at the end of the semester, but he hadn't told his mom yet. He hadn't told anyone—just me. I didn't find this amusing. For kids like us, who had it hard, what we needed was found in college, even if we didn't know what that was yet.

His parents weren't together, and he lived with his mom. His dad was around, but there were a lot of years when he was not. They don't talk about it, and it made Chaquille mad. When he talked, he sounded rough, and he pushed out his words with intensity. As he shared about his dad and his future, more syllables spilled out that seemed to anger him more than the ones before.

He brooded about being jumped. All he wanted to do was spin records and make people dance, but his parents and now these goons, he really wanted no beef with, wanted his head. His phone buzzed all night, and I saw at least three girls' names pop up on his phone. He glanced at the phone and sat it back down, returning to our conversation. Who was calling him? I wanted to know... I wanted his full attention even though I had it already. The deep coarse curls and black bush of hair framed his face. While he spewed heated words, I reached over and palmed his chin, taking in a fistful of his chin hairs. I massaged them babies and I let the oils from his beard seep deep into my hands. I couldn't keep my hands off him.

Chaquille stopped talking. He rested his head back on the couch and closed his eyes. His words were no longer cross. They were relaxed and easygoing. With one touch, I had calmed his spirit. He smiled and leaned in closer, staring at me. I didn't move back, and he was so close I could smell the balm on his lips.

I leaned in close and said, "thankfully I was there to save you. Sounds to me like you need to get some security, Tekashi."

"Maybe I can hire you," he chuckled. With that, we commenced into a fit of giggles again. Chaquille asked me about

my future plans, and I told him about my penthouse dream and magazine. I told him about Ez and wanting to make sure he was squared away. I even told him about Mom and her shenanigans. When my own words became bitter about my family and angry tears threatened to spill, Chaquille said, "you have to find what works for you. Make sure you have options."

"Options for what though?" I frowned.

"Everything. Just make sure whatever you want to do, nothing is holding you back. You're good at defending the little guy, I noticed that about you."

I blushed under Chaquille's words.

"And you know what I noticed about you?"

"What?"

"Those bags under your eyes. Titus got you stressing?" I joked.

Chaquille's face broke into a smile as I swatted at his leg and laughed.

Everyone was coupled up in different corners. The snacks, a few joints, and lots of music trivia floated around the room. My heart was full of so many things. Fight and all, I was glad I came out last night.

Some hours later early into the morning, I pulled out my phone and emailed the Wellness Center hopefully for the last time.

> *Hello, my name is Indigo Lewis. I had two appts with someone, and I also emailed previously to schedule another session. I would like to see if someone else was available for another session, and if not, can you refer me to somewhere?*
>
> *Thank you,*
> *I. Lewis.*

I clicked my phone shut, sat it down, and leaned into Chaquille. He passed me a tiny joint without inhaling and a silly grin spread across his face. I would go back to the Wellness Center and try one more time. I couldn't give up on me.

CHAPTER 21

"YOU MAKE SURE you open and close those curtains like your life depend on it. Ms. Muffit is in a tizzy today." Harper nodded to Chaquille and I. Her many bangles on her wrists jiggled as she warned us. "And the next time you try to miss days of work, let me know so I can cover for you! I get no appreciation around here!" Harper huffed.

"I'm sorry, Harper. I-I wasn't feeling my best," I settled on. It was technically the truth.

"It's okay. It's just, you guys are like my kids. I worry about you. When I texted and you didn't respond, I got worried. Just let me know something." Harper shifted in her seat and placed her elbows on the desk.

"I will." She was a proverbial single, female, cat lady. With no biological children of her own, she still had the maternal gene. My phone vibrated in my pocket and when I checked, I received a confirmation email from the Wellness Center. I had an appointment today for another counseling session. I was still shaking my head at the last two, but I had to try again.

Harper said, "umm, Indigo. They switched the location of the Libra Festival this year. It's usually held in Texas, but

SOMEONE MORE LIKE MYSELF

they're holding it in the Big Easy. New Orleans baby!? Can you still make it?"

"New Orleans? Why the switch?"

"Well, like I said, heifer. If you would come to work, one of these days I could fill you in. I don't think they gave a reason, they just like to switch things up every few years." She rolled her eyes and sank her hand into her palm like she was exasperated. "You and Chaquille will be responsible for the dressing competition. Whoever can dress and undress their actor the quickest wins. This is including make-up and hair."

I was wide eyed listening to what sounded like a bunch of college misfits and an old school camp style obstacle course. "They have awards for everything these days," I grumbled.

"So does that mean I can put you down on the list?" Harper asked, sounding more like a statement.

"Yes, for New Orleans," I huffed.

"Perfect! Everything will be covered by the school, including your hotel room. You just have to show up with your pretty little face and kill 'em dead."

Kill 'em dead, she said. She didn't know the half of it.

Harper had a large paper with boxes and grids, and she scribbled in my name in the last remaining box. Her tongue was slightly out of the corner of her mouth as she concentrated. She pushed her glasses up on her nose. "The track team will be in town as well if they keep up this winning streak. They're holding the state championship the same weekend!"

Chaquille leaned against Harper's desk and flashed his signature smile. His mouth was still slightly swollen from when they snuck him in the face and his left eye was also a nasty bluish-purple color. I toyed with a braid as I glanced him up and down. "How are you feeling?" That night would be one I would never forget.

"How are *you* feeling?" Chaquille returned the question without answering mine. "You coming to the party tonight?" he pressed.

I searched Chaquille's eyes. He hadn't said two words to me since the fight and now he wanted me to attend another party? I texted him a few times and his responses were short and choppy. Had I missed something? As dazzling as his smile was, I didn't want to be caught up in things that may or may not really be happening. I thought we shared something that night and when I didn't hear from him, I guess that told me everything I needed to know. Maybe it was all in my head. Maybe maybe maybe.

"I don't think I can make it. I have class and an appointment I have to get to." And with that, I said goodbye to Harper and exited the building without looking back at Chaquille.

I zipped my jacket up as I made my way to the Wellness Center for my next appointment, pushing Chaquille from my thoughts. I checked in at the front desk, and seconds later someone greeted me.

"Hi, I'm Trenita Jenkins, follow me." She extended her arm, and I followed behind her. I caught a whiff of her perfume, and the scent tickled my nose; she smelled like honey and a touch of Mama Jackie. I sat down in her office then she closed the door. I studied the certificates on her walls. There seemed to be so many of them. She was certified to do a little bit of everything. Her shelves were lined with all different shaped books and most of them were dog-eared and old, like she pulled them from the shelves and read them. They weren't just for show. I squirmed in my seat, trying to get comfortable. Trenita turned on a low humming sound device outside of the door. She saw me give her, and the weird looking contraption, a funny look. "It's to drown out our conversation. For privacy."

I had been here twice before and no one else turned on this machine. I sat down and picked at my nails. Would she see the voices? Would she hear them too? "I've done this before," I blurted.

"I read that in your file," Trenita said with a half-smile. She sipped from a large mug. She stirred it with a spoon and then sat it down on a table next to her chair.

"And what brings you in today, Ms. Indigo?"

I crossed my legs and looked around the room. "Isn't that in my file too?"

"The file says one thing—yes. But I like to ask anyway. If you had to describe why you are here, what would you say?"

I shifted in my seat and glanced at Trenita's large window. I was here for a reason, and I wanted a normal life. I wanted one that didn't involve killing and enjoying it. "Sometimes, I hear voices." I waited for Trenita's eyes to bulge out of her head.

They didn't.

I continued... "It's my mom's voice, but sometimes others."

"Do you hallucinate as well?"

"Hallucinate?" I questioned.

"You hear these voices, but do you see anything?"

I shook my head. "No, I don't."

"Okay, continue." Trenita sipped from her mug.

"That's about it, that's why I'm here."

"How do you think your previous sessions have gone?"

"I did the two sessions with your, uh, colleagues. But it didn't end well. I think it was my fault though."

"Why was it your fault?" Trenita paused and scrunched her eyebrows together, the steam from her hot cup rising.

"I don't know. I went to two counselors, and it didn't work out. Maybe I didn't do it right or something."

"Indigo. There is nothing to do. You ever go to the grocery store, and you see dozens of different brands of bread? You have your favorites but there are so many other favorites too? But you still choose the one that's best for you, right?" Trenita leaned back in her chair. "It's the same with counseling. You have to find a therapist whom you feel safe with, someone you build a relationship with. And if you haven't found it yet, you keep looking. You try new bread. But it's nothing you did wrong. You did right, by even being here. A third time tells me we have to do better as a mental health clinic."

I sighed a little louder than normal. I fell back not realizing I was perched upright with my hand gripping the ends of the chair. I took a deep breath and relaxed my shoulders. They were tight against my chin. "So, it's not my fault? That I haven't met a counselor I like yet?"

"No, it's not your fault. Just like hearing voices isn't your fault either. When did that first start?"

I studied Trenita's cappuccino colored face. Her hair was cut short like Jada Pinkett Smith, and it was shiny at the top, like she had sprayed it with sheen. She was heavy set like my mom, and she carried it well. She wore a long-sleeved, black t-shirt that said, *Dope Black Social Worker*. I wondered if I could trust her.

'*Don't tell her anything, Indy. Keep her out of our business,*' a voice said in my head.

Before I could talk myself out of it, the word vomit set in. I told Trenita about Tunica Rivers. About Mom. About Ez. Sidney and Ms. Arletha, and even a little about Chaquille and Will. The session flew by due to my rambling. If words could really fill a room, this one would've been stuffed to the brim with the things I managed every day. I shed angry tears for Chaquille, and curious ones for Will. I cried a mess of confused tears for myself and a few for Jaxon. The one thing I didn't tell Trenita about was Jaxon. Ez was big on knowing his rights and he said doctors couldn't tell people's business because of *hippos*, or something like that. I wanted to tell her, but I knew better.

At the end of the session, I felt lighter, and my chest was no longer tight.

"Here are a few release forms I need you to sign. I usually have you sign these at the beginning of the session. Time got away from me as we talked, I apologize." Trenita was clicking on her computer and papers shot from the printer at the same time. She handed me a clipboard with a few papers and a pen attached. "This one is consent to services. It states that anything you and I discuss is completely confidential, I will only have to report something if you threaten to harm yourself or anyone else."

"Myself or anyone else?" I repeated. I held the pen in my hand and clicked the top back and forth.

"Yes, like if you have suicidal or homicidal ideations. These are crazy questions, I know. We have to ask anyway; they are part of the intake. Most mental health issues start to appear in college. Not all the time—but sometimes."

"They're not crazy. I guess you have to ask... You never know what people are capable of." I nodded and signed the paper.

I knew what I was capable of. But based on this consent to services form, and Trenita reporting me if needed, one thing we would not talk about was Jaxon Green, and my increasing thirst for Mr. Chestnut.

Later that night, I was feeling good after my session with Trenita. I laid in my bed, rubbing my feet together under my blankets. Theodora wasn't in our room, nor did she or Naomi respond when I texted them. I was desperate for a milkshake. I scrolled through my text messages and spotted my thread from Will. I smiled and without a second thought, pressed the phone icon and called him.

"Hey you," Will breathed. I could tell he was smiling into the phone.

"Hey yourself." I smiled back.

"And what do I owe the pleasure of this conversation?" Will asked. There was shrieking and what sounded like gears grinding in the background. I had to yell over the noise.

"I miss you!" I shouted. The words bounced off the walls in my room.

"I miss you too!" Will yelled back. "I'm at the plant in East Tunica."

"At this hour?"

"They had a water main break and I'm on-call."

"Can you fix anything right now? I mean, you're still in school for your certification?"

"Oh no, my instructor is here too. Say what's up, Mr. Shaud. This is my girl, Indy."

"Heyyy, Ms. Indy," I heard an older man hollering over the noise.

Will called me his girl.

The loudness stopped when Will went to a quieter place so we could chat. I started to tell Will I loved him. I didn't know why, but at that moment, the three words sat on the tip on my tongue, waiting to spill out.

Will and I exchanged I love you's many times before as friends. You know, the nice, friendship love. The thick kind that sticks to the pot. If I said it to him today it would sound different to him. Before the words flew out, Will said he saw Ms. Arletha at the grocery store. Dad and Ms. Arletha's baby seemed to spark a match in our home. Although everyone was sworn to secrecy, when she saw Will, she still held her stomach and beamed anyway. That made me smile. We were excited and couldn't wait to tell someone. Will was my someone.

"Are you still coming for Family Day?"

"I'll be there. I need to get away for a while, even if just for a day. This program is rough!"

"Yayy! I can't wait to see you. You'll love the campus. I'm going to ask my dad if you can drive with him, Sidney, Ez, and Ms. Arletha. Your hoopty..."

"Enough about my hoopty, woman!" Will chuckled. I heard the loud noise resume in the background. With that, Will and I said our goodbyes.

After our conversation, I was still salivating for a milkshake. I grabbed my keys and put on Theodora's Crocs. They were on my side of the room anyway. I hustled outside and fired up The Bus. When I turned the ignition it roared to life, waking everyone in its path.

I cruised off campus and made my way to the nearest ice cream shop. The windows were cracked, and a breezy, April evening felt perfect against my long-sleeved, Titus U sweater. I turned the old school dial until I landed on Mint Condition. I belted the song from my lungs and looked at my eyes in the rearview mirror as I sang. The song was loud and assaulted The Bus by bellowing out of the speakers and directly to me.

'Yeah, girl, this is my jam. Keep it here,' Mom sang along.

Together, we belted the song and let the beat pierce our souls. I stopped at a blinking, four-way red light and I tapped the steering wheel, still singing along with Mom. There was another car across from me and we both inched closer, waiting for the other to drive. I was in a good mood, so I waved the other car through and let them go first; however, a familiar set of eyes stared back at mine when we passed. Naomi sat in the driver's seat with Ivelisse next to her, stroking her cheek with love written all over her face.

When Naomi and I locked eyes, her face hardened, and on cue, Ivelisse stopped stroking.

CHAPTER 22

"**AND WHY WOULDN'T** you tell me?" I crinkled my eyebrows in confusion. A few miles and a lot of lies later, Naomi and I argued back in her dorm room. I never did get my milkshake.

"Indy, you are always in your own world. Half the time Theodora and I are wondering if you're even listening. What was I supposed to say?"

"So, are you and Ivelisse together? Like in a relationship?"

Naomi huffed and took a step back. When she and I locked eyes at the four-way stop, she texted me, told me to bust a U-turn, and go to her room to talk. She dropped off Ivelisse at her dorm.

"Yes, we're in a relationship." She looked at the floor and crossed her arms over her chest.

"Naomi, and you didn't think you could tell me? Did you think I would judge you?"

"Everyone says they won't judge—until it's someone they're close to. Then it becomes the thing that's swept under the rug."

"Naomi, that's not fair. You're the one sweeping it under the rug. You haven't even given me and Theodora a chance to... wait. Does Theodora know?" I fumed. If Theodora knew and they both kept it from me, how did I fit into this friendship?

"No, she doesn't know. I haven't told anyone. This is still new to me... I'm adjusting."

"New to you. Is this your first relationship with a girl?"

"It is." She sat down at the small table in her dorm room and a tear skipped from her face.

I plopped down across from her and placed my hand on her knee. "Naomi... you're ashamed. You don't have to be ashamed."

And with that, Naomi let out a deep wail, and her chest heaved up and down. She covered her eyes and rocked in the chair and muffled her own cries. "It's just that. I never thought something like this would happen to me. I've always been attracted to guys. Since I've come to school and met Ivelisse... she feels like nothing I've ever experienced. And I don't know how to take that. She sees me in ways I've never been seen, and she shows me parts of myself too. If there's anyone who I know for sure is on my side. It's her."

"Then why deny her? Why keep it a secret?" I was still confused.

"My mom is as religious as they come. She can't have a lesbian daughter. I can't hurt her like that."

It made sense now. She didn't want to disappoint her mom and who knew how she would react? I searched Naomi's face and saw so much pain. "But you can't keep living like this either, Naomi!" Sure, her mom may feel some type of way, but Naomi had to do what she had to for herself. And that should mean way more than disappointment.

'My, aren't we the pot calling the kettle black these days,' Mom tuned in.

This is different, I thought. *It wasn't the same. Besides, do you want me to tell people, about you?* I challenged Mom in my head.

'No, I don't. But I do want you to be honest with yourself. Don't blame me for your urges. You're only feeling what comes natural to you. It's primal and it's in you. That is all, my love,' Mom sang in her famous English voice.

"I was planning to tell her at Family Day," Naomi interrupted my thoughts. "But I just don't know if she is ready. I don't know if I'm ready. But Ivelisse deserves it."

"Are you ready for that? Do you think that's a good time? Family Day will probably be crazy."

"I know. I thought about that too. She won't go off on me in front of other people, so it might be the perfect time," she chuckled.

Naomi was right. The only time I knew for sure Ez would do his best to act accordingly was in front of strangers. "Are you going to tell Theodora?" I asked.

"Well, since you straight up caught us, and Family Day is this weekend I guess it's time to start letting the cat out of the bag." Naomi's face was red and stained with tears. She folded her hands together at the table and twirled a few rings on her fingers.

I placed my hand over-top of hers. She stopped twirling and I looked her in her eyes.

"Naomi. Let us be there for you. We're girls. You can trust us."

She wiped tears from her face once more and looked away from me. With another chuckle she said, "I know I'm in the hot seat right now. I get it—you straight up caught me. But same to you, Indy. Let us be there for you. Trust us too." And with that, she placed her free hand on mine. Naomi and I shared a moment in time, looking at each other, as tears now sat in both of our eyes.

I eyeballed the paper. B- it read. I received a B- on my first big assignment of the semester. The topic our professor gave us was mythical creatures in Greek mythology. I was always interested in mermaids, living on the water in Tunica Rivers. When I was a kid, I would go sit outside and skip rocks into the shimmering waves off our back deck. I talked out loud to the waves and although no one ever talked back, I felt someone or something listening. Maybe it was the mermaids.

This week I had made it a point to go to sleep and wake up earlier in the morning. I even blocked off time to study for each day this week and I attended all my scheduled sessions with Trenita. I was on time—on schedule—and on my shit. Sessions with Trenita were going well and I felt comfortable with her. So far at least. I told her about EZ, and she giggled at all his one-liners and listened intently when I explained we found out last year he was autistic. She was angry when I told her I went to the social services building to get help for him and what they said. She gave me a bunch of pamphlets for day programs and said she would make some calls for us. It was nice. I felt like she was on my side.

I was staring at the paper and walking onto the courtyard when Chaquille bumped me. "Every day? Really!" I said annoyed. Chaquille would make it a point to walk with me to the dining-hall for lunch daily. It was so awkward; he made small talk and it felt forced. I didn't know what we were or where we stood. I mean, what kind of person was he? We had a friendly conversation then he ghosted me without an afterthought. To think we had connected and he so easily friend zoned me. I didn't understand guys, let alone college guys.

"Hey, Indy! I like your little headband, is there some naps up under there we're hiding?" he reached up and tried to tug at my headband.

"Get off!" I yelped. I giggled and pushed him away from me, trying to keep some distance, emotionally and physically. Chaquille snickered and grabbed my head and hugged me between his neck and shoulder. I didn't have a chance to object, and before I knew it, his lips had brushed my cheek. I pulled away clearly confused and searched his eyes. They were shifty but stared back into mine. It was like he wanted to be in my presence, but only on his terms. I didn't know what his terms were or if I even agreed to them. Before I could shoot off questions, I heard a loud rumble and people screaming and clapping. Chaquille and I made our way toward the noise. I picked up a flyer that was flitting by on the ground.

I eyed the postcard style flyer. Her name was Laylah Capri, and she was some sort of feminist and Titus alumni. They were handing out free hot dogs and hot chocolate. What a combination, but in college, free was free. I took one for myself and one for Chaquille, but he grabbed four hot dogs, two for him and two for me. We found an empty bench and sat down to eat while Laylah talked.

"I have a question. Does everyone know that this is a patriarchal, white, male dominated capitalist society?"

Chaquille choked on his hot dog and scampered for a sip of his hot chocolate.

"I know those are really big words, but I'll break them down. Patriarchal means controlled by men, and so does male dominated; but I like the two phrases together. I think they packed more of a punch, so I'll go with it." She motioned with her hand like she was sprinkling something into a pot and stirring. She was animated. She smiled and moved her hands with each word. Her large, afro puff blew in the wind, and she wore stiletto heels and skinny jeans with a cinched camouflage jacket. "Do we know what that means? This land, this place of milk and honey, allegedly," she dragged out the last word like it was vile. She let it hang in the air and as several heads nodded and affirmations poured in her direction, she continued, "— this place was never made for us, Black women. It was never made for us. We weren't even a thought. So why do we continue to ask for a seat at their table? When do we create our own?"

The crowd murmured in agreeance. She was using her own voice alone and doing her best to scream her message, when finally, someone from the tech department got her a microphone. Now her message reverberated in my chest. My ears rang as her words pierced my soul. "We have to fight for each other, we have to network for each other. Let's start building our own tables!" Laylah screamed into the microphone. A few women in the front screamed and cheered her on.

"Shorty is dope," Chaquille commented, and took another bite from his hot dog like he didn't choke when she first started. He gave a seal of approval to Laylah with one head nod. I was intrigued.

My hot dog sat in my hands now cold. I was in a trance listening to Laylah's words. I pulled out my phone and followed all her accounts on social media she had listed on her flyer. She ran some sort of program on campus called Black Feminists Nation.

"If you are interested in meeting soul sisters like yourself, if you are interested in making a difference in your Black girl community, come sign up for more information. We have work to do, ladies." And with that, Laylah pulled her sunglasses off her forehead over her eyes, and strutted off stage. She never missed a beat in her heels and my heart stomped with her every move, praying she didn't ruin my fantasy by tripping and falling. But I knew she wouldn't, and she didn't.

When I stood up, my hot dog fell off my lap.

"Oh no, look what you did!" Chaquille bumbled around to grab the food off the ground, but I didn't care.

I jumped in place, trying to spot Laylah, but I couldn't see her anymore behind crowds of people. "Excuse me, excuse me," I shooed between people until I made my way to her table. I scribbled in my email address and checked yes; I'd like more information. I did want more information. I liked the way Laylah talked, and her words made me want to shout like I was in a Baptist church one hot July, Sunday morning.

"How did you make it over here so fast. I looked up and you were gone?" Chaquille was hot on my heels and upset I had taken off.

Spinning around, I said, "Chaquille, what's up with you? We're friends, then we're not friends. We're cool, and then we're not. I think we're on the same page, and you show me we're not. Why are you mad I walked away?"

I was feeling pumped after hearing Laylah talk. He looked down at me and took in each word. Gritting my teeth, I didn't enjoy talking to Chaquille like that, especially in front of this Black Feminist Nation. The vendors eyes darted between us, sizing up our interaction.

"You really gonna do this right here?" Chaquille asked through tight lips and a disappointed frown. The crowd had died down and he was trying to keep his voice even.

"Why do you insist on walking me to and from the dining-hall every day?" I pressed. The workers behind the table were quiet.

"It's not you. I just . . . have a lot going on. I don't want you to get involved."

"I have a lot going on too, hell, college is *a lot* going on. But you shut me out and then try to pull me back. What gives?" I questioned.

Chaquille stood there staring at me with a frown like I did something wrong. Whatever it was Chaquille couldn't get me involved with was not my concern, but all this back and forth had to stop. I picked up my hot dog and squished it between the buns. I would not allow Chaquille to have me confused ever again. Without another word, I dumped the cold hot dog into the nearest trashcan. My hand was now sticky and needed washing because of the gunk. I rubbed it onto my jeans. If they wanted a show, someone else would give it to them. I had to get to class.

CHAPTER 23

INDIGO,
My world. I am sorry we haven't been able to communicate much like we usually do. Things have been changing in here and quickly. Nurse Meanface has switched on us, girl, there is a new sheriff in town and she ain't no Indian, she's definitely a chief! Lights out at nine sharp, and if you're even a minute late for breakfast, you can't enter the dining hall. She had me and Ruth-Ann in solitary again because we wouldn't stop singing. Can you imagine? Being isolated for singing, for having fellowship. I don't know how much more of this I can take Indy; I know this probably means nothing to you, to hear me complaining about breakfast, but this will not stand. I have nothing but time in here to figure this out. I don't know if they are reading our letters or what. I would like to start talking on the phone instead. I will try to call you every Monday, Wednesday, and Friday. Make sure you are available by the phone in the evenings.

I received a letter from your dad. He said that he has a woman he is sweet on, and that she is having a baby? That's good, I guess. Your dad is a good man; he would do anything for me, and I'm grateful for that. I guess he shouldn't wait for me in here . . . They say I have another thirty years, but I've been praying to Yemaya, and I don't think it will be that long. Something will pull through, just you wait! Anyway, tell your dad that I am happy for him, as long as he is happy. But when my time comes and I do get out of here, she better hit the road, Jack!

Love, Mommy

Mom's latest letter was weeks later than her last one. I crumpled the paper and tossed it into the library's trashcan behind me and sighed. Monday, Wednesday, and Friday—I could never commit to that schedule. I had class those days and work at the theater. She said she wanted to talk at night, but still. That meant I would be anticipating her phone call all day, and who knew what type of mood she would be in. Hell, what type of mood *I* would be in. Plus, I didn't want to talk to Mom that often. She had a way of affecting my thoughts and my choices. Her voices in my mind were nonstop and they kept me up for hours, figuring things out without my consent and compiling the best way to take out Mr. Chestnut without it blowing back on me.

    I knew Mr. Chestnut had something to do with Mom being in solitary. What would it take to tip off the university or the police without *me* being involved? If I was going to turn someone in for a crime, I needed to make sure I had enough proof. This would put me out there in every way, and the last thing I wanted to do was expose Mr. Chestnut for the predator he was. Instead, I'm imprisoned for Jaxon's murder in the process. If I told what I knew about Mr. Chestnut, surely, they would find out I was being questioned about the disappearance of Jaxon and they would somehow turn it around on me. *Why are you coming forward and not Joya? Why do you care?* They would say. I needed enough juice on Chestnut so they would look past me.

    I pushed my chair from the table and walked to the Wellness Center for my session with Trenita. When I got outside, I spotted

a group of students standing in the campus center by a large oak tree. It was an unofficial meeting place for anyone with a message in their soul that needed to be shared. It was the poet's stage, where the dreamers and thinkers congregated. My heart skipped when I peered over the small crowd that had formed, and I saw Laylah Capri again.

"To close this out, ladies, I need you to remember who you are, and that you, and only you, are the breath of life." Laylah paced in front of the tree while the wind blew through her hair. "Many people will question you; many people will stand in your way because they don't want to see a woman. Particularly a Black woman, at the helm. But you remind them we deserve to be here just as much as anyone else. We're so busy building a life for ourselves and for others that we put our own needs on the back burner until it's too late. Ladies, don't let it be too late. Growth takes place when we start doing the things that scare us."

Laylah glanced around at the small crowd of women, and I followed her gaze. About a dozen of us listened, taking in every drop of confirmation needed. She transfixed us with her words, and we let them settle into the parts of us where it was needed the most.

"Don't get so caught up caring for others that we don't care for ourselves. I come to college campuses, and I talk directly to you, black and brown girls. Titus University is home for me. This is where I grew up, where I became a woman in a lot of ways. I speak on it because I know what it's like to not feel heard. To feel like you are a dot in a world full of men, intent on telling you what to do with your life. Take care of yourself, your body, and your mental health. And keep all three safe from men who want to exploit it. Have a good day, ladies!"

While we clapped, Laylah nodded in appreciation. The group dispersed and she picked up her water bottle and bags sitting under the tree. Her teams were behind her, cleaning up her vendor table. I ran my hands through my hair and smoothed my eyebrows before I tapped her shoulder.

"Ms. Capri?" My voice was above a hush.

She turned around. "Please, call me Laylah."

I glimpsed her face up close and personal. She was the same shade of coffee when you put in too much cream. Before Mama Jackie passed, she loved her cup of coffee every morning with more cream than coffee. Ez used to tease her. I thought of them and smiled. They would have a field day debating how much cream it would take to make Laylah's beautiful skin tone. Her hair was shiny, thick, and long. I scanned the top of her head for lace and found none. I also looked for wefts and saw none of those. The last time I saw her, she wore her afro loud and proud. Today, I saw just how real shrinkage was because the girl had inches and her hair was all hers.

She looked genuine.

"Laylah," I repeated. "I have to get to an appointment, but I just wanted to say I enjoy your podcast, and I even purchased your book! Thank you for your powerful thoughts," I continued speaking from my heart. "You give me hope. I can take care of myself. I am safe."

Laylah beamed. Her straight, pearly teeth shone on this sunless day. "My pleasure, queen. We have to challenge each other to be better, while not being disrespected in the process. I'm glad you took what resonated. Now, go change lives, sis. And remember, don't let anyone disrespect you. Anyone."

I thanked Laylah and hustled to Trenita. I wouldn't let anyone disrespect me. Or show up to my dorm room or deal with me in any way that was less than my worth.

No more.

A few minutes later, Trenita and I stared at each other.

"Excuse me?" I repeated. I wasn't sure I was hearing her correctly.

"Your voices, what exactly do they tell you?" Trenita blinked a few times. Her phone rang, and I hoped she would answer it like all the others had done, but she didn't. She stood and reached over her desk, swiping at one button before the shrewd, cold ring stopped.

I picked at the corner of the loveseat I was sitting on. There was already a tiny hole, and I dug my nail into it, making it larger. How many butts had sat here before me, telling her about voices they heard? Not many, I bet. I started slow. "They don't tell me to do things, they kind of comment on my day." Yeah, that felt right. And it wasn't a full lie.

Trenita looked at me over her glasses, and I had to stop myself from giggling. The way she leaned forward and squared her face reminded me of Harper. Whenever I said something they didn't understand or agree with, they both pushed their glasses higher on their faces as if seeing better would help them figure things out.

"Comment on your day?" She frowned.

I shifted in my seat and pulled cotton out of the couch. Her eyes darted between me and the white mass rolling between my fingers. I said nothing. I wouldn't make this easy for her.

"Walk me through a typical day in your head." Trenita changed gears. How did I put it into words without giving myself away? But that's why I was here; to get better. To talk about the voices. I had to tread lightly with my words.

'It's okay, honey. You can talk to her. I like this one,' Mom breathed. Her voice was low, and it reminded me of Ms. Arletha when she talked to Dad with interest and soft eagerness.

"And can you lay off my couch? I do have to stuff that cotton back in there when you leave for the next person."

I snickered at her words and relaxed my shoulders. "I don't know. They get on me when I don't want to go to class or work. Encourage me to have fun and stand up for myself. Stuff like that."

"That doesn't sound terrible," Trenita commented. She crossed her legs and clasped her hands over her knees. "Anything bad?"

"Define bad?"

She unhanded her knees and draped her arm over her chair. "Do they tell you to hurt anyone or yourself?"

My hand twitched, resting next to the gaping hole I picked in the couch. I had the urge to pick even more.

I resisted.

This was a moment I knew would come in counseling. The one I dreaded but nervously waited for. Anything I had to say in this moment could and probably would be used against me in a court of law.

"Indy?" Trenita gazed at me. She repeated my name once more, probably thinking I didn't hear her or the question.

I heard.

I waited one second longer for Mom to give me an answer that would suffice, stacked against a therapist who'd been to college for these sort of things. I cleared my throat. "When someone does something to me, yes, they tell me to do bad things."

Ms. Trenita raised an eyebrow but didn't make a move. Neither did I.

"Indy, have you hurt anyone? Has anyone hurt you?"

I paused a second too long again, waiting for Mom to come. She didn't.

The things I wanted hidden the most were the same parts of me I needed revealed. Instead of finding the syllable, the adjectives, and all the persons, places, and things that contributed to how I was here today, I chose something more

guttural. Deep wails escaped me, and one small tear fell into the hole. One more drop fell, this one larger than the rest, and before I knew it, hot tears spilled from my eyes.

Ms. Trenita handed me a tissue. I continued crying as my tissues got smaller and smaller from my tears and snot. Ms. Trenita handed me more tissues and then the entire box.

"No, I haven't hurt anyone. But people have hurt me," I coughed out. I lied to Trenita, and I felt like I had been gut punched.

"Are you ready to talk about that now?" Trenita asked softly. I shook my head.

"You know, I remember you saying you had trouble focusing and staying on track in college. We have . . . medications. They may help stabilize some of your moods," Trenita whispered after my whimpers settled down. "I really think you may benefit from something. To help you get acclimated to college and assist with some of these thoughts."

"Do you think it will help?" I gave Trenita wet and quizzical eyes.

"I do." She was sympathetic, but I wasn't sure I wanted her sympathy. More than anything, I realized I needed her to listen.

"If you think it will help, I'll try it." I wiped my face for the last time.

She inspected me once more with a long and intense gaze. Her face was serious, and her eyes were darker than I had ever seen on her beaming face. She exhaled and gave me a notepad for an appointment with the school's psychiatrist.

CHAPTER 24

THERE ONCE WAS a couple who lived on Beauregard Road. They looked happy to all their neighbors. They smiled when they were supposed to and waved when they went to get the mail. They walked their dog at the same time every day and brought along a little scooper and bag to pick up the shit when the dog did its mess. The shit didn't even have a chance to stink because the couple was so careful to pick it up before anyone caught a whiff. I'm eighteen years old, and lots of people have many more years than I do. But even I knew everyone's shit stank. Everyone. No matter how much you tried to hide it.

Finding out where they lived wasn't hard. I tailed him one day when he left track practice. I laid low a couple streets over until I felt brave enough to peer into the windows.

'Make sure you're quiet. You almost set off those damn motion detector lights last time,' Mom hissed in my head.

My hair was wrapped up, secured under my bonnet and I wore my blackout sunglasses. My all-black Nike tracksuit was tight on my skin, and I felt like Halle Berry in that movie,

Catwoman. I still had on my studded silver earrings; I forgot to take them off.

Trailing him and Nurse Meanface, or better known as Allie, was becoming something Mom wouldn't let me rest about. I was on medications for about two weeks now and although Trenita said I shouldn't feel any side effects of the medication just yet, I begged to differ. I was so-very-tired and sleeping through my alarms. People were knocking on the door, and I was snoring my life away. I even slept through a fire drill the dorm had, and thankfully Theodora was there to shake me awake.

I crept to the back of the house where their bedroom sat. I stood on my tiptoes to listen. This conversation was spicy, and I held my breath, making sure I heard things correctly.

"Gregg, I'm just going to go back to Tunica Rivers. I'm tired of all the whispering about you and the students. We tried to make a life here. We left everything behind. I have to drive almost two hours to get to work. I don't want to do this anymore."

Mr. Chestnut paddled around their bedroom with a thick towel wrapped around his waist. His chest was littered with light, brown hair and a small old man pudge poked from his midsection. His hair held little speckles of water. He ran a hand through his tossed, blonde locs swinging water in Nurse Meanface's direction.

"Allie—what are you going on about now? I told you I will handle the mortgages. I took on the dorm rep position, so we had more money coming in. You can put in a few more hours at Trochesse, you know. I mean, how selfish are you? I'm paying for this house and our house in Tunica Rivers and you're questioning me about other women? Get a grip, woman."

Nurse Meanface's face reddened. She piled on make-up when I saw her in Trochesse. I didn't think she was much to look at with her slender straight frame, protruding chin, and pointy nose. That was how she got the name Nurse Meanface. As Mr. Chestnut slipped into pajama pants that had Titus U's Track and Field emblem, I peeped at Nurse Meanface, and noticed the sunspots that peppered her bare face and her damp from the shower hair.

"They're not just other women, Gregg," Allie hissed. "I don't know who you think you are dealing with, but I won't stand for this. Why would you be in the car with high school girls, Gregg? Yes, you coached them, and I get that. Big bad Mr. Chestnut, all the girls coo and make kissy eyes at you. I look past all of it for you. But this is enough!" she shouted.

Mr. Chestnut squinted at Nurse Meanface. With a curled lip, he hauled back and flung everything off their long, rectangular dresser toward his wife.

"Ahhhh!" Nurse Meanface shouted as she shielded her eyes. Her perfumes and lotions shattered on the wall from the force of his rage. "What is wrong with you!" she screamed and pushed back on their large bed. I could see the whites of her eyes from here. She held her arms up in a defensive stance, and Mr. Chestnut laughed. Like he really leaned in, snickered, and smiled in her face.

"Let me say one thing and say it good," he started.

Nurse Meanface said nothing. She looked like she was holding her breath. Shit, I was holding mine too. My eyes were wider than hers, and I was hoping I wouldn't see something that would keep me up at night. Mom and them did that enough.

"You aren't going anywhere. We are married and we'll figure this thing out. You didn't see what you think you saw. We had to leave Tunica Rivers because of accusations just like this one that you are making against me—my own wife. The school board almost didn't let us leave without forfeiting my pension and leaving quietly. Over accusations! That they

couldn't prove! If you think I'm going to lay my head next to a woman who also doesn't trust me, you've got another thing coming." Mr. Chestnut's face was so close to Nurse Meanface's that I saw her reading glasses fog up.

"So, are you denying that you are sleeping with teenagers, Gregg?" Nurse Meanface's voice was squeaky, and she hardly made out the question. I almost screamed from the window, *'speak up!'* I didn't want to miss a second of the conversation that I would never be able to process with anyone else. I took brain pictures of it all.

"I am saying that I have done nothing that would bring dishonor to you, my wife," Mr. Chestnut quipped. He backed away from Nurse Meanface and stepped over the mess he made by tossing the dresser's contents. Perfume scents wafted in my direction in the window and before I knew it, I felt like someone had smacked me directly in the nose and a pinched sneeze expelled from my nostrils.

"You can continue on with your whores or whoever you spend your time with. I'm done, Gregg!" Nurse Meanface didn't hear my sneeze because she stomped out of the bedroom and over the mess on the floor. She was trying her best to play tough, but I smelled the fear from here. Maybe that was where my sneeze came from.

She didn't hear me beyond the window, but Mr. Chestnut heard something. He frowned, looking out into the darkness. I ducked my head and covered my mouth.

'See what I mean, she's an amateur,' a voice whispered.

I cursed them in my head. What was the point of medication anyway? They made me tired, and the voices were still there, critiquing every move I made. I dropped down to my knees and crouched in the flowerbed. I heard light and precise footsteps moving closer to the window. A shadow appeared over the windowsill. I held my breath as Mr. Chestnut stood there and looked outside. I smelled his cologne just a few feet away and I wanted to vomit. After what seemed like minutes, Mr. Chestnut slammed the window shut and I heard the lock click.

Carefully maneuvering back to The Bus parked down the street, I kicked myself for coming out here. I was itching to climb in my bed and figure out all that had happened tonight. I had the information I needed. He was forced out of Tunica Rivers by the school board but instead of holding him accountable for his actions, he was quietly let go. It wasn't fair what men were capable of and the levels that went into protecting them.

The buck would stop here.

I would write an anonymous letter with all the information I heard tonight. Although he didn't directly incriminate himself, it would surely open an investigation or something. The thoughts feverishly swirled in my head.

About thirty minutes later, I entered our room and Theodora had her hot comb out, pressing her hair. I heard the familiar sizzle of hair meeting a little grease, and I winced for her.

"Hey girl, you okay?" She eyed me up and down in my blackout outfit.

"I'm straight. Had to work late at the theater to get ready for the Libra Festival," I said as I peeled off my clothes and changed into my pajamas. My hands were shaking, and my words were even less convincing talking to Theodora, but she pressed on.

"The Libra Festival! What time is that again? I want to make sure I'm there to support you and Chaquille open and close the curtains," she giggled into the mirror hanging on the back of our door.

I climbed into bed and couldn't help but chuckle at her jab. I snuggled into the blankets and tried to stop my body from shaking. "Shut up! The real question is what time is your big meet so I can see you against some actual opponents?"

"I know, right? Everyone we've run against has been so basic. It's such a shame," Theodora joked in the mirror with a fake sad face. "Since this is the state competition there should be some real talent; we'll be running all day just about. Mr. Chestnut said only the best girls can compete." I winced hearing his name and knowing what I had just saw.

"What time are your parents getting into town for Family Day?" Theodora asked.

"They're all driving together—Will too. Knowing my dad, he'll probably be here first thing in the morning. What about yours?"

"They'll be here super early in the morning. They don't want to miss a thing," Theodora replied with a sigh. I caught her eye in the mirror. It was the same thing I saw in Naomi's face when we talked about telling her mom about Ivelisse. Nervousness.

I gazed around the room and made a mental note to clean up in the morning. I drifted off to sleep, my body giving out from the events. I sank deeper into the bed and wrapped myself in my comforter set tight enough to make a human burrito. For hours, I slept and slept. Mom and the voices let me rest and I knew it was probably the medication working on me again because as soon as I opened my eyes, I closed them back.

"Indigo? Indigo?" a voice mumbled.

"Mom?" I croaked. My throat was dry.

"No, it's not your mom. She's still in Trochesse. It's Mr. Chestnut and Theodora."

My eyes popped open, adjusting to see Mr. Chestnut standing over me with Theodora next to him. He had the same lip curled up and smirk he gave to Nurse Meanface the night before.

"Ahhh!" I screamed as I flailed my arms in Mr. Chestnut's direction.

"Indy, Indy, calm down." Theodora stepped in front of Mr. Chestnut. He locked eyes with mine and he was cold as ice. His face was hard and if I blinked, I would lose the trance he and I shared. He would be hell bent on showing me his reach and his ability to invade my space.

"Why is he here!" I shouted at Theodora. I squeezed my legs together and prayed I did not wet myself right here the second time this man descended on my room.

"I told you my family was coming early. I left to meet them this morning, but I forgot my keys. I called your phone over and over. I even called the landline in the hallway. You didn't answer. I had to get Mr. Chestnut to let me into the room, he's the rep on duty in the mornings."

I grabbed my phone and saw I had eight missed calls—all from Theodora. There were even a few text messages from her. My hand balled around my blanket as I slowly released it. I had slept through my alarm, all of Theodora's phone calls, and her bringing my worst enemy into my room.

"Sorry, Indy. Maybe don't sleep so hard next time," Mr. Chestnut said in my direction with his same sinister, wide smile. He was as fake as they came, and girls ate this shit up.

"It's Indigo, don't call me Indy."

"I have to run. My family is downstairs. Thanks for letting me in, Mr. Chestnut. I'll see you later in the quad for Family Day." Theodora searched around the room for her jacket and keys while Mr. Chestnut loomed over me and I laid in the sunken place in my bed; my alleged safe space, under his

power. Theodora would never see what I saw. He and I had a history she just wouldn't understand.

"I would love to meet your family, Theodora. Yours too, Ms. Indigo. Will your mom be attending?"

"No." I cleared my throat. "She won't be attending. She has prior engagements," I gritted through my teeth. But he already knew that. He just said she was at Trochesse. Asshole.

"I really have to go. Can you guys talk later?" Theodora poked her head back into the room and motioned to Mr. Chestnut. I was glad Theodora didn't grab her jacket and leave me alone with him.

Girl code for the win.

Mr. Chestnut flashed his million-dollar fictional smile at me and Theodora. "Sure, Ms. Theo, I'll walk down with you. Oh, one last thing. Ms. Indigo, I found something I believe belongs to you."

He leaned down and placed a small silver stud earring on my nightstand beside me.

I gasped and instincts made me raise my hand to my left ear. That earring usually got caught in my braids and would pull itself out. The back was still there, but the earring was missing. He said nothing else, but we both knew I had been outside of his house. Fire flashed in his eyes.

It was game on.

CHAPTER 25

Q UICKLY SHOWERING, I tried to scrub away Mr. Chestnut's ugly face and coffee-stained teeth from my mind. Every few minutes I checked my phone to see if Dad or Will had called. No missed calls which meant I still had some time to get ready. Racing around the room, I made our beds and fluffed our pillows so the room looked presentable. I shoved the letter the financial aid department had mailed to me. This time, they wrote the words *Second Notice* on the front in red ink. I would talk to Dad about it later. He could help make some sense of it.

'*Or you can just go down there, Indy,*' Mom said. I shoved that voice away.

I stood in the mirror and gazed a myself. The lines where Dad's face began, and Mom's dimples stared back. I blinked, and I saw Ez in front of me. I blinked again, and I saw Sidney and parts of Mama Jackie's face.

My phone buzzed and I rushed to my bed and answered. "Hello?"

"Hey, Indy Lindy!" Ez bellowed. "I reckon we about 15 minutes out."

"Are you driving?"

"No, ya daddy driving, girl; I don't be fussing with these roads. I leave that to the women," he chuckled. I heard Dad's voice in the background but couldn't make out what he was saying. We were on the phone for three minutes and Ez already called Dad a woman. I hoped they were on their best behavior.

"Where is Will?" I asked.

"I'm here, Indy," Will's voice perked up. I exhaled hearing his smooth tone.

"Oh, she asked about him, not about us," Sidney quipped from another corner of the car. Everyone began talking at once and I couldn't tell the voices in my head from all the voices in the car.

"Anyway—we'll see you soon, Indy!" I heard Dad huff. I stifled a laugh as I thought about him gripping the steering wheel and bickering with Ez at the same time.

I pulled on some tights and laced up my boots. My phone buzzed again, and I thought it was another call from Dad, but it was a text from Chaquille.

> **CHAQUILLE:** Wya?
>
> **ME:** My room. Waiting for my family. WYD?
>
> **CHAQUILLE:** I'm downstairs. You like those girly coffees with all the foam at the top and shit, right? I got you one.

I looked at my phone and smiled even though I didn't want to. After my outburst with Chaquille at the Black Feminists Nation table, we seemed to be starting over. I'm not exactly sure when it happened, but Chaquille had learned my favorite drink. I grabbed my Bath and Body Works lotion off my dresser and slapped some on my knees and ankles. I couldn't be ashy with him downstairs and all my people in tow. He was trying these days and I guess that counted for something.

'*Make him wait a little, honey. Just a few minutes,*' Mom whispered in my head.

"But why?"

'*No reason. A man should always wait for a woman. She should never come running for him.*'

I sighed out loud and started doing my hair. I sectioned my braids off into two handfuls and twisted them together until they made a pretty braided twist around my head. I secured it in place with a few bobby pins, my moon broach, and I took out an old toothbrush and I laid my edges down to perfection. I added in extra gel today, just in case I started to sweat, which was likely knowing me.

I grabbed my windbreaker jacket and looked myself over in the mirror once more before I barreled out of the door. Once downstairs, I was cursing myself for listening to Mom and waiting those extra minutes.

Chaquille was out front of my dorm building, holding two iced coffees in his hand and he was eying Will—who was giving him eyes right back. Ez was sitting on a bench, watching Will and Chaquille, clearly amused. Dad, Sidney, and Ms. Arletha unloaded the car. They were only staying for one night at the hotel in town, but they had packed a cooler full of chicken wings, potato salad, and cans of soda. Ez and Sidney even had Lunchables, their favorite.

"Chaquille," I breathed. I panted a few times to calm my heart rate. Seeing Chaquille and Will there together, when I felt some type of way about them both, almost felt like I was creeping. But how was that? I had done nothing with either of them. We had many opportunities, me-and-Will,

me-and-Chaquille. Even a few times when I thought the deed would go down, but ultimately... it didn't.

"Indy," Chaquille said coolly and handed me my coffee. "This your dude?" He pointed to Will, wasting no breaths. I gazed at Will awaiting my response. Ez waited too as his head shot back and forth between me, Will, and Chaquille. My coffee dripped down my hands; the ice quickly melting under the heat of the three of us.

"Will, have you met Chaquille? He's my friend from school. Chaquille... this is Will. He is my friend... from home." My words echoed when I said them out loud, and I hoped I didn't sound unsure, even though I was. Chaquille and Will said nothing to each other and continued squaring off. Will stood with his hands in his pockets and Chaquille had his arms folded at his chest. Ez broke the silence and let out a deep, belly laugh while the picnic table he sat under shook.

"Indy Lindy! You got the mens fighting over you! That's right, my girl. You see them but they don't see you. You see this, Jackie?!" He cackled to himself and spoke to Mama Jackie.

"Nice to meet you, Chaquille, is it?" Will glared at Chaquille, and he removed his hands from his pockets.

"Yeah man it's Chaquille. Nice to meet you. I've heard a lot about you." He uncrossed his arms and extended a handshake to Will. They embraced and I gulped down my iced coffee. I never mentioned Will to Chaquille, so that was a lie. But why would he say that? Was he trying to be smart? I caught a smirk from Chaquille as he cut his eyes then backed away from me and Will.

He *was* trying to be smart.

I cleared my throat and took another long slurp of my coffee. The sweet liquid poured down my throat, and it felt refreshing since I was standing in the hot seat. How did they even get here together? And why did I still feel like I was doing something wrong? As if reading my thoughts, Ez chimed in.

"Ya daddy took the highway and we got here a little early. That boy over there went and talked to them people. They were about to let that boy go on up to your room, but Will heard them as we were getting out of the car. Will said, 'ain't nobody going up to Indy's room' and that boy looked him up and down and said, 'who are you?' And then Will said it again, but he put some meat in his voice this time, and said, 'ain't nobody going up to Indy's room. I don't know you!' And then that boy over there was still holding them coffees, and I know his hands was cold, and then Will"

"Okay, Ez, I think that's enough. Indy Lindy . . ." Dad sat the cooler on the front curb as a few other families made their way in and out of the dorm's check-in process. They eyed Dad's cooler, leaking ice water from the bottom. With Chaquille being a student, all he had to do was flash his ID and check-in before making his way upstairs. This time Will stood in his way.

"I'm going to head out," Chaquille said. Before I could cut in, he headed off behind the dorms to the campus center where the first event of the day was held. Ez continued to chuckle while my chest tightened, watching Chaquille walk away.

"Got anywhere for us to put the cooler? 'Letha put too much ice in here for the watermelon slices and now we've got a little leak," Dad said. His shirt was wet and little speckles of black watermelon seeds were stuck to his collar. Ms. Arletha shrugged behind Dad and gave a sheepish smile.

I handed Ez my iced coffee and he sucked it down. "Is this one of those French coffee latto's, Indy? This is delicious. I can taste the sugar in my brain. Mmmm." He closed his eyes and slurped.

This was my family.

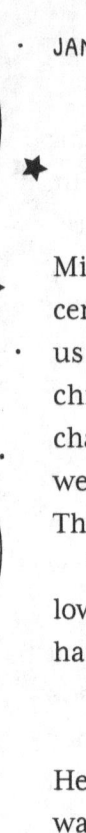

Minutes later, the gang and I made our way to the campus center. There were students and their families walking with us in the same direction, trotting toward the smell of free chicken and canned soda. There were so many voices and chatter, I wondered if I was hearing them for real, or if they were in my head. I looked around at everyone's loved ones. There was a lot of happiness today. I took brain pictures of it all.

"So, is that your dude?" Will asked, with his head hanging low. Sidney trotted behind with Ms. Arletha and Dad in tow, hand in hand.

"No, he's just a friend."

"She say he just a friend..." Ez sang in front of Will and me. He didn't look back but continued with his song until my face was beet red.

"If you say so. I'm just saying—don't let me be the last to know if anything changes."

"Excuse me?" I retorted. I stopped dead in my tracks and glared at him. Sidney almost ran into the back of me before she scurried out of the way.

"Don't be fussing with him, Indy. The boy been loved you since ya'll was kids." Ez took a seat on a bench and pushed Sidney toward the food line. He barked out his food order and sent her in search of something sweet.

Anger welled inside of me when I whipped my neck around and gawked at Ez. "And what does that mean? I have to put my life on hold?"

"C'mon, Indy," Dad interjected. "Nobody is saying that. They're just saying, if you were seeing that boy, you could have told Will."

"But there is nothing to tell! Why aren't you guys listening to me?" I was so frustrated; I couldn't think straight. My temples were pounding, and the look on Will's face was enough to make me call off the entire day and send them all home. All the men in my family were upset with me for what really? For being a girl and having options? Will had twelve years of us being best friends to tell me how he felt!

Will stood in a straight line with Dad and Ms. Arletha, while I brooded. They all looked at me as if they could see the voices and the words swirling in my mind and they were trying to make sense of it all but I couldn't make sense of it.

"Hey, Indy!" Theodora's raspy voice sounded.

I spun around and Theodora was standing in front of every single person in her family. I searched their faces and got lost in a maze of noses, eyes, and lips, all somehow resembling Theodora's. I had never seen so many family members together at once like this. My few people were here with me, but Theodora came with an army.

"Indy, you remember my mom, right?" She stepped back and positioned herself so her mom and I were facing. I swallowed, trying to push the lump in my throat further down. With a plastered smile, I leaned forward to hug Theodora's mom, but she swiftly moved out of the way. I lost my footing when she moved, and I stumbled into her shoulder.

"My . . ." her mom gasped as she shoved me off her.

"Oh, no she didn't," Ms. Arletha sputtered and took a step forward. Dad held her and her protruding second trimester belly back.

"Mom?" Theodora squinted.

Before Mrs. Nwosi could say anything, Naomi and her mom waved and made their way toward us through the crowds. "Hey ya'll." Naomi gave a little wave not knowing the iciness

before them was colder than a snowboard to the forehead in Tennessee.

"It's nice to meet everyone. I'm Carol, Naomi's mom. I've heard so much about the down south, Indy, and the beautiful and smart, Theodora." Naomi's mom smiled and waited for the usual pleasantries that came with meeting the parents of your children's friends. I had a feeling it wouldn't come with Mrs. Nwosi.

"Hello, uh, I'm Indy's dad, and this is my lady, Arletha. This is Indigo's grandfather, Ezra, Indy's uhh . . . friend, Will. And this is Indy's youngest sister, Sidney," Dad stepped forward and extended a hand to Naomi's mom. He turned and extended another handshake to Mr. Nwosi, but Mr. Nwosi cut his eyes at Dad.

Will frowned, hearing Dad linger on the word friend. Family Day was going great.

Down South, Indy, I reflected . . . Theodora got to be beautiful and smart in Naomi's tales. I glanced at Naomi, wondering what she thought of me and told her mom. Why didn't I fall into that category? I wondered if she also told her mom about her beloved Ivelisse yet?

No one in Theodora's family waved back, and it sounded like one of Theodora's aunts made a grunting noise as she eyed Naomi and her mom, both wearing matching sneakers, jogger suits, and large gold hoop earrings. Ms. Carol was a lover of Christ and shoes according to Naomi. She made it a point to say she was from Jersey, but she was from North Jersey—closer to New York. That distinction was important, I guess. Theodora's family was not impressed nor amused.

"Theodora, honey. I thought we would get a chance to meet some of your professors, ehhh, even your track coach?" Theodora's dad asked gently. The rest of their family gaped at the swarms of people around them.

Hearing mention of Mr. Chestnut made the lump in my throat return. I stiffened in place, remembering his beady eyes roaming my body when he stood over me this morning.

"Can we go now?" Sidney leaned toward me and whispered. I wanted to move away from this awkward scene myself.

"Enough with all this small talk. Ya'll got any more food around here?" Ez hopped up from the table and tossed his cup of water ice in the trash. His eyes searched the area and before I could say anything, he marched his way through Theodora's family, sniffing toward the BBQ.

"Wait for us, Ez!" Ms. Arletha trailed him. Like penguins following their leader, Dad and Sidney hustled behind him.

"Nice to meet you all." Naomi's mom flashed a tight smile and turned on her heel, following the food smells and better energy.

My stomach growled, and I was ready to follow suit and find some food when I spotted Dylan through the crowd. He fixed his eyes on Theodora. His blond hair blew in the wind and his cheeks shared a hint of pinkness as he moved through the masses, walking tall with determination. With a flash, I spun around and gave Theodora large eyes. I scrunched my face and mouth, trying to get her attention and alert her to the large, white boy barreling toward us.

"What? What's wrong with you?" Theodora crinkled her nose. She gazed over my shoulder, and her eyes widened to what we knew was about to happen.

"Theo... what's up?" Dylan rushed us and grabbed Theodora in a bear hug.

Mr. and Mrs. Nwosi's mouths fell open and gave an incredulous stare. Her family stood behind hushed behind her.

"Hi Dylan. Mom... Dad... this is Dylan. My friend... from school... my friend from school," Theodora breathed. The words came out choppy and forced. Theodora said them like she was trying to convince someone.

No one looked convinced.

"Friend?" Dylan repeated. He backed away from Theodora and looked her up and down in confusion.

Theodora closed her eyes and took a deep breath. "Mom... Dad... This is Dylan. My boyfriend."

Mr. Nwosi stepped forward and placed a hand around Theodora's back. "Young man... it was nice to meet you. If you don't mind, we're going to get something to eat. Good day." He cocked his head at Dylan. He disregarded Theodora's admission.

"No, Dad. Seriously. This is my boyfriend, Dylan."

"Really, Theodora? I can't believe you're doing this! On today of all days," Mrs. Nwosi fussed.

Theodora's cheeks were deep red now and Dylan stood beside her and clasped her hand. I noticed his collar was stiff and pressed. His oxford, boat shoes looked new and were a far contrast from the usual sneakers or slip-ons he wore. Dylan preferred comfort. He was dressed to impress for Theodora's family.

"Young man! We have spoken. Good day," Mrs. Nwosi raised her voice.

"No, Mom! Dylan and I are dating. He loves me, and I love him. I want to live my own life. Please listen to me," Theodora's voice cracked but she stood tall in front of her family.

"Fine, my headstrong daughter," Mrs. Nwosi was curt. "Dylan, you say? Are your parents here? We shall have dinner tonight," she commanded.

Dylan ran a hand through his hair and paused, looking at Theodora. So many questions and answers passed between them when they defined what they were for a group of people who didn't support them. "Yes, they are here. Dinner sounds good." He gave a nervous smile.

I stood next to Theodora, not wanting to leave her side. I don't know why, but I didn't want her to be alone in this moment. She gazed up at me and her eyes looked sadder than I've ever seen them look before. Theodora was so many different things to different people. I wasn't even sure who she wanted to be. I could tell by the tear forming in her eye that whoever she wanted to be, it wasn't this person.

CHAPTER 26

A GRILLED CHICKEN THIGH and corn on the cob later, Will and I stood watching the AKA's step in the campus center. A circle formed around them, and a clan of pink and green girls were chanting and performing for us. Every time they stepped, they wowed me. They moved in unison, but each girl had their own flair. I wondered how long it took them to practice their moves.

"This is amazing," Will chimed in.

"I know, right?" I smiled. Now the Zeta's had swarmed in with their royal blue and white. They had bullhorns to liven up the crowd around them. I glanced over at Ez grasping at his ears. The bullhorns were too loud for his sensitive hearing. I walked toward him as I saw him slinking out of the crowd and backing away.

"I got it, Indy." Sidney held my arm back. She held her head high and her tight, natural curls shone against the sun as she trotted toward Ez. Ms. Arletha encouraged Sidney to step away from her flat iron and embrace her naturalness. She looked so much older than her thirteen years, and I wondered if that was

because Ez was becoming a full-time job. He led her through the crowd, clasping her hand, but she was leading him.

My eyes were still on Ez and Sidney when Will cut in. "Listen, Indy. I know we never really established what we are. So... what are we?" Will had his hands in his pockets and I could see him flailing them nervously. His forehead was dotted with light beads of sweat.

He was asking me? I didn't have an answer for him, and I didn't know how to say I didn't have an answer. As much as Chaquille's back and forth confused me, I had to admit I liked him.

Figuring out what to do about Mr. Chestnut, passing my classes this semester, worrying about Ez... and Mom... It was just too much. "Will... I... we..." I couldn't get the words out over all the chanting, music, and people around me. Others surrounded us and Will's eyes bored into mine, searching for answers I didn't have. "I don't know about that right now. I have so much going on. When we're at home, we're good. But when I'm here... It's just different. Maybe when I'm home this summer we..."

Before I could get out my last statement, a bullhorn sounded, and I jumped. The Titus University marching band was making their way into the campus center with a moving float behind them. "Let's go over there." I motioned under a tree and shouted into Will's ears. He squinted to where I pointed and took my hand, leading me through the crowd just like Ez had led Sidney.

'The key is, let 'em think they in charge,' Mom whispered in my head. I tightened my grip around Will's hand.

"Will, I love your family... I... I love you," I confessed. The emotions came from somewhere. As much as I loved words, I just couldn't find them for what I felt. I did love Will. I did. I loved him as a friend and much more.

But more wasn't an option right now.

JANAY HARDEN

I held onto him and leaned into his shoulder under a tree with scores of people surrounding us. "Will, can we take things slow? College is ... a lot."

"Indy, you know me better than that. Come on, we're always going to be friends. But just let me know what's up, *that's all I ask of you*," he sang the last part in his best *Tony-Toni-Tone* voice, and we both cracked up laughing. I placed my chin on his shoulder. I stood on my tiptoes and lightly brushed my lips on his collarbone. I looked up at him, exploring his face and slanted eyes.

"Don't be trying to love up on me now, girl." He smirked with a fake eye roll.

Will and I chuckled. A loud horn sounded, and I jumped out of my skin. I spun around and saw Mr. Chestnut and the track team, including Theodora, making their way to the campus center on a large float. I seethed, seeing him and Nurse Meanface up there. He wore a customized Titus University coach uniform. I eye-balled the crowd, searching for my family. I saw Dad and Ms. Arletha sitting with Naomi's mom. They were stifling back laughs and slapping their knees. Sidney and Ez had found an ice cream stand, and they were close to Dad and Ms. Arletha, licking from large cones.

"Titus University? Are ya'll ready for another win in New Orleans?" Mr. Chestnut shouted over the mic.

"Yeaaaa!" the crowd shouted.

Nurse Meanface stood in the back, smiling at her husband. Her arms were crossed, and her purse was tight to her chest. If uncomfortable had a name, it would be Allie Chestnut. I wondered why she chose to stay and not return to Tunica Rivers like I heard her say.

"My girls are ready to represent you, Titus University. They are the fastest and the brightest. Once we take on the New Orleans Relays next week, next stop will be Nationals!"

Theodora clapped, standing next to Mr. Chestnut with her teammates. Her family was behind the float eating up every word Mr. Chestnut spewed while Dylan stood off to the side with his family, staring lovingly up at Theodora. I moved closer, with Will not far behind me. I just couldn't believe his wife and these people were taken by his bullshit like this. My hands began to shake. I tightened my coochie muscles to be sure I wouldn't pee on myself this time.

"If anyone had any doubts about my girls. They will crush them! Just you wait. Titus University, we are here to restore your destiny as the greatest track and field, D1 school in the nation!" Mr. Chestnut was inspiring and dignified up there.

I looked around at everyone captivated by his lies and pearly white teeth. Nurse Meanface slinked to the furthest corner of the float where the least amount of people stood. Mr. Chestnut was larger than life and had a personality and a dazzling smile that hypnotized people. Mrs. Chestnut-Nurse Meanface-Allie, played her part to the world as the dutiful wife. But to a girl who spent the past few weeks staring inside their window—I clearly saw the cracks.

"And now I'd like to turn things over to a special guest. I've not had the pleasure of meeting this woman before, but I just love what she represents. I think you guys are in for a treat. Coming up, we have Laylah Capri!"

The crowd roared when Laylah made her way to the float. She extended her hand, but Mr. Chestnut frowned and lifted her into a bear hug. The crowd was magnetized, and I guessed Laylah was too. My interest piqued. I recently joined Laylah Capri's local chapter for Black Feminists Nation, and whenever she spoke, it stirred me. Laylah smiled and waved to the crowd. She wore a white pants suit, which hugged her body in all the right places. She turned around to wave at the crowd off to the side and on the back of her jacket written in red lettering said:

JANAY HARDEN

Michelle
Stacy
Kamala
Tamika
Me

"How's everyone feeling?" Laylah started. She placed her hands to her ears as if she was listening to the crowd. We ate her up.

"Are we ready? I have a story to tell..."

The crowd hushed when Laylah began. Will and I leaned on the back of the float. Laylah fascinated us. "Did everyone know this campus is sixty-five percent female? And from that number, forty percent are Black women? That makes me proud. So many of us are going to college. But do we have what we need here? Do we really know what to do about financial aid or mental health services, or those infamous Thursday night parties? I know, I know, these issues aren't specific to Black women, but why is it that these social issues seem to affect us at such a disproportionate number? One of my chapter members in Florida, was kicked out of school simply because she reported to her counselor that she was depressed. Said she didn't want to live. She went to a counselor and shared her deepest traumas. Since they didn't have the services to accommodate her depression, they put her on academic probation and kicked her out of the dorms instead. I'll ask you guys; do you think she finished college?"

"No, no, she didn't," the crowd shook their heads and murmured.

"Gate-keepers!" someone shouted.

"We need better services for us. Us! The Dean of Student Affairs has been gracious enough to let us start a chapter here. They see a need for more inclusive services for our female students. Let's give him a round of applause." Laylah waved toward the dean's table. They were all sitting at a long table high on a hill. They looked hot and stuffy in their suits and formal dresses. "I would like a few people from my chapter here at Titus University to come forward. I didn't announce that I would be here, so I'm sure it comes as a surprise to my chapter members. But I wanted to thank you in person for doing the work and being committed to our collective healing of the community." She looked around for anyone to step forward.

"That's you, right? Go up there!" Will hissed. I sent Will an episode of Laylah's podcast a few days ago and told him I joined the chapter. I was kicking myself for telling him now as my mouth felt chalky, and my underarms began to sweat. "No, I can't go up there, Will," I tried to whisper.

Hearing the chattel behind her, Laylah whipped around. She flashed her smile and said, "I didn't forget you! Come on up here." She motioned toward me.

This was happening, this was really happening. *If there was ever a time when I needed you Mom, now is the time,* I prayed, hopping onto the float.

"This is one of my newest chapter members, and please forgive me, I am terrible with names but never with faces. What's your name again, sis?"

"Indigo, Indigo Tina Lewis," I sputtered. I hoped my voice didn't crack. Why did I say my middle name?

"What a beautiful name, Indigo. Can you tell us what it means to you to be a Black feminist at Titus University?"

I looked at the audience. Theodora's family blankly stared. Mr. and Mrs. Chestnut cut their eyes, and both looked irritated because she chose me. Ez and Sidney were grinning from ear-to-ear, and Dad and Ms. Arletha were watching, waiting in anticipation of what I was about to say. I was not the same Indy that had left for college months ago. "Being a Black

feminist at Titus University to me, means freedom. It means freedom to make mistakes, without the fear that my life or my livelihood is at stake. Mutual respect for staff and students," I said, my voice now raising. I glanced around at the hordes of faces, black and white, and all the colors in between, staring back at me and cheering.

They were feeling what I was saying.

I continued. "We need people to stand up for us. We need allies. Don't pin us against each other, we're the generation that's going to make the change. It's not our parents, and it's not our grandparents, it's going to start with us! We ain't with the shits no more!" I shouted.

The crowd responded with a resounding *hell yeah* and pumped their fists in the air. "No more to financial aid being the biggest gang on campus! No more work-study jobs that pay pennies! No more taking advantage of others because you think they're weaker!" I turned and looked in Mr. Chestnut's direction. "No more!" I pumped my fist in the air.

Laylah Capri came up behind me and placed her arm on my shoulder. She gave me a big hug, and she smelled like vanilla. "You go, girl," she whispered.

I nodded at Laylah as tears formed in the corners of my eyes. I waved to the crowd as they cheered me on when I walked away. I hopped off the float in a daze by what just happened. The electricity it sent through my body was like nothing I had felt since, ironically, I had killed Jaxon.

"Wow, Indy! You were amazing up there!" Ms. Arletha exclaimed. She rubbed her protruding belly. "Looks like your big sister is an activist." She grinned.

"You were Indy! Just amazing!" Dad had tears in his eyes.

"Indy, that was great!" Sidney said excitedly, repeating some of my words back to me. "No more! We ain't with the shits!" she shouted. Dad frowned at her words but let it slide. Sidney had come out of her shell and the only thing she needed was consistent love. Ms. Arletha gave that to her.

"But why you was doing all that hollering, girl?" Ez's voice boomed.

We giggled and before I knew it, they had enveloped me in a hug and congratulated me for my speech. I knew exactly what I needed to do with Mr. Chestnut. He couldn't live anymore; plain and simple. I was about to be the Black Robinhood, and it was what it was.

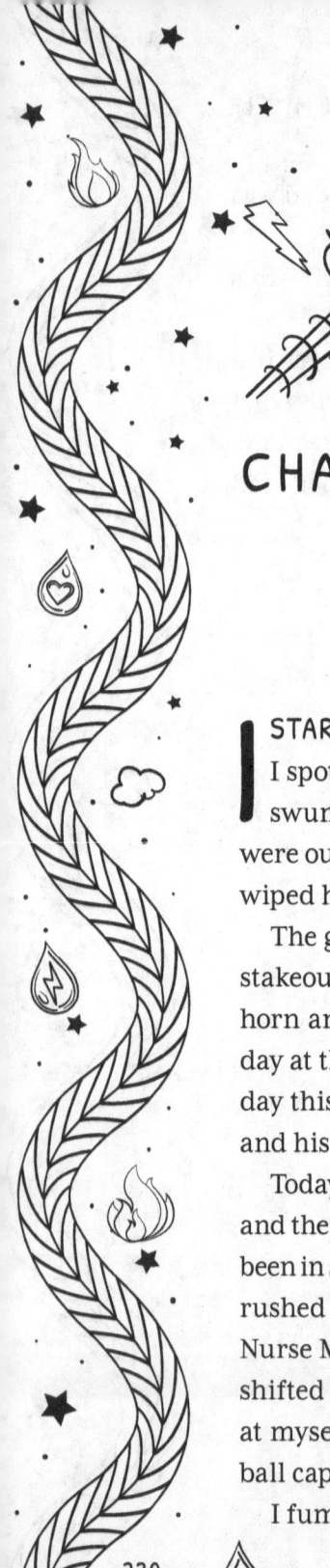

CHAPTER 27

I STARED AT HIM from The Bus way across the parking lot. I spotted Theodora. She was tall, graceful, and her braids swung every time she took one hurdle. While the other girls were out of breath when they finished, Theodora smiled and wiped her forehead even though it barely looked wet.

The girl was bad, and if I wasn't on another Mr. Chestnut stakeout, attempting to be *incog-negro*, I would've beeped the horn and cheered for her. Theodora practiced every single day at the same time. It was so easy to find them, and every day this week I spent scoping out Mr. Chestnut on the track and his house.

Today, a letter from Mom rested on my lap. Nurse Meanface and the others were still making life for her hard, and she had been in solitary confinement. Mom was angry. Her handwriting rushed and messy. She believed she was targeted because of Nurse Meanface's outburst. She never mentioned her own. I shifted in the car, and I adjusted my mirror, stealing a glance at myself. I shifted my black-out sunglasses and pulled my ball cap tighter over my head.

I fumed.

Was Mr. Chestnut commanding his wife to lock up my mom? What did Mom have to do with anything? She had been there for years with Nurse Meanface and while they weren't close, they had certainly never taken Mom to solitary. She used to act like it was beneath her and only those *bad ones* went to that place. She used to say, *'I can sang my ass off and they need some inspiration around here, I'll never go in there.'* It made little sense, but I had a feeling he had something to do with it.

'That's all-right Indy. We'll get him.'

"I'm on it, Mom," I said, peering at the track and field practice across the hazy grass. My window was cracked, and an older, white woman eyed me from her car next to mine. She never shifted, and I faintly heard her locking her automatic car doors. She was scared. Good, she should be.

My buzzing phone made me jump. "Hello?" I answered, clearing my throat.

"Hi, uh, Ms. Lewis?"

"This is her."

"This is the Titus University financial aid office. We sent you two letters regarding an outstanding balance. I just wanted to let you know that we received payment and your account is currently all caught up. It was just in time too; we would have had to readjust your award package."

I gritted my teeth. I forgot all about that letter . . . those letters.

"Next time please reach out as soon as possible, things like this can affect your enrollment status, Ms. Lewis."

"Yes, I uh, forgot to call the office. Sorry about that." They must've received payment from Ms. Montague's studio back home. I'm glad it worked out because I surely forgot about it. There was so much going on. I sat my phone back down and no sooner than I did; it rang again. I sucked my teeth. Why was the financial aid office calling back? As I looked closer at the number, it had our hometown area code to Tunica Rivers.

I answered with a rushed, "Hello?"

"Indy, everything is okay, but Ez... can you come home?" Sidney's voice sounded pressed.

"I'm coming," I slammed my phone down on the passenger's seat without another word.

I fired up The Bus and roared out, leaving dust in the parking lot, and the woman next to me still staring. I raced down the highway, wondering what Ez had gotten himself into this time. Sidney could exaggerate, but I didn't like the way her voice sounded. During the ride, I was angry with myself for being selfish and attending a school three hours away. Ez needed me.

I found Laylah Capri's podcast channel, and I listened to it while burning rubber on the road. She said, "women, do ya'll feel heard? Vindicated? Do we own our power? Do you have it in you, to take back your power? I'm taking mine back right now, by not cowering. I will not apologize for being a woman. The best parts of me are feminine, and that's my superpower. Ladies, we can create our own realities simply by choosing us first. Have an honest to God, actual conversation with yourself. What are you good at, effortlessly? Those are your superpowers, ladies."

When I pulled up to Ez's house, I saw an ambulance. I wondered what my superpower would have to be. Ez's house was boarded up from the outside. Police tape sectioned off the driveway. It was now dark, but they had so many ambulances and firetrucks out front lit up like a crime scene gone wrong. I saw the large, red letters **condemned** over the front door. I threw the car in park and searched around for Ez. I heard him before I saw him.

"This here land got my daddy blood on it and it's mine! I reckon ya'll might want to leave before things don't end smoothly for ya'll cop-folk kin-folk!" Ez was shouting from the back of the ambulance. When he saw me, he leapt off the ledge and the ambulance bounced back up like it was sighing under Ez's weight.

"Mr. Ezra, I understand how you feel, however you cannot live here anymore." This person's voice sent a chill down my spine.

K. Jamison.

Why was he back again?

"You don't say anything to him!" Dad yelled. Him, Sidney, and Ms. Arletha stood on the other side of the property. I ran to them. Ms. Arletha took me into her arms as I trembled under. We watched Ez hop around his front yard angrily.

K. Jamison was on the bullhorn talking to Ez. "Mr. Ezra, please settle down. We had to board the house so you can't get in, it's not safe. If you need to retrieve your items, please make arrangements to do so in a safe manner with city hall tomorrow." Jamison's voice was robotic and flat.

His officer friends nodded their heads in approval of the script they all knew by heart. It must've been cop 101 basic training they all had. Make people feel like they always had an answer, even when it was recycled bullshit. Maybe it was a man thing. It didn't work on Ez though. He pulled down the police tape that tied one tree to another. He raced to his house and almost fell when his knees buckled in the divots of the uneven ground under his feet. He ran up to his house and with his bare hands, pulled a large board off his window. He moved to another one and he pinged another board from the window. He flung them like they were toys and his grunts told me how much anger he had inside of him. Maybe it wasn't Mom I got my thoughts and anger from. It was Ez.

"I'm not leaving!" Ez's voice echoed off the trees. I shivered as the wind blew and whipped through my light jacket. Dad came over and placed his arm around me as we looked on.

"Mr. Ezra, again. This residence is no longer safe. You cannot stay here," Jamison screeched from the bullhorn.

Sidney leaned to me and with wide eyes, said, "he's been like this for hours. Running back and forth into the woods and trying to get into the house. We thought we could talk him down, but when the sun started to set, he became more upset because he said he was missing Wheel of Fortune. I knew we had to call you."

With a soft voice I said, "Ez, let's go, you can't go in there."

He stopped running around the house and stood in the middle of the driveway. He glanced around at the people, noises, and commotions. He made a face, as if he was just seeing and hearing everyone for the first time.

"It's too much, it's too much."

He covered his ears and squeezed his eyes shut. Ez dropped down and sat cross-legged in the driveway, kicking up dust around him.

"You can't stay!" Sidney screamed.

Ez's head was down, but he soon raised it and I glimpsed tears in my grandfather, Ezra Campbell's, eyes. "Jackie," he said and looked to the skies. And with that, his shoulders bounced up and down while he cried.

CHAPTER 28

A FEW HOURS LATER, we checked Ez into a nearby motel. He refused to stay at the house with Dad and Sidney. He said real men didn't sleep on the porch, and he gave Dad a little dig for even suggesting the likes. When I offered my room, he said he sometimes had nightmares and didn't want to sleep that close to Sidney.

When I asked what his dreams were about, he flatly said, "the water."

When we entered the motel, Dad sat the large key on the rickety dresser. A flat screen tv was the focus of the room, and everything, including the bedsheets and furniture, were different shades of tan and white. Ez held one small suitcase duct-taped at the side. He hadn't needed a suitcase in a long time; he stopped going to places requiring them after a while.

He started, "Look at these here windows, they don't even open. And look at this bathroom, how am I supposed to feed the cats . . ." His voice trailed off. I guess he remembered the cats were still at the house. "Do this tv get my stories? Do this tv tape my stories, Indy? Ms. Know It All?"

I sighed. "Ez, that was at the house. This tv does not dvr. I'm sorry, if you are not here to watch your stories when they come on, you'll miss them. Hopefully, you won't be here long until we figure something out. But for now, this is the next best thing."

"Naw, Indy," he croaked. "This ain't no best thing." Ez glanced up at the ceiling and the dreary walls.

"Would you like one of us to stay with you tonight, Ez?" Ms. Arletha stepped forward.

Ez paced the floor. "Naw, ya'll head on home, but be here first thing in the morning. I ain't staying here long, you hear me? I ain't staying here long. They look like they got the roaches." Ez sat on the bed, and it sank under his weight.

Dad went up front and instructed the manager to call us if they had any issues with Ez. I checked my phone and had one missed call and a text from Will checking on me. It was late into the night and starting to rain. I wondered if Will was still up since his messages came through hours ago while we got Ez situated. I replied to his message, telling him I was in town and what was going down with Ez. I wasn't expecting to hear back from him, then my phone buzzed.

> **WILL:** I didn't think you were still up. Come through.

> **ME:** To where? Your house? It's late!

> **WILL:** It's cool. No one is here.

I held my phone to my mouth and pondered for a second. It was a late Wednesday night. Why was Will home alone?

> **ME:** Give me a few...

SOMEONE MORE LIKE MYSELF

> **WILL:** Cool

By the time I headed home, showered, put gas in The Bus, and trekked across town to Will's house it was after midnight. I didn't spot Mr. or Mrs. Simms cars in the driveway, nor did I see Dominique's. I heard low grumblings of thunder in the distance, and it was still sprinkling. When I hopped out of The Bus, I paused and stared at the moon. I inhaled and took in cool air. Something caught in my throat. My head ached, and I couldn't breathe while my chest heaved up and down, up and down, up and down. Feeling dizzy, I leaned against the car and closed my eyes. I ran my tongue against my teeth, and it tasted sour. No food or drink for hours. What was this? Was I having a heart attack? It smelled a tad rubbery outside; the scents bouncing off the Simms' blacktop driveway.

The wind whipped through my hair and I tugged at my jacket tighter, trying to bring myself down from whatever this was. Will stood, waiting with the door open. I could tell he was barefoot. He wasn't smiling, and he had a strange look in his eyes. I took a few deep breaths and bent down pretending to tie my shoe. When I rose, I said, "where is everyone?" He held the door open for me to enter.

"My parents caught a late movie and Dominique is out."

When I took my jacket off and spun around to face Will, he still gave me a strange, serious look.

"What's wrong?"

"How is Ez?" Will's eyes searched mine.

"He . . . he . . ." I started to lie, but that feeling came back to my chest and I clutched at my locket of Mom I kept around my neck. I started to say Ez was fine, and we would take him to more appointments, and specialists, and doctors, and we would clean the house, and we would keep researching and figuring things out since the day programs didn't work out

237

either. I started to say I would drop out of Titus University and move back home and go to City College. I started to say all the things I knew would make Will raise an eyebrow with pleasant surprise. I couldn't lie, not to Will. He knew me better than anyone. A lump formed in my throat and before I knew it, fat tears rolled down my face.

"Come here," he said. And with one step, he had me in his arms; my head between his neck and shoulder. I cried for Ez. The sobs escaped me, and my stomach heaved in and out and up and down and all around me. The anger for the things I couldn't control consumed me. I was grasping at straws, trying to take the reins in my life. I wanted to bury my head under a blanket and wake up to Mama Jackie in the kitchen cooking pancakes and Ez on the water rowing and singing. I wasn't sure if I would vomit, but I was glad I showered before I came because I was starting to perspire.

"I'm sorry, I'm sorry." I wiped my face and exhaled a few times.

"Don't be sorry, Indy. It's me you're talking to. Don't ever be sorry."

Will and I sat on the couch. I told Will about Trenita, the situation with Ez, and what we were up against. I told him about how hard college was and trying to manage everything at the same time. He admitted he wasn't doing well in his plumbing courses, and he wasn't sure he wanted to be a plumber anymore. He just couldn't focus this semester.

Man, did I ever understand.

"You should meet us in New Orleans for the Libra Festival. It's going to be fun!"

Will sighed. "I need to put some space between me and Tunica Rivers. I'll be there!" He smiled. He leaned in and kissed me, and I kissed him back with the same intensity. Will and I shared wet and slippery kisses before he skimmed his hand up my shirt. I jumped under his chilly fingers. He ran his fingers over my breasts, and I grabbed his shirt in a fist, pulling him closer. In this moment, I wanted my best friend, and I wasn't running from it.

Will and I were necking heavy when I pulled away from him and stood. I wiped my lips and leaned over him on the couch. "Let's go to your room," I mused.

He smiled and rose. He took my hand and led me down the dark hallway illuminated with candles. As he closed his bedroom door, he looked me in my eyes and said, "mine?"

"Yours," I breathed back without second guessing it.

And I was. I always was.

CHAPTER 29

ONE WEEK TURNED into two, and then three. It was never completely cold in Louisiana, or maybe there was a chill wherever I was. I did my best getting to class every day and on time. I went to work, and I tried to bury my head in my books as best as I could. Ez was still staying in the motel. He had made it his own and patrolled the grounds around the perimeter daily with a hatchet. It scared people when he first moseyed around the camp style buildings in his straw hat with the Tomahawk gleaming. They've added him as their marketing ploy, and they told the people staying there he's security. Ez seemed to like that title too. Ez paid them no mind, and walked, huffed, and chopped at the brush he never let get too high.

Ms. Arletha's face was bright; the baby was making her glow from the inside. They were waiting until the birth to learn the sex. "You have to do it old school," Ms. Arletha instructed. "That's how my momma and her momma and her momma did it." She never talked about her family. She said her mom passed away when she was young and she had issues conceiving, hence why she was older with no children. I wondered if she worried about mental health? How could she bring a life into this world knowing what type of problems and destruction already lived here?

Dad was open to whatever she wanted, and with that came them trying to figure out how to make room for a baby. The obvious choice was to clear out my bedroom, but the house was already bursting at the seams. I didn't think it could withstand one more person, let alone a baby and all the gadgets one came with. Despite my obtuse worries, we were excited. A new face! I was team girl myself. The way I saw it, this family was doing fine with girls. It was the men we had to worry about.

"And what makes you feel like your mom is your project? And Ez?" Trenita asked. She jarred me out of my thoughts and my eyes returned to the chill of outside, forming on her windows. We were back in the Wellness Center late one afternoon.

I tugged on a loose braid in my head. I needed Theodora to give me a touch up. The last thing I wanted to worry about was my hair looking a mess. They were looking more busted every day and my headband wasn't cutting it anymore. "I never said they were a project. I just think, they, you know. Need help sometimes." I shifted under Trenita's serious gaze and thoughtful eyes.

"And when do you need help, Indigo? What does that look like for you?"

Trenita's words sounded vile, but the truth sometimes did when you didn't want to hear it. I wanted to argue with her. I wanted to say *'uh-uh lady, you're wrong about this one. I don't need no help, and the kind of help I do need is why I'm here.'* I wet my lips and rubbed a hand across my eyebrow, pausing before I said, "I know where you're going with this; I'm not saying I don't

need help. I'm just saying they need it more. I'm younger, I can figure things out. They're kind of . . . stuck."

Trenita leaned forward and her eyes danced as if she figured something out. She started. "But that's what I mean. You need just as much help as you say they do. You talk with your dad and discuss their problems, Ez and your mom, but never your own. Why is that?"

"I can talk to my dad about my problems," I scoffed. "I just haven't lately. He has other things to worry about." I still hadn't told Trenita anything about Jaxon and even though I had wanted to clear my conscience, I just couldn't work up the nerve. I kept hearing the same thing in my mind—homicidal. Jaxon was the main thing I ached to talk about, but I held back. She spoke as if she knew I had done something. Was that some weird voodoo therapy crap, or did she really know?

"Hmmm interesting. And you don't see yourself as something else for him to worry about?"

"No, I can take care of myself."

"Yes, you can, but is that teaching you how to trust other people? Or to depend on someone?"

I was confused and shook my head with squinted eyes. "Why would I *want* to trust other people? Why would I *want* to depend on someone?"

"Well, isn't that what we all want? Maybe to live in our truth, and to love and be loved while doing it? What is your truth, Indigo? And once you get through that—isn't love on the other side?"

I sat back in my chair and glanced outside again. The trees were swaying, and I shuddered thinking about the wind whipping through my sweater I wore with no undershirt. "The Libra Festival is coming up and maybe I can talk to him before we leave town. Even about our sessions here." I picked at lint on the couch and kept my eyes low.

"I like it," Trenita said. "And make sure you are speaking your truth, or at least learning how."

"I can do that!" I perked.

I studied Trenita's eyes for approval, and she gave a confident smile. My sessions with Trenita had become important to me, and most days I couldn't wait to see her. I felt clear; like there was no cobwebs muddying up my thoughts. Trenita called it challenging my negative self-talk, but I called it a success. She would do most of the talking and then when our time was up, I would head to my room and stew on all the things I should have said, and the funny innuendos I had missed at the time. I wished I could go back and laugh when I didn't or give an agreeing nod when she paused. I wised up and began writing down everything I wanted to talk to her about, so I didn't forget. Man, did she start hitting me hard once I did that. Trenita had become my life coach in some ways, and I valued her opinion. It took me this long to find her but when I did, was she ever worth the wait.

When my session was over, I checked my phone and I had two missed calls. One from Will and one from an unknown number. I called Will back first.

"Hey, you." He picked up on the first ring.

I smiled into the phone. "Hey, Will."

"What are you doing this weekend?"

I paused. Naomi and I were planning to attend an event held by Laylah Capri. I didn't want to miss it. "I'm actually busy. What did you have in mind?" I said carefully.

Will sighed into the phone and I could tell he wasn't expecting me to say no. His words strained. "I just thought, I could come up and visit, like we talked about."

"Yeah, I like the sound of that. I just can't this weekend." I cringed, hoping I wasn't hurting Will's feelings. "But listen, we have the Libra Festival coming up."

"I haven't forgotten. Message me the details for your hotel. Am I staying with you in your room?"

"I don't think that will work. The school is footing the bill and they already have us paired up." I was bunking with June, and I just found out a few days ago. She was decent at work and hopefully she would be just as amicable in a new city.

"That's cool. I'll make sure I'm at least in the building," Will chuckled. "Indy," he paused. "I can't wait to see you."

I smiled, knowing he couldn't see it, but he could feel it. "I can't wait to see you too."

After I hung up with Will, I called the unsaved number back in my phone. It was local to Tunica Rivers, and it was probably about Ez.

"Hello, this is K. Jamison," a male answered, and the chill returned to my spine.

"Uh, Mr. Jamison, this is Indigo Lewis. I had a missed call from this number."

"Yes, Ms. Lewis, a few things. Your grandfather, Mr. Ezra, has been breaking into the residence and stealing items. Can you please remind him that it is condemned, and he cannot retrieve anything? I know this may be difficult for him and he may see the property as still his, however it is not. If this continues, we will have to station an officer outside of the home at all times to monitor for safety and security."

I gritted my teeth. "Did you call my dad?"

"I did, Ms. Lewis, and I told him the same."

"Then why are you calling me, Mr. Jamison?" I asked with more annoyance in my voice than I usually reserved for anyone. This one continued to question me, my family, and I had enough.

"Well, I do have one more question for you, Ms. Lewis," Mr. Jamison's voice became hushed, and I envisioned him looking around, making sure no one saw him talking.

"We were able to review the tapes from Dennis and Sons Funeral Home, you know where you worked before you left for college?" he said it as if I had forgotten.

I didn't.

"I'm not sure if you know this or not, but Mr. Dennis only had the basic surveillance system, and so his cameras only clicked on and began recording after a certain time. Interestingly enough, when I pulled the tapes to see if I could spot Mr. Green's bike, The cameras picked you up coming out of the building, and you looked disheveled and out of place."

"And what does that mean?" I gripped the phone tighter.

"We checked Mr. Green's cloud accounts but didn't find anything there. We did find a few burner phones he used to contact people, and we were finally able to track one of them. He posted and deleted on a social media site that he was going to meet with his Honey Girl. Good thing we were able to recover it. Now, who would that be?"

Honey Girl? What does that mean? And why was Jamison referencing me and that phrase and the cameras together in the same sentence?

As if reading my thoughts, he said, "let me tell you what I think. I think Jaxon was referring to you as his Honey Girl. Come on, Jaxon dates white girls. Who else would he be referring to? So, I figure I would call you and ask. Did something happen that day? Did you see Jaxon Green that day? Did he come to see you at work?"

I couldn't breathe.

'Add him to the list, Indy,' a voice said. This one was low and pressured.

Mom added. *'You know, honey, she is right. This fine specimen of a man has to be added to the list.'*

While they debated his existence, I couldn't formulate anything to say; nothing that sounded better than his theory.

JANAY HARDEN

I looked around and wondered if I confessed right here and now what would happen?

"Ms. Lewis? Are you there?"

"I'm here," I breathed. "I didn't see Jaxon that day. You should ask some of his other friends," I managed to choke out.

He was quiet for a while before he spoke. "Like I said, I just wanted to see what you thought. "Please don't forget to talk to Mr. Ezra about the house. You have a good night, Ms. Lewis. I'll be in touch. You can count on it."

CHAPTER 30

THEODORA DABBED AT the edge control on her fingers. It was tacky and slippery between them. She fingered the gel into my braids and with a flick of her lighter; she sealed the ends by burning the tips.

I studied my hair in the mirror and ran my fingers over the smooth and neat detail. This morning, when my trusted headband stretched too thin and snapped while I was snoozing away, I rolled over in bed, snatched my bonnet off, and pointed at my edges. Theodora was yawning and just waking when she saw my silent distress and giggled.

She laced her fingers together and moved them in my head so fast, it took no time to have me looking and feeling good. I snapped on a pair of earrings and studied my face once more.

A few minutes later, Naomi traipsed down from her room and was popping gum in front of us as she scrolled through her phone. "Indy, is Will still meeting ya'll in New Orleans for the Libra Festival?"

"Yep!" I grinned. "Apparently there's also some sort of plumber's convention that weekend so he'll be there for that too."

"And the plot thickens." Naomi rose to her feet, giving a loud and obnoxious stretch. I spotted a deep *purple-ish* passion mark on her neck.

Theodora's eyes were wide as she swept up hair from the floor. "Damn, girl, has Ivelisse been sucking on your neck like that?"

I stared at Naomi waiting for her reaction.

"You knew?" Naomi gasped and looked from me to Theodora. I threw my hands up.

"Wasn't me!"

Theodora giggled. "Girl, I been peeped that. I figured you would tell us in your own time. Ain't nobody tripping off that. Do what makes you happy."

Naomi sat crossed legged in a desk chair and her body seemed to sigh. "I love you guys."

"Love you too!" I chimed in. I turned to Theodora, and I sat up on my elbow. "What's up with you and Dylan?"

A fire flashed in Theodora's eyes that looked familiar. It wasn't happiness or sadness. She tapped her pencil on her notebook and leaned her head against the cinderblock wall. "My family is slowly, and I mean slowly coming around. Nana just about fell out when we were discussing the menu for an upcoming family dinner and Dylan asked what was pounded yam."

We chuckled hysterical.

"But they are at least talking to me again, I'm happy about that." Theodora wiped tears from her eyes. I couldn't tell whether they were happy or sad tears.

"Ain't nobody tripping off that. Do what makes you happy." Naomi smiled.

"The fifth floor?" I asked, holding up four fingers at them both as I slipped on my shoes to head to work.

Theodora and Naomi grinned and in unison they said, "fifth floor!"

"On another note, Theodora, I forgot to tell you. We can't be roomies for the Libra Festival. The theater is putting us all up at the same hotel, and when I checked, they said the track team stays at a different hotel uptown." I looked at Theodora through the mirror.

"Yeah, I meant to tell you that. We're big time," Theodora chuckled. She fanned Naomi away like she smelled funny, and Naomi giggled. Different funding came from different pockets. The theater crew and I were staying at a regular hotel by the airport further out. Theodora and the track & field crew bringing in most of the funding and all the ticket sales—were staying at the five-star hotel in the city.

"I wish I could go with you guys, but I have to check out my brother," Naomi griped.

Her brother was coming home after deployment for the past three years. She hadn't seen him in all that time and there was even a situation when his platoon was bombed and her family lost contact with him for a few days. He turned up at a hospital a few miles away from his camp. Shell-shocked, but alive. Naomi needed to lay eyes on him for herself, and I knew the feeling. Theodora and I were sending her home with lots of love; second chances didn't come too often.

"Hi, Indigo. Come into my office and take a seat." Rita pointed to a worn-out office chair, which looked like it had seen many behinds. Meeting my boss for the first time after working there for months was weird. The year was almost over, and she seemed off on the days when I worked or away making some

big theater purchase. My main contact had been Harper, and she was out today. This meeting came as a surprise.

Rita clicked on the computer and her perfectly manicured nails clacked over and over. I grit my teeth. I shifted in my seat. What could she want with me? "It looks here like you've missed a lot of time." Rita stared at the computer as she spoke.

Clearing my throat, I started slow. "Yes, I had some family issues and other things going on. I wasn't here when the year first started, but I am now. I've been here every week at my scheduled time."

"I see," Rita said, still examining her computer, looking for something more interesting than this conversation. Her hair was pulled up tight in a French roll and I could see where her foundation met her hairline. She had small, simple pearls, and a matching necklace. Did women still wear pearls? Rita looked every bit the part of a theater person. With her nose so high in the air, she must've believed herself to be one.

Butterflies churned in my stomach, and I feared my omelet Booker whipped up for me this morning would come back up. That was another reason I had missed work. A nasty food poisoning spell sent shockwaves through Titus and although it didn't hit me too hard, I had missed a few days of work. Shit, I had missed a lot of days of work. I sank in my seat, hoping this conversation wasn't heading in the direction I thought it might be going. "I can make up the time." I leaned forward and gripped the edge of the seat.

"I'm sorry, Indigo. The Board is making cuts and by you missing so much work, you've showed them they really can make do with three stagehands and not four. You can finish the semester since we only have a few more weeks until the end but we will not be renewing your contract for next year."

Angry tears came to my face in front of Rita, but she didn't know me enough to care. I cursed myself for being in my own way.

"Indigo? Are you okay?" Rita eyed me. The way she looked at me, I wondered if she saw my shame. My fears. My anger. My rage.

"What do you suggest I do, Ms. Rita?" I asked earnestly.

Ms. Rita's eyes softened and I knew she saw one thing. An 18-year-old girl unsure of what to do next.

"Pay a visit to your academic advisor. And don't wait. I'll try to see what I can do to hold your position. That's the best I can do for now. And Indigo?" Rita paused. "Don't let college get the best of you. Know what you can do—and do that."

"Thanks," I mumbled.

My jacket flew open as I hustled across the campus to the academic advising office. When I got there, I was out of breath and panting. I was sure I looked like a crazed woman. I pulled the door open to find it locked. I looked into the glass and noted a sign on the door which read: **Academic Advisement Office In -Service. Office closed all day.**

"No!" I banged on the glass door. I ran to the building next to academic advising. "Hi, uh. I'm looking for my advisor?" I asked the receptionist.

"This is the Bursar's office. But what's your last name, honey?" she asked.

"Lewis," I panted, still out of breath.

"Oh, your counselor is Ms. Wilkerson, and unfortunately, she is out on medical leave."

"So, who do I talk to when I need help?"

The receptionist searched through her file drawer under her desk and retrieved a clipboard. "Here, fill this out. We have to schedule you to see someone, and the next opening I have. . ." The woman moved her mouse around her desk again. "Is next Thursday."

"I can't do that day. I'll be away for the Libra Festival! Can't you squeeze me in somewhere?" I snapped. My tone was much

sharper than I meant. My hands shook as I gripped the counter and waited for this receptionist to tell me my fate.

She leaned back in her chair and examined me. Her tone matched the energy I was putting out. She coolly said, "well, we don't have anything before Thursday. The next appointment after that would be the following Tuesday."

"But that's almost ten days from now!"

"I'm sorry. The counselors are really busy, especially with Ms. Wilkerson out right now."

"Fine," I uttered, taking the appointment card from the woman.

I woke up this morning excited for Libra Festival and the possibility I had a solid plan for what to do about Mr. Chestnut. Now I didn't even have a job. Man, when I screwed up—I really did it in the worst way.

CHAPTER 31

I TURNED DOWN BEAUREGARD Road and slowly passed the perfectly manicured lawns with evenly trimmed hedges. The full moon above glowed brighter and suspended even more shine than usual. I saw someone outside with a pair of trimmers, hacking away at the bush, not caring who saw them. Good, I needed the darkness.

On Beauregard Road sat a small blue house with large arched windows. White curtains stopped at the top of the windows and looked directly into the house like a large set of eyes. Even though I was sitting a few houses away from theirs, I cut my lights off and exited my car. I crept to the front of the house and smashed a few tulips planted in the yard. Fuck those flowers, they would be the least of their worries soon enough.

A car lurched by, and the music bumped, making me jump. I yelped and kneeled before the car lights could hit me. My heart was beating so fast, I thought it might jump out of my chest right there. I walked as swiftly as I could, trying not to make wind or noise around me. I stayed low and walked to the first window, peering into the living room. Although I could see lights on in the house, it was too high up for me to

see bodies. The window was cracked, and I heard their voices as I craned my neck to listen.

I made sure to take off all jewelry beforehand, and I focused on the corners of the house, praying they didn't have any new cameras. I didn't see any. I pressed forward.

"Were you able to appeal the grievance she filed against you?" Nurse Meanface asked.

Mr. Chestnut didn't answer at first and a nervous laugh escaped him. "No, I have not. These are kids, Allie. I don't want a grievance to mess up their chances of getting their degrees. It was just a misunderstanding, and she's mad because she didn't make the team. Nothing more nothing less."

Allie sighed and flopped onto the couch. She pressed her hands into her face. "I just don't know if I want any of this anymore, Gregg. I was thinking, maybe I could move in with my mom in Tunica Rivers for a while. We still have the house, I know. But I don't want to be alone. Work is still a mess. That Sonia has been causing a rebellion at Trochesse. She's got the other clients thinking they need to break out. She's acting as some sort of martyr and convincing everyone the staff is against them. They just let her out solitary." So much angst intertwined in her words, and I wondered if marriage was the ultimate sacrifice as a woman.

Coming out of solitary. A team member had filed a grievance against him. I smoldered in the quiet darkness of their front yard, tucked away behind bushes. It was happening exactly how I thought it would. They were at Trochesse torturing Mom because she was standing up to them.

"Good. We don't know what those people are capable of. I just want you safe at work. There's no reason to move in with your mom, we're figuring things out here. Have you thought more about a transfer for Sonia?"

"We talked about it in the morning meeting today, but the

only obstacle is her family. The committees don't like to split up families who live close by."

"You have to advocate for yourself, Allie. Don't be such a pushover. If you don't feel safe anymore, she has to be transferred."

"Yes, you're right," Allie choked out, throatier than I wanted to hear.

Mr. Chestnut spent the next hour serenading Allie with more things for her to correct, including her clothes, home decor, and even the inside of her car. It wasn't up to his cleanliness standards. Allie sat on the couch with her hands buried in her face, looking more dejected as each moment passed. Their interaction transfixed me. The more I listened, the more I raged. He convinced her so easily she was wrong; she was the problem, and if she changed things about herself, their relationship would be better. She ate it up like a lapdog needing scraps of food and never really challenged him. She knew students had filed grievances against him and they had left Tunica Rivers like a thief in the night, and yet she still believed him to be true to her. I didn't like Nurse Meanface on account of my mom, but I especially hated the desperation that was rampant through their house. Did the woman have no friends? No backbone? Was this what love was all about?

I crept back to the car, knowing I heard enough and disgusted to listen to a word more. He easily got away with everything. Well, not anymore.

My plan was coming together. Right after Libra Festival, I would collect everything I had gathered and send it to the police station in an anonymous letter with the conversations with Nurse Meanface and Joya. I wrote down every time I saw him out with a player, and they seemed a little too comfy, cozy. I was going to bring up this grievance I learned about tonight, and him being pushed out of TRHS. I was going to

use my writing chops and send in a letter to Titus University so compelling, they wouldn't have a choice but to open some sort of investigation.

That's how these things worked, right? I couldn't prove that he was coming to my dorm room simply to torment me without outing myself, so I would have to leave that part out. If I implicated myself, that had the potential to catch me up in something related to Jaxon. People always questioned women in these situations and their reasons for coming forward. It would work itself out. I was helping women. I had to kill Jaxon. It differed from Mr. Chestnut and his perversions.

Men had oppressed people since the beginning of time, and it was exhausting. It was ingrained in our society. They convinced women that we had to nod and smile when a man looked our way with hardly anything appealing to offer. How ironic it was some of those smiles we gave men were done out of safety. It was the awkward request which had the potential to leave a woman bruised and bloody if she answered the wrong way. Mr. Chestnut reminded me of those men. I scowled at the thought of all the ways he had gotten over on us girls, simply because some of us chose to keep quiet out of fear.

I wouldn't have to lie or explain to anyone what I was doing out at this time of night with a fly ass hairdo, feeling like a million bucks, but really hanging on by a thread. No one would get it. They never did. Getting rid of Mr. Chestnut and possibly Nurse Meanface, was a family matter. At this point, I had to put her on my personal honey-do list because I couldn't count on her as a woman to stand up to her husband. Her lack of self-esteem was affecting my mom, and I couldn't let them send her away to some faraway place where we had no chance to visit her. If marriage required blind faith, it was something I wanted no parts of.

'I get it, honey, Mama gets it,' Mom said in my mind. *'She has to be watched too. Get home and let's brainstorm.'*

I started the car and headed back to campus.

PART 3
KARMA

CHAPTER 32

BEFORE I HOPPED on the highway heading to see Mom, I stopped to put gas in The Bus and when my phone rang, Trochesse's number popped up.

"Hello?"

"Hi. Ms. Lewis? This is one of the nurses from Trochesse. We are reaching out to everyone who frequently visits your mom, Ms. Lewis. She is in solitary confinement until noon and is not permitted to have visitors for the morning session."

"Excuse me? For what?" I shouted.

"We can not disclose that information, but I can have the head nurse, Mrs. Chestnut call you."

Nurse Meanface.

"You do that! I'll be there for the afternoon session!" I hung up. The *afternoon session* which Mom hated on account of all the families and noisy children who came. These people were really playing with me and my family.

I sat in the car, now all gassed up with nowhere to go. Will had called me over earlier for a *house date*, as he called it. After working at the theater and attending my classes this week

without being late, I thought I did damn good. Starting the car, I headed in his direction.

A few hours later, Will and I were sitting on his front step. The ice cream truck just left, and he spent a whopping six dollars on a Choco Taco for himself and a Strawberry Shortcake for me.

"What's wrong?" he jabbed. "This is fine dining over here; and next time when we go out, I'll even let you take the salt and pepper shakers."

So many things floated through my mind, but Will and I fell into a fit of giggles. I tapped at my arm where a mosquito was tasting my melanin and I wiped sweat from the back of my neck. It was seventy-four degrees in Tunica Rivers and the sun was setting almost the same shade of indigo.

Shades of Indigo.

The cicadas hissed and walls of trees lined the driveway. I smelled something spicy cooking in the distance and it tickled my nose.

Will and I were what we've always been. Best friends. And that was something I needed right now.

"So, what did you do when all that water shot out?" I giggled.

Will was sharing his latest adventure from plumbing school, and he hopped around imitating himself. "Have you ever seen the movie *Coneheads*? When the mom's water breaks, and she goes into labor? Remember when all that water gushed out? That's how this basement looked. We couldn't do anything with it." Will cleared his throat, pursed his lips, and imitated, "Eventually my boss said, 'we're charging extra for this, Sir.'"

We fell out laughing, knee slapping each other.

If this was real love—God, I loved it.

I wiped my mouth. The strawberry shortcake crumbles scattered down my shirt, and I brushed them away. My ice cream was dripping down my hands, and its stickiness wrapped around my wrists. Mr. and Mrs. Simms were in the house cooking and from what I could see through the open screen door, bumping butts. Their love was as old as they were, and they were still crazy about each other. I heard their voices followed by laughter, and I wondered if that's how it could be with Will and me.

Someone and me.

On cue, Mr. Simms opened the front door wider and said, "uhh, young man? Here's some money, take your lady friend out. Ice cream ain't no date." He handed Will a wad of cash and glanced in my direction.

Will snatched the cash from his dad. "Up for a real date?"

I was totally up for an official outing with Will, but my day was already jam packed. "I have to get going, anyway." I stood and grabbed my keys. "See you Thursday, in New Orleans?"

"The yearly plumber's convention, the Libra Festival, and an old-fashioned track meet. Only thing missing is ComiCon," Will chuckled.

I hugged Will and promised to drop my location to him once we were there. A text message came through from Ez, and it read: *come to my home at your earliest convenience.* I giggled. Ez must've been doing the voice to text option again. Ever since Ms. Arletha showed him how to do it, he became a voice typing maniac.

I turned into Ez's long driveway. He and Dad made a deal with the city to allow a professional cleaning company to come and clear out Ez's property and home. They made an effort to let him keep his house, but Ez still grumbled and sometimes barked at the team trying to clean. I think he understood these days it meant the difference between keeping and losing his home, so he dealt with them begrudgingly, but accordingly.

Ez was outside, sitting on his porch, holding a long dish towel, and cleaning his gun. The weapon gleamed against the sunlight, and it was long and oddly shaped. It reminded me of one of those old western movie guns when they challenged each other to a duel. Ez with a gun made me nervous. Guns made me nervous.

I parked and hopped out carefully while eying him. "Ez, what are you doing?"

"Nothing, girl, I'm just cleaning this here gun. Them rats been up in the attic again and I think some of them been doing they business right in here." Ez leaned the gun toward himself and looked down the barrel. "I got it all out though. Let me go put this up. You stay here, now," Ez shuffled inside the house and the porch's screen slammed behind him. I sighed, watching Ez pull down the attic door from the living room ceiling and placing the gun back in its rightful place. He returned with a paper in his hand. "Here, girl." He shoved a letter in my direction. "This letter came from Trochesse about your mama." He tossed a white envelope in my direction.

"What's this?"

"Open it, crazy girl," he fussed.

I opened the envelope and read it over. They were transferring Mom to a women's facility in Upstate New York, clear across the country. They signed the paper, Allie Chestnut at the bottom. I crumpled the paper and balled my hands. "They're trying to transfer Mom."

"I know'd it." Ez grumbled. He said it with an ominous tone, and I wondered if he thought the same things as me. How would this affect our family? I had to go to Trochesse and talk to Nurse Meanface myself, woman to woman.

"I'll take care of it, Ez."

"Don't go getting yourself in no trouble or nothing, girl. You know you don't know how to sit still sometimes." He gave a stern face. My hoarding, cat loving, hole in the roof living, water loving, gun toting grandfather was dishing out advice. I couldn't help but chuckle at his warning.

"You know, before you went to that loud behind school, your dad had me sign some kind of promise note to help pay for it if you ever needed. They sent a letter and said that you was behind on your payments and it even said they sent you a letter and they hadn't heard from you. Is everything okay? What you doing up at that school, girl?"

I bit my lip as tears welled in my eyes. I couldn't hold back my feelings, and I laid it out to my grandfather through sniffles and sobs. I told him about Mom and the voices; I told him about the financial aid office and my work-study job. I told him about how hard my classes were, and I had trouble keeping a schedule, going to work, and managing everything. I told him about the medicine I was taking and how it made me so tired. I didn't tell him about Jaxon. There were some things parents and grandparents shouldn't know about their kids, and this was one of them.

"I know'd it, girl. I know what you mean," Ez commiserated. "The voices be getting me too. You have to let it out. You have to talk to someone."

I didn't understand what Ez was saying. Did he see a therapist? "Who do you talk to, Ez?" I asked through sniffles.

He smiled. "My Jackie! She is all up and through these woods and waters. We talk all the time! That's why I won't leave this here house. She is here." Ez shuffled inside and came back with a small mason jar filled with the darkest liquid I had ever seen.

"What is this?" I asked through my snorting.

"It's hootch. Made it myself," he said smugly.

"I don't drink, Ez," I lied and handed it back to him, careful not to spill the thick mixture.

"Oh, I don't believe them lies." Ez gave a chuckle, like I had told a joke. "I know'd it, girl. You like the hootch, it's in your blood. Just take a few sips, it's good for the soul and it will make you feel better."

I took a deep breath and swallowed the liquor. It went down hard, and I was sure there was battery acid or something in it.

"Just give it a few minutes to work its way through your body. This the good stuff, it don't take long! It's so strong, you don't even need to wear a jacket at night. Just a teaspoon of this set you straight and keep you toasty," Ez said proudly.

After a few minutes, I felt hot. I sat back and rested my head on the chair as it rocked back and forth. Ez and I took in the land; his land he loved so much, now partly controlled by the city. We were quiet as the hootch took us over and we inspected the acreage.

"Now about these here voices, you say. You gotta tell your daddy. But, Indy Lindy, you know your Mama Jackie heard the voices too. She used to say it was the ancestors speaking to her. She used to go sit right over there on that small inlet and bury her feet in the sand. I said, 'woman, why you got your toes in that nasty sand?' You know I can't stand the sand, that mess gets everywhere, in your clothes, in your mouth, in your brain. She said, 'you have to ground yourself, so the ancestors hear you better.' Your mom heard them too, but I don't know about hers. Hers seem different," Ez grumbled.

"And what if mine are like hers?" I looked up at Ez with red eyes.

"You got Big Ez here, girl. I won't let nothing take my Indy Lindy. And Sidrock too." Ez leaned closer in his rocking chair, and it stopped creaking. He whispered, "you have to let them know you're the boss. You are the prize, Indy. They don't get to tell you what to do! Sometimes you have to go to the dark side to find the light." Ez shook his head and looked out to his front yard. It was littered with crime scene tape from where the city said no one was allowed to walk because of the caving ceiling.

When I quieted down and listened to Ez's words, he gave a smug smile and looked pleased with himself. "Did I ever tell you about your Mama Jackie, and how she used to love her some mermaids? She used to say they was in these here waters," Ez extended his hand over the water. I listened to Ez and although I had heard this mermaid story a million times—I leaned my head against Ez's shoulders, wiped my tears from my eyes, and listened to my grandfather. The time passed by quickly and shortly after, Dad, Ms. Arletha, and Sidney came to visit.

Dad stepped out of the car slowly and took in the surrounding sights. Ez's property wasn't in better shape than before the professionals got involved. Ez's front yard was filled with junk car parts, lawn furniture, old office equipment, and tons of other things.

Ms. Arletha made her way around the car. I smiled, watching her glow. Her skin was shiny and thick, and it radiated against the sun. Pregnancy agreed with her, and she welcomed it like the love she longed for. I watched her help Sidney out of the car and run her finger through Sidney's curls. She had been water to our starving family; her guidance, pound cakes, and love helped us grow.

"What ya'll up here talking about?" Sidney asked. She plopped down on the other side of Ez and wrapped her arms around his large leg.

"I was telling my Indy Lindy about Mama Jackie and the mermaids," he slid his hootch container under the rocking chair and out of sight.

"Tell me again, please?" Sidney looked up at Ez. Her large, brown eyes piercing his. Sidney would forever have Ez's heart.

"You know, Mama Jackie used to say the Black mermaids swam right up over there." Ez pointed to the small isle again.

"Why over there, Ez?" Sidney craned her neck to see the isle, like she had never heard this story before.

"She said that's where they love. That's where they love."

"What's that mean, Ez? That's where they love?" Ms. Arletha asked, patting her belly. Dad pulled a chair from the other side of the front porch for Ms. Arletha to sit down.

"You know, I don't really know. She just said if anyone Black wants to find themselves that we should look to the water. Our souls are scattered in all the oceans, and rivers, and lakes across this here world."

"You know, Ez. I don't think I ever found out how you and Mama Jackie met?" Ms. Arletha leaned over her armrest and got a load of Ez.

He broke into the largest smile I had seen on him in . . . in . . . I don't even know. It's been that long since I'd seen Ez smile. The thought of Mama Jackie did that for him.

"Awww, now, if you want to know how me and Mama Jackie met. I have to go whip out my Blues music. Because that woman put her mojo on me, and I been here ever since."

Ez ran in the house, and in a few minutes, I heard the husky and thick sounds of Howlin' Wolf. Ez strolled out of the house, imitating Howlin' Wolf's voice. He crooned and used his broom like it was a guitar and pranced around the front step as Sidney clapped her hands.

"What ya'll know about the Blues?" Ms. Arletha snapped her fingers and danced along.

"I know me, and my Jackie fell in love to the Blues in an old jukebox café. She came in for the Farina and she left with me." Ez tapped his hand on his knee. "You hear that pain? That ache? That's how it feels without her here."

I licked my lips, and my heart skipped a beat. God, I missed Mama Jackie. She had been gone now for about four years, and memories of her were everywhere in everything.

"But ya'll don't be sad, no ya'll don't be sad. My Jackie sees us. I like to think that she's right over there with them mermaids, anyway." He pointed to the small isle. Ez turned the music up louder and he sang with intensity and fever while he played a fake, broom guitar. He could hold a tune, and for all his quirks, he really could sing.

I looked at my phone and then at my family. I had to leave soon if I wanted to catch Mom before visiting hours were over. "Sid, are you sure you don't want to come to Trochesse with me?"

"I'm okay. Dad took me last week. She's been asking for you anyway."

I swallowed. I didn't want to leave my family and this moment we were having, but Mom was family too, and she beckoned for my attention. I sat back and enjoyed Ez's wailing a little more.

CHAPTER 33

MOM WAS TALKING so fast I could barely understand her. She had that white stuff sitting in the corners of her mouth where she had eaten five Tums. She loved Tums. I watched my mother intently. I studied her face, which was slightly shaking back and forth. With every word she twitched, and the white foam sat unmoving in the cracks of her mouth.

"And look here, Indy. You see this here? They are trying to put things in my skin. They said one day this week we'll go to Mount Shasta. You know that's where the aliens live anyway. Have you ever been? I know you always wanted to go to California. So, your daddy is having a baby with that woman? He said she has an enormous bruise on her head, but she ain't ugly. Is she prettier than me, Indy? You can tell me. I never thought he would go and get himself a candy girl. A baby. What that man know about a baby?"

"Mom enough!" I hissed.

Dad had already told Mom about the baby, but she was rambling on anyway like it was her first time hearing the news. I was trying to keep my voice low while I scoped out

Nurse Meanface and her punk posse sitting in the bubble in the center of the visiting hall at Trochesse. Her gaze burned a hole in the back of my head, and I felt flush, knowing she was peering at me the same I was at her. Did she know how many nights I spent gawking into her dining room window? Was she aware of how many tulips I had crushed while listening to their conversations and disagreements? Why did married people disagree about so many things anyway? At what cost would she continue to let him rule over her life?

Her pride.

The cost would be her pride and it was a sum far greater than imagined. My letter to the police and Titus was about ready. I had it tucked away under a floormat in The Bus to make sure no one found my evidence.

Mr. Chestnut and the track team were staying in center city New Orleans at one of the expensive hotels. Theodora already told me if they win, he was treating the team to dinner and a round of drinks that night. If I knew Mr. Chestnut's old tricks, he would celebrate with a PYT. He seemed to have a girl waiting for him in every city he visited, and I had a feeling this one would be no different. If I could somehow get video or pictures of them together, I could include them with the letter. As much as the voices wanted me to off him and parts of me craved that feeling too, I knew I couldn't. I couldn't. Murder was wrong. But with Jaxon, it felt so right . . .

"Ms. Arletha is nice, and Sidney loves her. Please don't talk about her like that." My tone was soft. It was the first time I objected to her theatrics, but Mom was wrong on this one. Ms. Arletha had done a lot for our family when we needed it the most.

"And you're defending this? My dear daughter wants a new Mammy, everyone. A new Mammy," Mom proclaimed in an English accent. She stood from the table and waved her hands

around the room, waiting to be noticed. Minister sat at a table next to ours with a younger Black girl who resembled him. Ruth-Ann and Cordelia huddled in the back of the visiting hall and had parked themselves on a bench where they were eating water ice from small wooden spoons. They eyeballed Mom as her voice rose but continued with their treats. Minister shifted in his seat and cut his eyes in our direction. He turned his back away from us, scowling so he couldn't see Mom anymore.

Mom was a master performer. Realizing her band of misfits had enough of her shit, she lowered her voice and sat back down at the table. "They've done it . . ." she whispered. "They've turned my people against me."

"Mom, no one is against you. Don't see it that way. We just want you to feel your best. You're not okay."

"I am just fine. It's you all who should be in here. They are reading our mail, and they think they can stick me in the hole because I have a voice. I will not be silenced. Not by you or her, or anyone!" Mom shouted. She pointed to me and Nurse Meanface. Mom's eyes were dark, black, and ablaze with anger. "You'll see. You all will see. When I am caged in like this, I come out swinging. Just you wait until I'm not here anymore, then what will you do? Have you talked to Ez? He still doesn't sound okay when I talk to him. And are you still stringing that Will boy along? Keep him eating out of your hands, Indy. But don't let him eat until you know he can handle a full plate."

I listened to Mom's thoughts. I tried to remember it all, but she jumped around so many different topics, my head throbbed. I could never keep up with her, and if this was how I looked to people when my thoughts got the best of me—I wanted no parts of it. "Mom, have you been taking your meds?"

I braced myself. I wanted so much to tell her about the medications I was taking. She still believed they were reading her letters and therefore we could only talk on the phone. That made no sense either because if they were reading her letters then surely they would listen to her phone conversations. That part blew right past her as she dialed my phone, raging about Trochesse and whatever they did to offend her that day.

"So, you think I'm crazy too, huh, Indy?" Mom lamented with sad eyes. She didn't raise her voice like she normally would. She slumped into her seat, and seemed to collapse into herself when she said *crazy*. Staring into Mom's eyes and seeing someone I didn't recognize was the definition of crazy. She jumped up and moved around the table and shouted at Nurse Meanface. "You've turned them all against me. You did this!" she bellowed. Nurse Meanface shot me a look.

"Mom. I have to go; I have to get ready for my trip." I stood and turned away.

She grabbed my shoulders and stared me in the face. "You can't escape it. It's fate. Death is inevitable. Heads will roll. One match will start the wildfire." Mom let go of my shoulders and leaned forward to kiss my forehead. "I won't be here long," And with that, she turned on her heel and marched away; her long blue terry-cloth robe flitting behind her. Minister rose from his seat and ended his conversation with the girl he was sitting with. He followed behind Mom, as did Ruth-Ann and Cordelia when they got closer.

I quickly grabbed my things and rushed out of the room before I heard, "Ms. Lewis, Ms. Lewis." Nurse Meanface caught up with me right as I was leaving. "Your mom—"

"I know, she's not doing well right now," I interjected, not wanting to hear it or talk about it with Nurse Meanface. I had the urge to place my hands around her neck and make her pay for all her husband's sins. A low growl escaped my chest, and I had to be careful she didn't hear the eruption threatening to flow from me.

"That's not it. Your mom has been in solitary quite a few times. She continues to be a behavioral problem at Trochesse. Listen, I will look past a few things, but I will not tolerate her threatening me."

"She threatened you?" I contended.

Nurse Meanface paused. "She said she knew a special place for me to go, in the water. Also . . . " she looked around . . . "The hospital board has decided to transfer her to another facility. I will have to call your dad so we can schedule a family meeting and discuss discharge planning."

I grimaced upon hearing what I already knew. I walked outside to my car as the skies opened up and rained on my life.

Later that night, after I returned to school and packed my bags for the festival, I waited for Chaquille to come over. He had been visiting each night and we watched tv. Tomorrow we were driving The Bus all the way to New Orleans. The school provided transportation via their own chartered bus, but Chaquille and I opted to drive together in case we wanted to sightsee.

Naomi finally talked to her mom about her feelings for Ivelisse, and they seemed on the mend. She said her mom was religious, but she was also a mom who wanted her daughter to be happy, and so with that came acceptance. It was beautiful to fully *see* Naomi. She looked happy these days.

I straightened up the room and tossed some dirty clothes in the closet. I swept up the floor, which was littered with black, popped rubberbands. Our room was filled with hair products like Afro Sheen and hair grease. I lit a candle and sat on my bed. I smoothed out the comforter and fluffed my pillows. I was nervous and waiting on Chaquille made it worse. Just as I was about to text him and cancel, a knocked rapped at the door.

"Hey you." I grinned.

Hey yourself," Chaquille returned an equally wide smile. He wore a long-sleeved cotton t-shirt and gray sweatpants. Yes, those gray sweatpants. I gulped, forcing myself not to look down and sneak a peek. Chaquille carried a small white bag, and I smelled something delicious wafting from it.

"I got you some ice cream," he shoved the white bag in my direction. "The way you were snapping about your grandfather dropping your butter pecan cone at Family Day brought out a side of you I don't want to see again."

I snorted a laugh and almost choked on my cone of awesomeness. Mama Jackie loved butter pecan. I used to be a mint chocolate chip girl myself, but one day we ran out and Mama Jackie offered me some of hers. I've been hooked ever since.

People say the way to a man's heart is through his stomach, but why was it the men who benefited in these stories? The way to a girl's heart could be found in food too. Most men knew that. At least Chaquille did. I settled onto my bed with my fuzzy socks and pajamas.

Chaquille brought a fish platter for himself and was cracking open ketchup packets, licking his fingers. He sat on the foot of my bed and kicked off his Jordans. He grabbed the remote and pressed a few buttons before the Netflix icon popped up. "What are we watching?"

"How can you eat that at this time of night?" I asked incredulously.

"I'm hungry all the time. Don't be coming for me, you're always hungry too," he retorted.

Ice cream dripped down my cone and before I could lick it, Chaquille leaned in with his tongue extended, doing what

I didn't get a chance to. His large, pink tongue licked where the ice cream had threatened to fall.

"Chaquille! That's gross!" I shoved him.

He broke into a sinister smile. "I was just trying to help, there seemed to be a need." His shoulders bounced up and down as he tried to get the words out without laughing.

Snatching the remote from behind Chaquille, I rolled my eyes and turned on *The Fresh Prince of Bel-Air*. It was the episode when Will Smith's dad showed up and Will was emotional. I watched this episode with a heavy heart. It reminded me of when Mom went to Trochesse. Licking my cone slower, I glanced over at Chaquille, and he was shoving French fries in his mouth and watching the tv with the same intensity I was.

"Chaquille, where's your dad?" It had occurred to me that Chaquille and I were spending more time together, but he never mentioned his dad—like ever. Maybe it was the wrong question because Chaquille choked a little and grabbed his soda, taking a long sip.

"He's... around. I guess. Still lives in the city."

"He lives in New York? Do you see him?"

Chaquille stopped eating and rested his head against the cement wall behind him. "Not really. He was never really interested. When I was younger, I overheard him telling my mom he didn't know what to do with me because I was sickly, as he put it."

"Sickly?" I squinted.

"Yeah, I mean. He was never around much, anyway. He took me and my sister to the park and bought us some kicks now and then. But there were a lot of things I couldn't do when I was younger. My epilepsy wasn't managed well at the time, not like it is now. He wouldn't take me anywhere. He was afraid that I'd seize, and he wouldn't know what to do. I think he just didn't want to be seen with a weak son."

"But you're not weak!" I interjected.

"Well, thank you. I don't think so either. But he wasn't there with m mom and me, going to appointment after appointment and being picked and poked. I just know when it's my turn to be a father someday, I'll do better."

Chaquille's words burned inside of me. I studied his face and his deep forehead lines. I moved down to his tiny ears and his full, straight out of Africa lips. Chaquille's dad had missed out. He was missing out on this beautiful specimen of a man with so much determination.

"Anyway, your turn in the hot seat. Talk to me about your mom. What's one of your favorite memories of her?

"She's not dead," I huffed.

"I know that. I'm sure you have a memory that stands out to you."

Leaning against the wall behind me, I thought and thought and thought. There were so many memories of Mom in everything. Theodora wore a perfume, and it reminded me of Mom. Naomi was into '80s rap and she kept Slick Rick and Doug E Fresh blasting the same way Mom did. Harper was dramatic and expressive, and bits of Mom shined through her too. Mom was in every aspect of my life, there was no denying her.

"You know, when Sidney and I were younger, Mom and my dad took us to this dock where we would go fishing and crabbing. It was right outside of New Orleans and there's a small hole in the wall restaurant attached to it. You could go fishing, bring back whatever you caught, and they would cook it right there for you. Dad was the fisher, and us girls were on lookout duty. We used to scream, *'over there, Dad, there's another one.'* He would whip his line all around the dock in whichever direction we pointed until we had enough fish for all of us. We used to have a good time. That was before Mom went away, back when Mama Jackie was still alive." The memory

brought tears to my eyes and before I knew it, one had escaped down my face.

Chaquille didn't say anything, but he wiped it away. After a few seconds, he said, "sounds to me like we need to take a fishing trip, just like I said weeks ago! See what all the fuss is about." He did an exaggerated eye roll.

"Do you even know how to fish?" I giggled, thinking about our last conversation on the subject.

Chaquille feigned hurt and placed his hand on his chest. "That one hurt. Of course I know how to fish. And fry it too!" He shoved more fries into his mouth.

"Maybe," I shrugged with a giggle.

Chaquille whipped out a weed pen and before I knew it, we were laying on our backs, staring at the ceiling.

"I thought you don't smoke weed?"

"The pen is safer than putting that mess on your lips." He shrugged.

The Fresh Prince of Bel-Air was watching us as I told him about the mermaids, Ez's house, and the new baby. He listened while I talked and laughed when I mentioned Mom and her Trochesse performances. I told him about Trenita and the medications. The meds subdued the voices but when they weren't subdued, they wanted to talk about one thing—Mr. Chestnut. I didn't tell him that part, though.

I talked for what felt like forever. Taking a deep breath, I was about to tell him about Jaxon . . . about what really happened. I looked over at Chaquille, ready to bear my truth and unload my shame, when I heard soft snores escaping him. I sighed and closed my eyes too.

My plan was perfect. A few more days and the deed would be done.

CHAPTER 34

CHAQUILLE AND I rushed around the first morning of the Libra Festival, preparing for a day of opening and closing the curtains. His room was right across from mine in the hotel and the night before I was in bed staring at the ceiling, wondering if I should make my way to his room. Let him open the door and without a word, hold it wide and welcome me in. I wanted to welcome him in. Tell him all the things I've been thinking and let the chips fall where they may.

Instead, he rapped on my door. For deodorant. A lost sock. Toothpaste. I wondered how men survived. They needed women for almost everything.

Thoughts of Will danced in my mind. He had claimed me as his and I agreed, but I didn't know what I wanted. I didn't know how to tell him that. He texted me this morning and said he would be at his plumber's convention most of the day. We were meeting tonight for the big track and field party. Will and Chaquille would be there together, and I wasn't comfortable with that at all. I played out the various scenarios in my head about what could happen, and each of them ended with bloodshed or someone thrown in the river. Maybe that

was my imagination getting the best of me, but these days it wasn't that out of the ordinary.

New Orleans sang and danced around me. Chaquille and I opened and closed the curtains at the Libra Festival against dozens of other colleges in the South, and just as we suspected it was a snooze fest. Rita and Harper were there orchestrating it all, and we were so studious in our matching yellow t-shirts. Chaquille and I giggled through the whole event and when it was over, we scored second place in the stage breakdown category, thanks to me and Chaquille. We were a good team—him and I.

After that, we strolled down Bourbon Street before Theodora's track meet started. A few kids had set up camp on a four-way corner. They were dancing and doing flips. A crowd formed around them, and people were dumping dollar bills into a bucket, grateful for their entertainment. I wondered what it was like to live in such a big city like New Orleans. Were the people happy? They certainly looked it as I stared into their smiling faces. Could I be happy here? I know happiness was an inside job these days, but I had so many people trying to help me inside as it was.

I noticed Chaquille shifting out the corner of my eye, and when I glanced over, he was leaned back. He had pulled his fitted hat over his eyes and was dancing along with the kids on the corner. I moved out of his way and smirked. A smile broke across his face and he grabbed my hand, twirling me on the street. "It's like we're in a Julia Roberts movie or something," I giggled, as Chaquille dipped me in comedic fashion.

"Well, in that case, are you going to be my pretty woman?" Chaquille held me close as he whispered the words. His hands moved from my shoulders and rested above my waist. While the world bustled around us: tourists, their fanny packs, and wide eyes didn't pay attention to us. They didn't pay attention to me.

Chaquille did.

Something caught my eye over Chaquille's shoulder. Mr. Chestnut's presence made my blood boil. The snake that he was, hiding under all that Titus University paraphernalia must've sensed trouble because his eyes caught mine. His lips curled into an entitled, *ugh-this-girl-again* smile.

Yep, motherfucker, this girl again.

"Young man. Ms. Lewis." Mr. Chestnut brushed by us. He placed his hands on the small of my back and scooted behind me where Chaquille's hands had been moments earlier. My skin burned from his touch, and I seethed. Why did men think that was okay? You keep your hands to yourself at all times. When you slide past a girl, you don't have to touch them. But to some men, this was too much like asking for consent.

"Indy, you good?" Chaquille frowned. Mr. Chestnut stopped a street man who was selling flowers by the dozen. He flashed a wad of twenties and peeled off one and handed it to the man who patted and kissed Mr. Chestnut's hand.

Man, he was good.

"Let's head back to the field," I kind of asked, but kind of insisted to Chaquille.

"Is that an order, General Lewis?"

"Are you in formation?"

Chaquille grinned and locked his arm around mine and led me through the crowd. I don't think a man had ever led me anywhere, but I happily trotted behind him; my sandals slapping against a new city.

"Chaquille, I'm gonna hit that porta potty over there." I pointed. "You go ahead and meet the taxi driver."

"What? I'm not leaving you." He sat down on a curb.

I snorted back a laugh. "No, seriously, it's right over there, and besides, the taxis don't play in NOLA. If we're not there when they arrive, we'll get left like last time."

JANAY HARDEN

The taxi had already left us this morning and what a fiasco it's been trying to find parking and decent rides. Even though I drove The Bus, the town was packed from multiple events happening and driving through the city wasn't an option.

Chaquille considered my words and nodded. "Yeah, you're right. I am not trying to chase a ride down another seven blocks." He shuddered. "I'll call you as soon as I flag one down. Don't get lost."

As Chaquille walked around the corner, I ducked down a busy street where shop doors were open, and alcohol was everywhere. I saw a fishing store sitting between a Madam Laveau shop and a ninety-nine cents souvenir cafe. I had taken brain pictures of it when Chaquille and I walked past earlier. I bought two of everything; two used fishing rods and pre-made kits the store had already assembled when out of towners like us wanted to go fishing. Grinning, I grabbed and searched the shelves, gathering everything we would need for an impromptu fishing trip on the same docks I used to go with Mom and Dad. The shop had a sign that said it would hold our purchased items behind the counter until needed so we didn't have to carry them around Bourbon Street.

"Do you know where you're going to use all of this stuff, lil lady?" the older gentleman asked. "Looks like you got a lot with a little understanding of it. And we close at 8 p.m. You'll have to be here before that time for pickup." The older man leaned over the counter and shook his finger at me.

I glared up at him, not letting even his misogyny take the happiness I was feeling. I stared between him and his finger before I growled like a dog. The throaty gnarls escaped me and paired against my fresh braids, stud earrings, and face beat down—he wasn't expecting the delivery behind the package. His eyes widened, and he looked confused.

Good.

Not one more man would question my understanding of time or events. "Yes, I know exactly what I'm doing. Mind your business, you'll live longer. I'll be back before closing to pick up my fishing gear." I snatched my change off the counter and walked out to meet Chaquille. The welcome sign illuminated in front of me, but I felt anything but.

After some intense internet stalking, I was able to find the spot where Dad took me and Sidney fishing as a child. There was one lone posting for it on Google and it was one of the few spots in the state which allowed fishing at night. Harper recommended it. She said her family used to go there as a child and throw rocks off the sand mounds and imagine who was at the top of the old lighthouse next to the water. Tonight, I would go to the docks where the small inlet was located, I would place the fishing rods and supplies there, and after the big meet, I would surprise my New York City boy with an old-fashioned night fishing adventure. I was giddy just thinking about it.

A few hours later, I watched from the stands as Theodora and her team brought home gold medals. The track team formed a circle around Mr. Chestnut, and the large, javelin throwers with huge muscular arms, lifted him on their shoulders. He waved and cheered like he was the king of the castle. The track team won their state championship after all.

Theodora ran to me, breathless with a broad smile.

"Is it always like this? All these people? You were amazing, Theodora!" I squealed. I meant every word. It was my first time seeing Theodora run, and I was floored. She was long, leggy, and graceful. Her chocolate arms extended, and her plump muscles pounded forward with grit. When she bowed and

crossed the finish line, her team surrounded her and cheered while Mr. Chestnut slapped her butt.

I cringed at that part.

"I can't believe we won! I mean, I can believe it—but I can't! We have to celebrate tonight! Are you coming to the party?"

"Of course! I wouldn't miss the last big party, especially after today!" I put an arm around Theodora's shoulder and squeezed.

My friends were really dope, and I was ecstatic they were mine. Knowing Mr. Chestnut was going to be there excited me in ways I couldn't describe. He would be there, and I would get more information I needed to take him down. Just then, Will texted me and asked what time we were getting together.

If I picked up the fishing gear in enough time and got on the water at a decent hour, we could make it back for the party by at least eleven. I was pushing it, especially having Will and Chaquille breathing the same air again. Armed with a camera and an axe to grind, I congratulated Theodora again before making my way out of the crowd to head to my room, clean up, and take the fishing items to the docks so I could surprise Chaquille.

As I pushed my way through people, I felt someone watching me. Out of the corner of my eye, I gazed at Mr. Chestnut staring. Hoards of people were around him, and he nodded and gave me a sinister smile; the same smile he gave me earlier.

'Game on,' Mom said in my head. 'Game on.'

CHAPTER 35

I CHECKED THE TIME on my phone and tried to hurry. Chaquille was waiting.

I want to show you something tonight, I texted him. He sent back eyeball emojis, and I laughed out loud.

Will crept into my mind while I placed the fishing items in a small lockbox in the park where Chaquille and I would fish later. I had told Will I was his girlfriend. I loved him. I did. But I committed prematurely. I watched his parents love each other out loud and I wanted those things too. But right now, something kept drawing me back to Chaquille and I couldn't deny it. Will meant too much to me to string along. I would talk to him this weekend.

A swig of the hootch Ez insisted I take with me warmed me up on this balmy night. The park kept small lockers for anyone needing to store items during their fishing sessions. The area was overgrown with grass and old pieces of two-by-four wood planks were leaned against the storage sheds. I grinned, thinking about Chaquille's face once he realized what we were going to do.

I looked around at the area and it was so different from when me and Sidney were kids. There was one boat sitting on wooden posts, and when I peeked over the sides of the boat, there sat a few life vests, a medium sized boat anchor, and a nylon rope. The water was so secluded. I cursed myself for not buying a flashlight. As I plopped back into my car and threw the gear into reverse to head back to town, I checked my rear-view mirror and saw nothing behind me on the gravel road. It was pitch black besides one light overlooking the water. As I gazed around, my heart skipped a beat. I saw him.

Him.

Mr. Chestnut had walked some distance, and my eyes squinted trying to figure out where the hell he appeared from. Was I seeing things? I saw a low light behind him and what looked to be a trail leading from somewhere with people. *Shit!* What was he doing here? And he was carrying a small to-go bag. He was dressed in his Titus University regalia and his phone shined in his hand.

He was waiting for someone.

One thing I was sure about, there was a reason we were both here, right now in this moment. I wasn't sure what it was. I was buzzed and damn . . . he was *right here*.

'*Indy, look how this worked out for you. Now is your time,*' Mom whispered. '*Do it now. Do it now. Do it now,*' she repeated. Her voice was comforting. If her voice had a taste, it would be rich, chocolate cake, and she wanted me to experience every morsel. My heart was beating so fast, and everything seemed to be happening in slow motion as I watched him scroll through his phone. I knew I hadn't had chocolate cake in a while, and I was famished.

Mom was there for me in her own little way. I often wondered how she felt when she hit that man with her car before she went to Trochesse. Why did she do it, and what type of person was she? And what did that make me? As much as these same questions ran through my mind, the choices were mine to make. The voices beckoned me. Wanting me. Chasing me. Following me. They were never too far away. As much as I wanted them to be.

In my mind, Mom was the pastor, and they were the choir. They each played integral parts in the makings of Indigo. There was one part of me that belonged to no one, and it was my thirst to right the wrongs of unscrupulous men. One way or the other, revenge would be mine for the taking. I could be that girl. The one who people never suspected. I could put my glasses on and be my version of Clark Kent. Only it wasn't Clark. I was Indigo Lewis. Indy Lindy to those who knew me best. But to men like Mr. Chestnut, I could be so much more. A thirst burned through me and my mom that was quenched by murder. Jolts shot through my body and my growl returned I had reserved earlier for the man in the fishing shop.

To be such a dangerous girl, I was so unassuming. Welp, you know what happens when you assume. It was time to decide which fate had already made for me.

Mr. Chestnut glanced up from his phone and eyed my car. He darted forward, thinking I was here for him. He walked up fast with authority, like he was so sure of himself. When he got closer, and he saw the whites of my eyes through my windshield mirror, he paused and sneered.

"Who do you think you're dealing with, girl?" With not one ounce of worry, he threw his head back and laughed at me. I wasn't the driver helping him get to his party across town. I was the reaper here to collect, and I wanted this as much as my mom did. Mr. Chestnut glimpsed me behind the wheel and the look on my face.

I originally crafted a plan that didn't involve dead bodies. I worked hard to put it together so it wouldn't blow back on me. But damn the plan.

Opportunity was knocking.

With my foot on the gas, I revved the engine and giggled. Ice Cube rapped on the radio about a *good day*. I took his words in and snorted. Maybe it was a good day... just maybe. Without thinking, I pressed my foot to the floor and my tires spun as they kicked up debris and thundered toward Mr. Chestnut. Within seconds, The Bus struck him, and he disappeared under the car with a crunching sound.

My lips formed into a smile.

I reversed one more time for Gloria Steinem. We just learned about her in one of my classes. Although Gloria didn't say you had to kill men to be a feminist—she didn't directly say not to either. When you came from a different stock and it was genetic, you did what you had to do. Besides, I was doing my part to keep the world free from men, who believed they could treat women any way they wanted. Laylah Capri would be so proud. "Take back your power!" she had urged. She was damn right.

I threw the car into park, hopped out, and searched around. The only thing I could see was the small, gravel pathway where he had walked from and trees disappearing into darkness. The path was wet from the earlier rain. He came back with a bag of food so clearly on the other side of those trees were people, also known as potential witnesses. My veins buzzed as fire ran through me. My heart was louder than ever. Mr. Chestnut was under my car and history had repeated itself. My mom had run a man over and now so had I.

'Good job, Indy!'

'She's getting so good at standing up for herself!' another one commented.

Mom came next. *'You know the drill, Indy. Let's finish him. What do we have around? What can you use?'*

I looked around as The Bus hummed behind me. Water, there was only water. According to Ez, that was all you really needed. I wouldn't be able to lift him and get him into my car. Even if I could lift him, what could I do? Take him to the police station and give them all my information and say, 'lock him up, boys?' No, I would go down too. Something would come out about Jaxon or the ways I had stalked Mr. Chestnut. It was their fault anyway, Tunica Rivers, and Titus University. Shit, Nurse Meanface too. The fact that they allowed it to happen for years, and no one had caught him yet. Nah, this was old-fashioned street justice. I wouldn't depend on anyone to take care of me or keep anyone close to me safe. I would be taking care of that from now on.

I pulled him from under the car with as much might I could muster. My hair had fallen and was wild in my face, swinging over my shoulders. I didn't see any blood under or around him nor did I see him breathing. I got down on all fours and grunted as I rolled and pushed his body, but he was so heavy. Too heavy.

'C'mon, Indy, you can do this! Mom encouraged. *Just a few more feet,'* she cheered.

"Ughh," I grunted, pushing his large body across the wet gravel top. I still had a way to go before he was on the dock. "This isn't going to work, Mom," I fussed.

'Try pulling him. Use both arms,' she instructed.

I did as I was told and rose to my feet. I heaved and pulled at his arms, while drops of sweat formed on my head. My eyes were stinging from the salty wetness dripping into them. It seemed like forever. I was sure I would pass out at any moment. I got into a slight groove of pulling his arms, pushing his body, and rolling him at the same time. A dog barked in

the distance, and I yelped, jumping back from his body. The impact had his arm twisted into a weird, ninety-degree angle but he was quiet.

My eyes were wide as I scanned the area for signs of life. Unless I was hearing things—which could very well be true, no one else was here. Trees lined the small island as far as I could see. The lightbulbs in the posts were blew out and had yet to be replaced. The shallow walkway, where Mr. Chestnut came from, was wild with weeds. It looked like only a small spot the locals frequented. Besides the low light, there was no signs of anyone.

With a few more grunts and tugs, me and Mr. Chestnut's body made it to the splintery dock. I stumbled out of breath onto the boardwalk. I stretched my back and it cracked loudly from hunching over.

He hadn't moved. Before I got any further, I ran back to the sitting boat and removed the metal chains. I tied the chain around his head and waist as best as I could. My hands were shaky when I grabbed the live bait container. Cringing, I dug my hand into the swirling fish and shoved them into Mr. Chestnuts pockets and mouth. Hopefully, something down there would see him as bait and take a bite.

I squinted down at the dark water, wondering what sort of fate would await a man who made it his business to objectify women.

Mr. Chestnut exhaled a loud noise as the fish made their way down this throat. He gasped and coughed. I inhaled, trying not to take on anything that wasn't mine and letting go of the things that were. I had control over my life. I would make it my business to handle them because I *could*. One thing I had learned from Laylah Capri was we all had to do our part in helping to heal the community.

This was my way of helping. Albeit different, but it was mine.

He coughed again and his eyes were large. Adrenaline was revving this engine. With one last burst of energy I could muster, I kicked Mr. Chestnut, and he rolled off the boardwalk with one arm outstretched reaching for something. Anything. Nothing.

CHAPTER 36

MY SHIRT WAS wet at the bottom and my hair was drenched from a rain soaked dock. I stood and wiped my hands on my jeans, and a few gravel pieces were pressed in deep, leaving indents. I darted around as the voices rejoiced and cheered in my head. They were happy, but I was worried. We were too wide open, and someone had to see something.

The water was still, and Mr. Chestnut's body sank down to the bottom. Hopefully the Gulf of Mexico, a metal chain tied around him, and a school of *fishies* in his pockets did what gravity couldn't. I sucked in a deep burst of air. My back was drenched in sweat, I knew what crack felt like without ever taking a hit. It was so dark, I had to adjust my eyes and be careful where I walked while I slugged my way back to The Bus. Before I made it, a shadow appeared from behind the green trash bin a few feet away.

"I saw you, girl. I saw you," an older man said. His face was dirty. He wore a holey hat, a flannel sweater, and work boots dogged and black.

My heart stopped. I inched closer and saw him leaned up against the trash bin. My chin trembled.

I was caught.

I knew someone would see something. Why did I think *we* could get away with this—again? Tears rained down fast and furious. They were angry and they fell on my face just as fast as I wiped them away.

"Excuse me? You saw what?" I leaned forward, examining the man who had the potential to be my undoing. I had to be sure he saw what I did, but I already knew.

"Oh, girl, you don't know how many bodies they drop off this block. I won't say nothing. What you got on you that you can give?" His toothless, gaped mouth curved into a sly grin. He looked me up and down and licked his nasty, chapped lips. I covered my chest when I noticed my t-shirt was wet, and my bra was showing through.

"Why you hit that man, girl? Then put him in that water? I saw you; I saw you," he laughed. He cackled like a crazy person who had nothing to lose and everything to gain by turning me in. He took out an old flip phone, and he pressed the nine number and then the one number while digits appeared on his dial screen.

"Wait!" I interrupted. My thoughts were moving fast. *What should I do, Mom? What should I do?*

'*Finish him*,' Mom whispered back. Her voice sounded eerily familiar in my head. This time it sounded like my own. '*We leave no witnesses, Indy.*'

"You got any money on you, girl? No, no. I don't want no money. What else you got?" he asked, his eyes twinkling. He studied my physique like he had just won the lottery, and even in his disheveled state, he tried to wield his maleness over me. His eyes danced over my body and whatever perverse thoughts

he had flashed in his mind, studying the curves and places on a woman he probably hadn't touched in a while.

Luck was not in Mr. Chestnut's favor, and it wouldn't be in this man's either.

I was already cold from my braids and t-shirt being wet, but the way he ran his eyes over me made me chilly to the bone. He wouldn't touch me, and he wouldn't look at another girl like that ever again.

I surveyed the area. There was a small two-by-four piece of wood leaned against the storage shed. It shined like I was being led to it. I sauntered toward the man, taking small steps, and making out more of his face. He appeared to be middle-aged and white. There were small beer cans littered around him. He leaned against the trash bin and struggled to stand and a bookbag was on his shoulders.

He breathed.

"Yeah, girl. I'm glad I came out here tonight! Come on over here. I won't tell as long as you gimme what you got." His breath was dank, and I smelled its sourness even just a few feet away.

I did as he asked and made my way toward him, picking up the two-by-four wood along the way. With one swift motion, I lifted both of my hands over my shoulders, and I smacked the wood down on his head. His body jerked and twitched as the board made a loud whacking sound. "I'm not your girl." I crouched down as he passed out and slid down against the trash bin, banging his head against the metal.

He was out like a light.

I took the small, fitted hat off his head and it felt warm and wet to the touch. Cringing from the foul smell, I scrunched it up. As quickly as I could, I shoved it into his mouth. I pushed it further and further until my thumb scraped his teeth. I winced from the pain, and the man's eyes sprang open. His body jerked. He tried to jump and began thrashing his arms and legs around. I straddled him and held his arms down. He was gasping for air, clawing at my t-shirt, and palming my breasts. I trembled under his chilly hands. I held him down tight. His eyes were wide with fear. His mouth was open, and I watched the hat lodge deeper and deeper into his throat, doing the work for me. He was pinching my waist, but I didn't feel the pain. He coughed and flailed his arms around me.

The hat lodged in his throat perfectly; I wouldn't be able to do it a second time if I tried. He had one last burst of strength and got stronger with each passing second. I was losing my footing beneath him. I placed one hand against the trash bin, and I steadied myself, getting a better stance. A few seconds later, he stopped shaking and went limp. His eyes rolled back in his head, and they turned a dark shade of black.

I squinted around and saw no one and heard nothing except for *them*.

'*You go, Indy. Two in one day! Our girl don't take no shit!*' they cheered.

The water was still my only way to get rid of him. I rolled and pushed his body to the boardwalk. I checked his pockets and found an expired license with a picture of him. His name was Freeman. Well Freeman, now you're really free. His body was skinny with oversized clothing, masking his lanky frame. He even had a few beer cans shoved in his pockets. I took the cans out because they were making it hard for me to roll him toward the water.

'*Leave them in. They'll weigh him down in the water,*' Mom advised.

I pushed hard and rolled him up the ramp. I stopped moving. I looked around and held my breath so I could see better, hear better. I needed something to weigh him down.

I rushed back to the boat on wooden planks and peered over the sides again. I grabbed the boat's anchor and grunted,

struggling to carry the heavy piece to the dock. Each step seemed longer than the next with sweat pouring from my face.

'They won't find bodies, Indy. They won't find bodies,' Mom reminded.

My back was aching and I tripped and almost lost my footing. I gawked down at the man. He was the one person who had seen my crime and could detail it with accuracy. He unknowingly traded his life so mine could go on. In the war of good versus evil and right versus wrong, I wasn't sure which side I stood. Maybe there wasn't even a side. Things happened for a reason, and no one would understand my reasons for why Jaxon had to go, and then Mr. Chestnut, and now this man except for me. I had enough of men. They did nothing but bring confusion and lies with them.

No more.

"I'm not your girl," I growled, looking down at the pitiful man who had the nerve to accost me for cheeks. I took the boat anchor and shoved it into his backpack and prayed it was enough to hold him down. I kicked him the same way I had done Mr. Chestnut, and he rolled into the water. Mr. Chestnut made a splash when he went in. This man didn't even disturb the water. He sank to the bottom quietly like it had been his plan all along.

A few feet away, The Bus purred. Mr. Chestnut's cell phone lay shattered on the ground and when I picked it up, I squinted through the broken glass and saw the Uber app was still open. He was getting a ride back to the hotel, and his ride was arriving in the next three minutes. I grabbed the phone and powered it off through shattered glass and tossed it into the water. I watched it sink into the darkness with its owner.

When I got into the driver's seat, I caught a glimpse of myself in the mirror and sneered a sinister smile only a bat-shit crazy girl would understand.

'Give 'em hell, honey,' Mom said.

Someone had to do it.

I drove to the other side of the lake with my car lights off, searching for where Mr. Chestnut had descended. I turned down a small, wooded road that was too small for more than one car to pass. I pulled over onto a side cliff and trembled as wind whipped through my wet t-shirt when I got out to walk the rest of the way. There was a small sign which said: **Backbay Cove, this way.**

I needed to make sure I covered my tracks, and when they came looking for Mr. Chestnut—which they would, it wouldn't come back to me. The one room restaurant was no bigger than a shack. There was a tiny window with a handwritten sign that said *to-go*. There was no place to sit down inside or outside. Delicious smells wafted from the small shack and besides the one lone light, I saw illuminating the tiny spot, the area was dark.

A Black man was inside, looking hot as hell and wiping sweat from his upper lip. He stood side by side with a woman around his same age, taking orders and collecting monies. I surveyed the area and besides the small pathway I walked down to get here, the area could only be reached by boat. No wonder I didn't see any cars. These people used motorboats or parked and walked around the small island like I did. I read a sign posted on a tree. People were permitted to go fishing on the lake and whatever they caught, the restaurant would fry it for them. *Make your own fish sandwich,* they called it. Access to this little spot was not easy, and yet men in dirty overalls *and* people dressed up in business suits waited in line.

Damn, the food must've been good.

JANAY HARDEN

My stomach growled from the aromas as I hunched behind a tree and took in my surroundings. I took brain pictures of it all. I shook my head and took a deep breath. The place I had visited as a child was still up and running, but they had moved the location away from the docks and into these woods. *Backbay Cove* transformed into some old-school, down south, mom and pop, hole in the wall, dive restaurant, and it was a small shed with twinkling tree lights. This was the low light I had spotted on the other side of the island off in the distance.

I watched for a few minutes while people got their orders and made their way back down the hill and into their motorboats, some big some small—in the opposite direction of Mr. Chestnut's watery demise. It made sense now. There was no parking at all up this way, and you either had to get here early to secure one of about three spots, or you could walk the short path from where I had spotted Mr. Chestnut into the woods. Forever the athlete, Mr. Chestnut chose to take the scenic route around the island and through the pathway. Hopefully, once his ride realized he wasn't there, they would drive off and forget about him like I was about to. One could only hope.

I crept back to my car satisfied. There was nothing here to see, just like there was nothing to see with Jaxon. I could take care of myself.

'You're a natural, honey,' Mom sang in her beloved English voice.

CHAPTER 37

WILL CAME AROUND the corner, strutting toward me from my left. He already wore a frown, and his walk was strong.

I turned my head, and I smelled his cologne before I saw him. Chaquille's stroll was smooth and told me I was a prize, and he was ready to claim it. Chaquille came from the other end of the hallway, heading toward his room. He had a pinched look on his face as well since I stood him up for a date.

The hallway seemed extra-long, and I felt their eyes on me, searching me up and down for answers I didn't have. To questions I didn't think I would have to answer an hour ago. I stood frozen in place and shivered under my still wet t-shirt, with my hotel room keycard in my hand, and my damp braids resting against the back of my jacket.

Chaquille and Will slowed down when they spotted each other, and they both scowled.

I *really* didn't plan this one well.

The three of us were here together again, only there was no coffee or Ez involved to intervene. I studied their faces in slow motion. They were here for me in different ways. One

was connected to my past and owned a space in my heart he had earned fairly through years of friendship. Will's love was enduring. I never had to question it.

I had met Chaquille this year, and he had almost run me down our first week of school. We argued. He confused me. He excited me. He turned me off. He turned me on. Our friendship—even in just the past few days had morphed into something I wanted to know more about. My breath deepened as they took steps toward me. I looked over my shoulder, and water dripped from my eyelid. I blinked it away, hoping they didn't see. Chaquille and Will glared at each other, both men intent on staking a claim to something that I wasn't sure I wanted anyone to own.

Thoughts of Mr. Chestnut and the other man swirled in my mind, while butterflies flitted in my stomach. I felt excited... aroused at what I had just done—again.

I turned back to Chaquille, and he glanced me up and down. I felt exposed when he looked at me. Like he saw parts of me I didn't even know were there. But he saw them, and he easily plucked them out. Was I that visible? Did he see right through me? Or was he the right one to see it all along?

And Will... my Will. He had asked me to be his girlfriend and I didn't object but I should have. I didn't want to hurt him, but I couldn't commit myself to something I wasn't invested in just yet.

I gave him another glimpse, and I saw his parents. I saw Tennessee. I saw ice cream dates. I saw him in the car with my family, who accepted and loved him. But would he accept me? The real me if he knew *that* Indy?

I held my breath when Will and Chaquille sandwiched me with questioning looks. I stood in front of my hotel door with the key in my hand. I was shaking and trying not to let the water dripping from my sleeve pool on the carpet. I needed to figure out what to do or who to do. I was turned on. Ending Mr. Chestnut and that man scared me and excited me.

Will's eyes were filled with love and concern. Chaquille's eyes with fire and wonder. Was I fire? Was I love? I was both at different times. The way they were sizing each other up, and peering over my shoulder, they wanted to know too. The inferno churning inside of me reminded me of a hurricane. I was in the eye of the storm, but I wasn't scared. I could make it rain too.

I was the storm.

Gone were the days when I let men take advantage of me and other women. We did not live in a time when being a woman was an advantage. Everywhere I turned, it seemed like it was used against me. I watched it hold others back from things they wanted. No more. But there was something I needed, and it took killing again for me to figure it out. As I gazed at him and exhaled, I knew who I needed right here and right now.

I glanced him over and licked my lips until they moistened. He returned my stare with knowing eyes.

"Indy, you good?" Will asked.

I was good. I was so good, so good, so good, in my *Destiny's Child* voice.

"I'm okay, Will, thanks for asking. I'm turning down for the night."

"Did you still want to go out tonight? I saw the team already at the party when I drove by." Will gave me confused eyes.

"No, I had something come up," I murmured. I continued eyeing Chaquille. He was leaning up against his room door, watching our interaction.

"Is that right?" Will whispered.

"Yes. I'm sorry, Will . . . I'm just not ready. I . . . I'll catch up with you in the morning. I'm sorry."

Will stood there glancing between me and Chaquille. He took a step back, breaking our holy trinity. "Don't even worry

about it. Whatever, Indy." He rolled his eyes. And with that, he walked away. I nodded in his direction but kept my eyes trained on Chaquille, who my body was now calling for. When I killed Jaxon last year, it electrified me. It turned me on knowing what I had just done. There was a time when I was quieter and people made decisions for me. This time, I was going for self, and *myself* wanted Chaquille.

Mom used to say, "when a man sleeps with a woman for the first time and she has on matching bra and panties, it's not him who made the choice." I had made the choice.

When I woke this morning, I took exceptional care and made sure everything matched. I wanted to let Chaquille see a different side of me. Chaquille waited for Will to turn the corner before he took two steps forward, leaned in, and wiped one lone braid out of my face. He cupped my chin.

"Indy, are you okay?" Will had just asked me that question, but when Chaquille asked it, those words sounded different.

"I need... you... now..." I breathed. And for the first time that night, I spoke my truth with no lies, no voices, and no indecision. Chaquille stared into my eyes intently, making sure this was what I wanted.

It was.

He lifted me off my feet. I surprised us both with a low moan and wrapped my legs around his waist. I handed him my room key, and he slid it into the door. Chaquille entered the room, carrying me and I collapsed into his arms, inhaling his essence. Chaquille took careful steps to the bed with us attached emotionally, and soon to be physically. The door shut softly behind him, and I placed my nose into the crook of his neck. Chaquille was an imperfect combination of many things. The embers burned between us, ready for what we knew was about to happen and realizing why it had taken us so long to get to this moment. To know him, I mean to really know him—all you had to do was listen.

Tonight, I was all ears, and other limbs too.

CHAPTER 38

"So, did you ever make it to the bluffs?" Harper asked over her glasses. "I didn't see you after the Libra Festival?"

I chuckled, leaning against the printers in the back office at the theater.

"Nope. We ended up seeing the town, just us." I left out the juicy parts with me and Chaquille. After I told both Theodora and Chaquille I hit a deer in the road and it left my car dented, they accepted my reason for disappearing and skipping out on the party.

I didn't mention the two men sitting at the foot of *Backbay Cove*.

I smirked at the thought when Harper answered the phone and gave someone directions to the theater. I popped a piece of gum in my mouth, took out a compact mirror from my purse, and examined my face. My skin was glowing and clearer than it had been in months. My freshly waxed eyebrows were lined perfectly, and I wore this cute, strapless black dress paired down with sandals. My pedicure exposed my bright pink toenails. I was bare under my dress. Naomi and I got Brazilian bikini waxes for the first time, and while I was sure I would pass out during the ordeal, I loved the way it looked. I was hoping Chaquille felt the same.

Chaquille.

I folded my arms; a small smile made its way to my face. I couldn't stop thinking about him. I couldn't stop thinking about Mr. Chestnut. That man. They all brought me a feeling of serenity and peace of mind that was hard to describe. Maybe that was my problem. I was always looking for answers and trying to figure everything out. With Chaquille, I could just be in the moment and let it take me wherever, whenever.

This morning, I took The Bus to the carwash and examined it for marks. There was a rather large dent under the bottom front, but it was almost under the car, and you had to bend down to see it. I hoped it wasn't visible to anyone else, but I still giggled at knowing what it represented.

Almost four years to the day, a delirious and mad Sonia Lewis, pounded down a busy street with her foot slammed on the pedal. She hunkered down as she hit a man crossing the street with full force and maniacal laughs escaped her lost spirit. It wasn't on purpose. I had every intention on turning Mr. Chestnut into the police, but fate intervened. If we were in a different space and time, Mom and I would be living parallel lives. I learned this from her. This shit really was genetic.

The voices were still there and ready for their next kill. In some ways I was too. What the hell? When I fought against them, I ended up tired and bitter. When I said, fuck it, and carried out their deepest desires, we both seemed happier. I wasn't opposed to the life, but the life chose me. Dad once told me cancer ran in our family and I believed him, but I was sure there was another sickness also running in our family. One that was filled with more sinister plans that afflicted me and Mom.

According to Theodora, no one had heard from Mr. Chestnut since the big track meet days ago. She said their assistant coach had stepped in for practice and they weren't sure where he was just yet. I said, "isn't he married? What does his wife say?" I had to play the part of the concerned college student.

Theodora shook her head. "Something isn't right. They said she moved back home after he didn't return home from the meet. But wouldn't she stick around and see about her husband? I mean if Dylan..." Theodora couldn't even fathom the idea.

This morning she was out with him again for breakfast. Can you imagine? A morning date? I wondered if Chaquille liked morning dates; I would have to ask him. The first time I killed someone, I worried about being caught and what I had missed during the cleanup. If I was going to do this work, I had to make sure it didn't happen in these haphazard ways that left me figuring things out on the fly.

It was a tough job, but I was up for the challenge.

My phone chimed, and when I looked at the alert, Titus University had posted some of my final grades. I scanned the email and smiled. I got a B in my English class, and A's in the others. "Look at this!" I showed Harper as she hung up the phone.

She took my phone and peered at it, tilting her head back like an old person. "Well, look at this, somebody just knocked out their first year of college!" Harper clapped and danced in her seat.

I smiled, and my heart felt so full. This year was difficult to say the least, and while I didn't think it would end this way, I would still consider it a win. "Yeah, you're right! I made it through this year!"

"You should be so proud! Stop being mean to yourself, Indy. You are the shit, baby!" Harper beamed.

I checked my phone once more, thinking I felt it buzz. I had been waiting for Will to reach out or return any of the dozens of texts I sent him, but so far nothing came through. *"Give him some time, Indy,"* Mrs. Simms had said when I called her to check on him. *"You kids will work it out."* I was hopeful she was right, but later that day, after I talked to Mrs. Simms, Will blocked me on all his social media accounts. I started to hop in my car and race to Tunica Rivers so we could talk but something held me back. While I had not lied to Will about my relationship or lack thereof at the time with Chaquille, I was sorry for the way things went down the night of the party. I wanted to apologize, but he wouldn't hear it.

I had an interview tomorrow with Synergy Publishing House. They had an internship available, and if I played my cards right, it could be mine. This summer, I was staying on campus instead of returning home. Chaquille was staying too. It would be the summer of love; I was sure of it. The thought made me giddy to think of us laying poolside with water dripping from his glistening skin.

I looked at my watch and noted he was late for work. We both had to be here at 4 p.m. for the closing shift and it was now 5 p.m. I shot him a text.

> **ME:** Wya?

A cold chill ran down my back, and before I clicked off my phone, it rang in my hand.

Ms. Arletha.

"Hello?"

There was noise in the background and I strained to hear. "Indy," Ms. Arletha breathed. "It's Ez. Come home if you can."

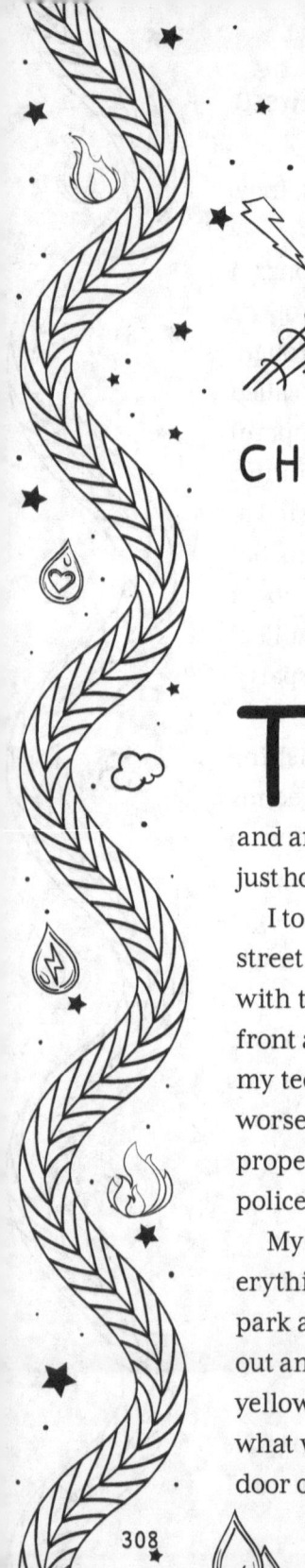

CHAPTER 39

THE HIGHWAY WAS clear tonight as I raced my way toward Tunica Rivers. *"Indy, come home if you can."* Ms. Arletha's words replayed in my mind. Her voice sounded pained and afraid. I didn't like it. I didn't even ask what happened, I just hopped on the highway. What could be wrong with Ez now?

I took my exit and raced through town. I turned down Ez's street and held my breath. There were at least six police cars with their lights flashing around his house. K. Jamison was front and center of the pack and he held a bullhorn. I sucked my teeth, hoping his presence wouldn't make this situation worse—whatever this situation was. I searched around the property, adjusting to the darkness and the bright lights the police invaded the neighborhood with.

My chest began to rise and fall as The Bus lurched and everything in the backseat flew forward when I threw the car in park and scrambled to get my seat belt unbuckled. I hopped out and ran to Ms. Arletha, Dad, and Sidney standing behind yellow police tape. I scanned the area, trying to figure out what was happening. Before I could ask, Ez swung the front door open and came barreling out with his shot gun.

My eyes widened.

"I done told ya'll before that this here is me and Jackie's house and I ain't going nowhere!"

"Mr. Ezra, we are trying to help you. We let you back in to collect your belongings, but it's not permanent. This house is not inhabitable. You cannot stay here. Please make this easy for all of us."

Ez sat on the front porch with his gun gleaming, ignoring the pleas from K. Jamison. "You can collect two-hundred dollars and go straight to hell!" he screeched.

"What happened?" I shouted over the bullhorn to Ms. Arletha.

It was Sidney who spoke. "The motel called. They said he's been agitated and mean to the guests. The city said he could get a few things, but he refused to leave so the neighbors called the cops. When we got there, he was already gone. That's when Ms. Arletha called you. Now he's back refusing to come out of the house."

Putting the pieces together in my head and looking around at the dozens of cats roaming the land and the never-ending piles of trash that grew leaps and bounds every week, I wondered what Ez was up to and if we had been wrong about this all along. Had Dad been right when he said Ez needed more than we could provide? We tried so hard to clean his house, take him to his appointments, and anything else he needed. Maybe if I didn't go to college . . .

"Is that my Indy?" Ez screamed from the porch.

"It's me, Ez!" I yelled back. We were so far away behind the police tape that my voice cracked as I shouted. "What's going on, Ez?"

"These people won't let me in my own house. They ain't got no say anyway. This is between me and my God. And Jackie, and my Jackie."

"Mr. Ezra, once again we are trying to help you. We will link you with one of our social workers to find suitable housing, but for now we need you to vacate the premises. Now."

I looked around at the officers. All white faces besides K. Jamison. Faces with families. Children. Vacation time. Hopes. Dreams. Fears. They looked like they preferred to be anywhere but here tonight, and one officer retreated into his cop car to check his cell phone. They didn't care about Ez. They just wanted to do their job, but Ez was family and to me—he was my job.

"I told ya'll ladies, I'm not going nowhere!" Ez belted. He hopped up from his seat on the front porch and jumped off the step with his gun by his waist.

"Mr. Ezra, take a step back! Or we will be forced to subdue you!" an officer screamed. Six eyes glared at Ez from behind the barrels of their guns. The house sat behind Ez, almost dejectedly. The place where I had spent long summer days and nights, looked like it was sighing under the physical and emotional weight of Ez.

"Oh, girl. Ya'll ain't doing nothing but working my nerves!" Ez yelled. With that, he jumped onto his bicycle and disappeared into the darkness, pedaling fast through the backwoods maze that he knew best.

"Uh, boss. Should we follow him?" K. Jamison asked another officer.

"No, we wait until he comes out."

"What is your plan here tonight, sir?" Dad stepped forward with his arms folded to the head officer in charge. His hands were in front of him where they could see. He squared his shoulders the same way Black men did when they saw the police. The rules were instilled in him childhood.

"Sir, Mr. Ezra has a large shot gun that he's been wielding around town. This has gone on long enough and with his size, he is a safety risk in the community. He may need to go to Trochesse."

"Trochesse!" Sidney and I objected at the same time. My phone buzzed in my pocket.

"His size?" I repeated, ignoring the hum from my jeans. They were threatening to send Ez to the insane asylum where his daughter was, just because his size made them nervous. My almost seven-foot, gentle giant, brash, grandfather was being profiled.

"My lands! That's the best ya'll can come up with?" Ms. Arletha rubbed her stomach and frowned. With all the chaos around us, I hoped we were all ready for the baby.

"He is not going to Trochesse!" Dad affirmed. His jaw was tight, and he looked small but mighty standing next to the cops. "We will find something for him!"

Three more cop cars entered the scene around the police tape. They walked with their hands on their guns and walkie talkies sitting at their shoulders.

"You didn't bring the recruits?" an officer asked.

"No, they weren't available this late. I told them they should come anyway; this would be the first mental health dispatch for them to see," the other officer replied.

Mental health dispatch, I fumed. Ez was nothing more than a case-study to them. Something for them to talk about in their trainings and back locker-rooms. I bit my lip and tried to keep myself from shaking. I stomped over to the cop, ready to give him a piece of my mind. Before I could, Ez darted out of the woods pedaling fast and his white t-shirt gleamed against the bright moonlight.

"You girls is still here?" Ez snarked at the officers and slammed his bicycle to the ground. He stomped toward his front steps with his back turned away from us. He moseyed around on his front porch, scooting cats and trash out of the

way. I held my breath and watched him and the officers with their fingers on their triggers.

"Mr. Ezra, once again. We need you to drop the gun and please exit the premises now. We are prepared to physically subdue you, if necessary."

"Physically subdue him? What does that mean?" I cringed.

I stood face to face with the officer and stared him down. I dared him to come up with some bullshit that would justify physically subduing, Ez. Sidney was next to me with her hands clenched. She stared straight away at Ez, looking so much like Mom. I had to blink twice. The concerned look Sidney gave Ez was the same one I had seen on Mom's face during our last visit. I wondered if I looked like Mom when I was worried. Sidney would be the Robin to Ez's Batman if she had to be. I didn't want her to be. I wanted her to be a kid, go to school, and play sports, but tonight she was ready for whatever with Lewis' blood in her veins; itching to go to war for Ez.

My phone buzzed again in my pocket.

"Subdue? Ya'll and them big words. Indy, you a big-time college girl. Tell them to talk regular."

"Ezra, once again this is your final warning. You must vacate the premises now. And please stop walking around with your weapon. Please don't give us a reason!" K. Jamison shouted. He sounded sincere for once.

Ez didn't care. He hopped off the porch and stomped toward the officers. His arms were so broad, and his skin was so dark, I almost couldn't see him if it wasn't for the flashing police lights and the bright moonlight. His voice roared though, and he unleashed a cuss-out worthy of an academy award directed toward the officers. His tongue was wicked, filled with contempt and he swore like a sailor.

"Ez stop!" I shouted. "This is serious! You have to go. You can't stay here anymore!"

"Ain't no white man in the Bible, and ain't no white man gonna tell me to get out my house. I think it's time we have us a fire!"

K. Jamison's finger flinched while holding the trigger of his gun. My eyes darted between the officers and Ez wielding years worth of anger and loneliness. His house was his last prized possession. His daughter was gone. His wife was gone. It was his only lifeline. I don't know why I hadn't seen it before. Ez would never willingly leave this land, and he knew it too. He would rather tear it all down before letting someone say he had to leave. I watched the events happening around me. I trembled in place. Sidney placed an arm on my shoulder and looked up at me. Her eyes filled with tears, and she knew, just like I knew, what was about to happen.

Ez wasn't going to make it out of this one. Even we couldn't help him.

With a sinister giggle, Ez lifted his bike, swung his leg around it, and disappeared into the woods again. He knew this land better than anyone else and if they wanted him to leave, they would have to search for him through the trails. Ez sang on his bike and his husky voice bounced off the trees, amplifying his thoughts and protecting him from their reach.

K. Jamison stomped to us. He walked heavy. Irritated. We were inconveniencing him. "This has gone on long enough. If you guys can't subdue him, we will. I don't want to do that."

"Ya'll ain't going to do nothing to Ez!" Ms. Arletha barked. "Let us talk to him."

Before K. Jamison could answer, I heard Ez's voice getting closer. *"Got my mojo working, got my mojo working,"* he belted. The land was so vast. I thought I knew it well but even I couldn't tell which direction Ez was coming from.

The officers and the rest of us quieted down and searched from tree to tree, trying to determine where he would make

his exit. Ez stopped singing and all we heard was the rustling of his bike under leaves. Like a flash of lightening, Ez shot out of the woods, peddling top speed on his bicycle from behind the house. *"I got my mojo working!"* Ez belted at the top of his lungs. His gun was still across his back, attached by a harness. He was coming up fast.

My eyes widened. "Ez no!" I screamed.

Everything happened in slow motion. I glanced over at one of the officers, who was sweating profusely and had already been playing with the trigger on his gun. He was the one who went to the car to check his phone. He had other things to do. When Ez cycled hard and directly in his sight lines, a deafening pop sounded when he pulled the trigger and struck Ez directly in his chest.

"Noooo!" Sidney shouted and ran toward Ez.

"Sidney no!" Ms. Arletha shouted. She pulled Sidney back and wrestled to keep her behind the police tape.

Ez stopped peddling and fell off his bike in front of his house. His cats purred around him and went to him, licking his face. In one swift moment, Ez growled like a bear and with a blood-stained white t-shirt. He stood. He was foaming at the mouth, and his eyes were afraid. Someone began screaming and the sound made every bone in my body rage.

It was me.

I was the one wailing as Ez made his way toward the crowd, blood leaking from his chest. Sidney's eyes glassed over as she watched him. He huffed and coughed. Ez peered around at the police cars and his eyes landed on the officer who shot him. The officer looked so young and unsure. His wrists shook as he held the gun, which now looked too big in his small hands.

"Ezra, back away!" an officer yelled.

"You." Ez pointed at the officer who shot him. With a last show of strength, his mouth twisted into a snarl. He lunged at the officer. "Do you want me to cry, girl? Do you want me to cry? I won't! I won't!" he screamed.

"Ez, heaven's no!" Ms. Arletha shouted, and more shots rang out around us, piercing through his body. One by one, I watched them light up my grandfather. He didn't fall. He stood strong, taking them all. Ez stood there with a blood-stained shirt, heaving. Blood seeped from everywhere now. I tried to speak but the words caught in my throat. Nothing came out besides screaming. I placed my hands over my mouth to hold back the wailing. Ez gasped. "Jackie... Jackie." He then fell to the ground.

A hush fell over the group and a few people sniffled. When I looked their way, it was the neighbors who were crying and rubbing their eyes, watching everything from behind the police tape. The same ones who started to call the police on Ez months ago when his land became too cluttered for their liking. K. Jamison was taking deep breaths when we caught each other's eyes. He looked tired. His back hunched under his thick vest as he watched his colleagues kill my grandfather.

The officer in charge slowly trotted to my dad and shook his head. "I'm so sorry that things took this turn. Ezra did not comply after multiple attempts at de-escalation. We didn't want it to go this way."

Dad was quiet and stared ahead at Ez's body, now surrounded by cats laying down with him. Ms. Arletha whimpered behind him into his shoulder.

"Young lady, step back!" another officer shouted.

My neck shot around, and Sidney was making her way to Ez's body. Her curls were wild and unruly. She waved away the officer yelling at her and she slowly walked to Ez. She laid down next to him. On the ground. Next to the cats.

My ears were sore and ringing from the sounds of the shots ricocheting off the trees. My hands were ice cold. Instinctively,

I pulled my phone from my pocket and saw I had five missed calls and many text messages. The first was from Theodora.

> **THEODORA:** Where did you run off to? Call asap. Chaquille is in the hospital. He had a grand mal seizure.

I placed my phone back into my pocket and closed my eyes. My heart sank. I was still here, living the hell on earth. That's what this had to be. Hell on earth. Feeling faint and with vomit threatening to come up, I leaned against The Bus as I heaved. Without thinking, I made my way to Sidney and Ez.

"Step back from Mr. Ezra!" the officer shouted. I glared at him, daring him to try me. He didn't know what I was capable of or who I really was.

"His name is Ez!" I cried.

They didn't even know him. The swirling red and blue lights didn't make me feel like anyone was here to serve and protect. They had taken the one thing most important to me. The one person who cared about me. Unleashing the dragon wasn't their intention, but that's what they got.

I laid down on the other side of Ez with Sidney on the right. She held onto him as tight as she could, his blood staining her clothes and forever embedding into her heart and mind. Tears streamed down her face. "Wake up, Ez. Wake up," she cried and tugged at his shirt.

All the voices inside unleashed at the same time, screaming at me and the sound was deafening. I wailed for all of Tunica Rivers to hear, while the tears flowed from my face and down onto Ez.

I was a granddaughter no more.

CHAPTER 40

TWO WEEKS PASSED. Sidney hadn't spoken since Ez left us. She ate a few meals and engaged in minimal conversation. She stayed in her bedroom, preferring to be alone.

Dad and Ms. Arletha languished around the house getting ready for the baby. It would be a few more weeks. Dad rarely took off from work, but he hadn't been to work since. He spent his time outside cutting wood and building handcrafted canoes. All things that Ez used to do.

Mr. Dennis, my former boss at Dennis and Sons Funeral Home, took care of the arrangements for us and I was grateful. One thing I couldn't do was plan a funeral for my grandfather when I felt like I couldn't even stand up. *"You don't worry Ms. Lewis, me and Tyson will make sure that he rests well,"* Mr. Dennis said. "I'll even add lavender to the water when we bathe the body." He winked at me.

Mr. Dennis believed that essential oils helped the bodies transition into the afterlife, and when I worked there, he was serious about fragrant water. When I watched him open his china cabinet and retrieve the expensive bottle of lavender

that he only used when the big whigs passed away, I lost it. My chest heaved and contracted as the tears dribbled down my chin. It was funny how life worked out. A little more than one year ago, I had killed Jaxon Green in this very place.

I knew the ins and outs of Dennis and Son's Funeral Home just like Mr. Dennis, and his son, Tyson. Never in a million years did I believe I would return to lay my grandfather to rest. Ez didn't believe in funerals and once Mama Jackie died, he refused to attend any more. He said, *"when it's my time don't put me in the ground. Let me live on the water."* After a quick funeral and cremation, his remains sat oddly out of place on the mantle at Dad's house in Tunica Rivers.

Today, the beeping sound of the hospital machines was blaring. I shifted in the hard seat and banged my knee against the equipment. It was freezing in the room. So cold. I was so cold.

Theodora was on the other side of Chaquille's bed, and her hands rested next to his leg. Naomi sat in a chair in front of the bed, sleeping. He was in a medically induced coma and had been for about eight days. After he didn't show up for work, Harper called his dorm rep and they found him in his room unconscious. Harper was the one who called the police and all the emergency contacts he had listed. His mom flew in from New York and also set up camp by his bedside. She was listlessly looking out of the window. She wasn't sleeping or eating. Neither was I.

"I'll keep watch, you head back and get some sleep," Theodora instructed.

I shivered in my seat and pulled my sweater tighter around my body, wishing it was a real blanket that could engulf me and take me away. I nodded to Theodora without saying a word. I wasn't tired, but I went anyway.

Heading back to our room, I was in a fog. In a matter of a few weeks, I had killed two people, broken a friendship, lost my grandfather, and possibly the man I liked. How could life be so cruel?

'Oh, Indy. Don't be so hard on yourself, my dear,' Mom reassured.

"Leave me alone," I grumbled out loud. A girl walking past me turned and frowned hearing me talking to myself. I glared back at her, daring her to say anything.

There was a full investigation into Mr. Chestnut's disappearance now. His wife was at the center of the inquiries. From what Theodora heard on the news, they had a rocky marriage stained with infidelities and domestic violence. After his disappearance, at least a dozen women came forward, alleging gifts in exchange for sexual favors and better positions on the teams. Joya wasn't one of them. One Titus student even told the news she was assaulted when he came into her dorm room one morning. She ended up leaving school shortly after and no one knew why.

Now we knew.

The world found out that Tunica Rivers High School had allowed him to keep his pension if he left town. Titus University was also in hot water for not investigating grievances filed against him in his brief time as coach. Even though Nurse Meanface was also a victim, according to public opinion she had motive to off him, and that was as good as guilty. Like everyone else, Theodora was shocked and made-up wild stories about where he might be. I told her. I tried to tell her. I tried to tell them all.

Once in my room, a flyer was taped to the door from the Black Feminists Nation. I signed up to be the secretary of the group and we were holding our first chapter meeting this

summer to discuss what the next school year would look like. I crumpled up the flyer, tossed it into the trash, then peeled off my clothes, and jumped into the shower. I didn't put a shower cap on, and my hair got heavier and heavier as the water soaked into my braids. I leaned up against the wall, visions of Ez's funeral yesterday replaying in my mind. I tried to shake away other thoughts, but Mr. Chestnut and the old man crept in. I stopped washing myself and stood under the searing hot water, and a small smirk found its way to my face when I thought of the way both men sank to the bottom of the water. Both were predators in their own way, and both deserved what they got.

'But look how it's made you feel, Indy,' Mom whispered.

"Shut up! Leave me alone!" I shouted back with red and puffy eyes. This was all her fault anyway. If Mom wasn't bat-shit crazy and she was still here, this wouldn't have happened to Ez; and maybe I wouldn't be walking in her footsteps as the next Tunica Rivers' killer. I turned the water onto the highest setting in the shower and I let the scalding water fall over my body. It felt like Hell.

Turning off the water, I opened my mouth and inhaled in the steam filled bathroom. Everything felt so heavy. My mind. My body. When I walked into my room, I noticed a large white envelope sitting on my bed addressed from the Titus University Financial Aid Office. I ripped it open Theodora must've put it there.

The bed creaked under me and all the extra weight I was carrying surfaced. I read through the papers in shock. My mouth fell open and I read the notice three times to make sure I was seeing right. My financial aid was rescinded due to me being on academic probation the first semester. They needed $10,000 to make my account current, and the due date had long passed. They had sent letters and emails requesting to meet, all of them went unanswered. I was too busy with the voices, school, and figuring out college; I missed something so important like how to pay for it. The last notice was the one that made me faint. The form said *paid in full by Ezra Campbell*. I checked the date and Ez had paid $10,000 around the same time they called and said my account was current. Ez paid to keep me in school. That's why he had asked about a 'promise' note as he called it. He came through for me in more ways than one.

My phone beeped but I let it go to voicemail. The number called back, and I still didn't answer. I was so tired and didn't have the mental space to add anything new right now. The number left a voice message, and I pressed a few buttons on my phone to play it. *"Indy! This is your mother, dear daughter,"* she sang in her English voice. *"I've just heard about Big Ez. My Ez."* She paused for a second . . . *"No one thought to tell me? I've had enough, enough of this place. You know what. I'll show you and I'll show them all,"* she cackled into the phone and hung up.

I laid down on the bed letting the towel fall to my shoulders and then waist. The papers and my cell phone fell to the floor, and I got under my blankets naked, curled into a fetal position and cried.

CHAPTER 41

SUMMERS IN TUNICA Rivers were the highlight of my childhood. Ez and Mama Jackie, especially loved the heat and sometimes she would get out on the water with Ez while he sang and let him row her around as she stared up at the vast sky with her sunglasses and straw hat on.

This summer was quiet. Ez wasn't cutting through the water in the canoe. Dad finally went back to work, and Sidney was at her dad's house more. I poked my head out of the back door, swearing I heard Ez's voice booming like it normally did first thing in the morning.

It wasn't him, and it wouldn't be him ever again.

I slammed the backdoor shut behind me and stomped to the kitchen. I planned to spend the summer back at school, but I just couldn't. My heart was so heavy, and I was afraid to be there alone. I stopped taking the medication Trenita gave me, and the thoughts were coming in heavy, reminding me that I could feel better if I killed again. I knew that I would feel better, but at what cost? I killed someone, and they killed my grandfather. It was a cost I didn't want to pay.

Trenita reached out a few times. She called and emailed, but I couldn't talk. I didn't want to and I really didn't have words for anyone right now. Madness. It was all around me. Later, I was supposed to go to the police station and meet K. Jamison to discuss what happened with Ez. They didn't really care anyway. He was big. He was aggressive. He was angry. He was cursing. He was yelling. He was a lot of things, but he was still my grandfather. I wasn't in the mood for the lip service and bullshit condolences they would offer.

'Don't go, Indy,' Mom said in my head.

Mom talked about Ez in my mind but no one had received a letter or phone call from her since she left me that voicemail two weeks ago. I summed up enough courage to call Trochesse and talk to Mom about Ez, but they said she was in solitary. I didn't have the energy to talk to her right now anyway, and so I quietly hung up the phone. I was too tired.

I was stifled between the hot confines of an incinerator and a damp lake. I was pissed off. How dare they kill my grandfather. How dare they! My heart raged and ached at the same time.

My cell phone rang, and I raced to my bedroom to grab it.

It was Ms. Arletha.

"Hello," I answered breathless. I hoped she didn't hear it in my voice that I had been crying.

"Indy. Are you okay, honey?"

"I'm okay," I lied. The lump in my throat hurt so bad from holding back tears.

"Indy..." Ms. Arletha started. "Your mom...she's out. She's escaped from Trochesse. They took her out for some appointment to get her ready to transfer to New York and she escaped."

The phone slipped from my hand and hit the floor as I fell into the wall.

JANAY HARDEN

"Hello? Indy?" Ms. Arletha shouted from the floor.

Mom's words replayed in my mind, *"We'll see. I'll show them all,"* she said. Did that mean she was plotting an escape? Where was she going and what was she doing? I stumbled into the bathroom, wiping my face, and taking deep breaths. I wanted to be free. I wanted to get rid of this weight following me and never letting me rest. I searched under the bathroom counter and moved cleaners and fresheners out of the way before I found a pair of scissors. Staring at myself in the mirror, I wondered if I should just end things. It would be so much easier to not have to deal with the voices and a world without Ez. I could put the scissors to my wrists, swipe down, and end it all. My life had taken so many turns this year and I had enough. My family needed protection and now with Mom on the run and Ez dead, who knew what that entailed.

I grabbed the scissors and instead of cutting my forearm, I took large sections of my braids and I chopped them off. I took even bigger sections and hacked away, not caring whether my real hair was being cut or not. I needed the monkey off my back. With my eyes filled with tears, hate, and revenge, I cut and cut and cut. I thought of Jaxon and him cutting my hair last year for the sheer fun of it. My eyes darkened as I remembered.

CHAPTER 42

"**M**S. LEWIS, I am so very sorry for your loss," K. Jamison acknowledged. Any other day I would try to comfort him, say it was okay, and shush him. It wasn't okay and neither was I.

He continued speaking when I didn't. "Also, I just want you to know. We are closing Jaxon Green's case; I won't be questioning you any further about it."

I was staring down at my hands in my lap, and I focused up at K. Jamison's last statement. I wanted to ask why? Why were you closing the case? Were you sure you wouldn't be questioning me any further? What about his parents? I had so many questions, but my body was giving out. I was so tired and could barely keep my eyes open. A broken heart did this to me.

"We still haven't found a body, and we don't have any clear-cut evidence that points to . . . anyone." He cleared his throat. "Once again, Ms. Lewis. I am sorry."

With my shoulders slumped and no words to speak, I nodded in his direction.

When I left the police station, I called Chaquille's mom to check on him like I had been doing for the past few days. This

weekend I was taking the three-hour drive and staying with him so his mom could get a break. He was still in a coma, and they were running all sorts of tests to see how serious it was. This was the first time I had ever *met the parents*. I never imagined it would be under these circumstances. We worked together to make sure Chaquille was never left alone. When I last saw him, his mom was on the phone with Chaquille's dad and she mentioned, *"Chaquille's girlfriend is here with him."* I didn't correct her—I *was* his girlfriend.

I hopped back into The Bus and on a whim, I made a sharp right turn onto a long gravel road. I had Ez's remains in the backseat of the car, unsure of what to do with them. I knew he wouldn't want to sit on a mantle in our house. I made my way closer to the inlet he often spoke about. Mama Jackie said she saw the mermaids right here and she loved to sit and bask in the sun. Exiting the car, someone in the distance rode by and I heard them blaring Nina Simone from their speakers, who wailed about being misunderstood. How fitting for a man who was misunderstood. My Ez.

With my hair short, in a Jada Pinkett-Smith cut, I glanced around the water shining so bright. The waves were calm. I knelt and felt the coarse sand in my hands. I took off my shoes and wiggled my toes. I grounded myself so the ancestors could hear me better. Taking out Ez's urn, I unscrewed the top and released his remains into the waters he and Mama Jackie loved so much.

I stopped at the corner store before coming here. An old woman with thick eyeliner and bangles on her wrists was mulling about outside. She grabbed my arm hard and said, "she's all fire, that one!" and walked away. It was the weirdest thing—but who knew that all along, my superpower had been fire.

Mom was out, and we knew exactly why. She wouldn't let anyone stand for killing her father and neither would I. I would burn it all down before I let that happen.

THE END

CAN'T WAIT TO READ MORE?

Scan the QR code below and receive a FREE sneak peek into Book 3 of the Indigo Lewis Series coming soon 2022!

OTHER WORKS BY JANAY HARDEN

Hey, Brown Girl

Forty-two Minutes (Book 1 of the Indigo Lewis Series)